THE WORLD BOOK OF GENERATIONS

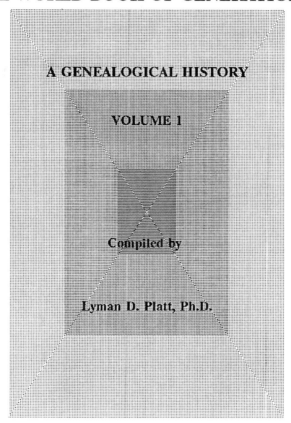

A GENEALOGICAL HISTORY

VOLUME 1

Compiled by

Lyman D. Platt, Ph.D.

The Teguayo Press
St. George, Utah
1996

DEDICATION

To my mother, Allie Lyman for nurturing me in the ways of God; for giving me a love of life and of my fellowmen. To my father, Gordon Leavitt Platt, for his love of knowledge, particularly history, geology, and astronomy. His example has been instrumental in the direction my search for truth has taken. To my wife, Linda Karen Petty, who is without doubt the most consistent lover of truth I have ever known. I have watched her in many, many situations where standing for truth was not popular, not convenient, and not safe, but she has stayed the course every time. Her training and abilities have assisted greatly in helping me as I have studied, sorted, and compiled this work.

Published by The Teguayo Press, 316 West 500 North,
St. George, Utah, 84770
Library of Congress Catalogue Number 96-070854
International Standard Book Number 1-888106-24-7
Made in the United States of America
Cover by Laura Taylor

Printed and bound by

CFP BOOKS
ST. GEORGE, UTAH
1 800 360-5284
1 801 628-7337

TABLE OF CONTENTS

INTRODUCTION   5

THE DEVELOPMENT OF WORLD CULTURES   14

Establishing an Accurate View of World History   14

The Patriarchs from Adam to Abraham   16

Dispelling the Theory of Evolutionary Time   21

Population Statistics   51

Chronology   55

The Limited Record of Civilization prior to
    the Flood, 4002-2345 B.C.   65

Mankind Spreads Across the Earth After
    the Flood, 2345 B.C.   72

A Preliminary Look at the Patriarch Abraham   82

**THE INITIAL DIVISIONS OF THE GROWING
    POPULATION, 2345-2245 B.C.**   92

The Basic Divisions of Mankind by Ethnic Designations   92

The Descendants of Japheth, Eldest Son of Noah   98

The Descendants of Shem, Second Son of Noah   108

From Unknown Origins   111

The Descendants of Ham, Third Son of Noah   112

A GENEALOGICAL HISTORY OF THE WORLD   117

Establishing the Birth Year of Jesus Christ   117

Establishing the Birth Years of Joseph and Moses, and
the Chronology from David to Joseph   123

The Controversy of the 430-year Sojourn in Egypt   155
Joseph, A Father to Pharaoh   158
Moses was the Pharaoh Akhenaten   176

Establishing the Years of Birth of Abraham, Isaac,
and Jacob   195

Chronological Information Regarding Abraham's Era   197
Primary Evidence   210
Secondary Evidence   210

Known Deaths Between the Beginning of Civilization
after the Flood and the Dispersion at the Tower
of Babel, 2345 B.C. to 1996 B.C.   212

Linguistic History of the Period from the Flood to the
Birth of Jesus Christ, 2345 B.C. to 2 B.C.   214

**THE DISPERSION FROM THE TOWER OF BABEL
AT 1996 B.C.**   234

Sample Dispersion Technique Employed by God:
The Jaredites   235

SUMMARY   242

BIBLIOGRAPHY   245

INDEX   252

INTRODUCTION

This volume is the first in a series that will uniquely identify all individuals possible, during the early history of the world, using proper research procedures and acceptable referencing standards. It is not presumed that all of the data recorded here is totally accurate. The reason for this is that original sources, and compiled sources, have incorrect information, some of which cannot be verified. Also, some purposeful inaccuracies have been created by record keepers of the past. Some errors have crept into *The Holy Bible* and other ancient works, either intentionally or by mistake. In the case of *The Holy Bible* these errors have thrown the chronologies contained therein off by ten to thirteen generations, or by as much as 307 or 407 years, depending on how the dates are calculated. In the cases of dynastic histories, there are serious chronological errors created by misinterpretation of archeological discoveries, the length of the reigns of many kings and pharaohs, the lack of knowledge regarding parallel dynasties ruling at the same time, and the misinterpretation of astronomical data. Typographical, transcription and deciphering errors, and mistranslation have created other problems. What is documented here is a record that is as accurate as possible. Unlike traditional historians, anthropologists, archeologists, and others trained in the modern school of thought, the author accepts several sources of proof which are not acceptable to most of these researchers. Although this position has as solid a basis in knowledge acquisition in its sphere as any of theirs, it is a procedure which most of the sectarian world does not use in its research process. This is not a criticism, just a statement of fact. Scientific methodology builds on foundation blocks called theories that may later become knowledge based on time-tested empirical data. That this process is flawed in some of its basic knowledge-building steps will be shown hereafter, thereby giving - if nothing else - equal claim for both methods to faulty thinking processes. Of course the claim of the author is that in certain circumstances the universal methodology used here is far superior to the scientific methodology because it includes all that is good in the scientific process, while drawing from *spiritually empirical data* for additional information.

There exists in the universe, a core of information that does not need to be verified, only discovered through the universal method. This information comprises what are called universal laws and eternal truths. These are constant over time, generations, and circumstances. It is, for example, an eternal law that truth is independent in its own sphere;[1] whereas falsehood is not. It is possible to find these universal truths and laws exercising a set of principles that are just as powerful and valid in their realm of reality as that set used by modern scholars in their pursuit of scientific truths, which in their purest form comprise part of the universal set of laws and truths. However, just because a group of professionals refuses to accept the set of principles used to find these universal laws and truths does not invalidate the reality of the process. *The Book of Mormon,*[2] for example, as a translated record from the past, contains information that can be accepted as truth, because arriving at that knowledge follows a set pattern, using the universal principles noted above. The disbelief of those who refuse to accept this process has no life of its own; *The Book of Mormon* does. Millions of people have put to the test the challenge contained therein and know with absolute sureness that it is an ancient record, of real people, written by inspired prophets. This method, although not scientific in its approach is, nevertheless, a proven universal method. Similarly, *The Doctrine and Covenants,* and *The Pearl of Great Price*[3] contain ancient

---

[1]*The Doctrine and Covenants,* (modern scripture published by The Church of Jesus Christ of Latter-day Saints) Section 93, verse 30, it is stated: "All truth is independent in that sphere in which God has placed it, to act for itself, as all intelligence also; otherwise there is no existence."

[2]Modern scripture of The Church of Jesus Christ of Latter-day Saints, translated by Joseph Smith, Jr. from an ancient record contained on gold plates given to him by the last keeper of these records anciently, the Nephite general and prophet Moroni, who appeared to Joseph Smith as an angel sent from heaven with the mission of restoring the knowledge contained in the plates to mankind in these latter days.

[3]"Sometime between the years 1818 and 1830, Antonio Lebolo, a native of Northwestern Italy's Piedmont region, received permission from Bernardino Drovetti (also a Piedmontese), to excavate in Gurneh ... [also spelled Gurna, located in western Thebes, in the Valley of the Kings, the houses of which actually penetrate the chambers of some of the tombs]. In his effort to find valuable antiquities, eleven mummies were discovered and taken out of Egypt by Lebolo." (Quotation from

James R. Harris, "The Book of Abraham Facsimiles," *Studies in Scriptures: The Pearl of Great Price,* [Salt Lake City: Randall Book Co., 1985], volume 2, page 251). According to one source, these mummies were from the end of the 18th dynasty ([given historically as] 1370-1305 B.C.). These mummies were obtained from about sixty feet below the surface and were found to be the family of Pharaoh, King of Egypt. ("Egyptian Papyri Re-discovered," *Improvement Era,* January 1968, page 14). Another source states that the discoveries were made in 1818 (Hyrum L. Andrus, *Doctrinal Commentary on the Pearl of Great Price* [Salt Lake City, Utah: Deseret Book Company, 1973, page 19]. This is more likely correct because the great discoveries in the Valley of the Kings were made between 1816 and 1818 for the most part.

Copies of the Book of the Dead vignettes (1567-1530 B.C.) with several originating during the 18th dynasty about 1567 B.C. were used to create the Joseph Smith Hypocephalus, of Facsimile No. 2 in The Book of Abraham. This literary form was peculiar to Egyptian history from 600 B.C. to Roman times. The illustration, therefore, could not have originated in its present form in the time of Abraham.

Some of the information given above is incorrect if Joseph Smith's following statement is correct. While showing a group of people the mummies then in his possession, he is reported to have said: "Why that was Pharaoh Necho, King of Egypt!" referring to one of the four mummies on display. (Josiah Quincy, *Figures of the Past* [1883], page 386) This would explain the use of the Hypocephalus of Facsimile No. 2, as Pharaoh Necho ruled from 610-595 B.C. However, the mummies being found in 1818 were not from that period, but mostly from the 18th Dynasty. Parley P. Pratt, who first published the Book of Abraham in England, stated that the papyrus scrolls were hid up with the embalmed body of the female upon whom they were found. And Joseph Smith at another time stated that they did not know who the pharaoh was, whose mummy they had in their possession. (Andrus, *op. cit.,* pages 12, 17)

"The record of Abraham and Joseph, found with the mummies is (1) beautifully written papyrus, with black, (2) a small part of red, ink or paint, and (3) in perfect preservation." (*History of the Church,* vol. 2, page 348). We will discuss in volume 2 the great significance of the family of Pharaoh wrapping scrolls around their bodies that were written by ancient prophets. It is the speculation of the author that the scroll were buried near the tomb of Aye, or Ephraim, son of Joseph, as shown later, and that the mummies in question were closely related to the patriarchal couple. In 1817 Giovanni Battista Belzoni, who had found the tomb of Pharaoh Aye in 1816, began working close to where he had made his earlier discovery. Over the next several years he found intrusive burials placed among the royal tombs, possibly the families of the priests who had taken such care of the royal dead. The discretion with which these burials were placed among the royal tombs makes it probable that they were put there by people who knew of the sacred nature of the Valley. The records that confirm portions of *The Holy Bible*, and allow for a basis upon which to build a core of historical knowledge. Unfortunately, none of these books was written to give us a clear view of history, even though they contain important historical events and settings; consequently, what is available in each must, at times, be gleaned carefully. This is even more true in apocalyptic literature and testaments. Two obvious examples that clarify history and prove the age-old question of the longevity of the pre-Flood patriarchs are obtained through the universal method. In *The Pearl of Great Price*, The Book of Moses 8:12 it states: "And Noah was four hundred and fifty years old, and begat Japheth; and forty-two years afterwards he begat Shem of her who was the mother of Japheth, and when he was five hundred years old he begat Ham." In *The Holy Bible*, The First Book of Moses, Called Genesis (hereafter simply called Genesis) 5:32 it says: "And Noah was five hundred years old: and Noah begat Shem, Ham, and Japheth."

Either the record in The Book of Moses is a new revelation of the ancient record, given in modern times to Joseph Smith, Jr., or it is not. Therein lies the basis of the eternal formula. The other example is in regard to the age of Enoch as explained in the footnote to the chart "The Patriarchs from Adam to Abraham," given on pages 15-18 below. It is accepted, based on this universal formula for establishing the accuracy of evidence, that *The Holy Bible* and the other books mentioned, contain actual genealogies of real people, even though they have been recorded with errors from time to time, and some generations have been left out knowingly. A professional review of the facts, based on analysis, and comparison, as well as use of the

---

description of the Lebolo discovery, and the conflicts that were had historically between Drovetti, his agent Lebolo, and Belzoni, suggests that after Belzoni's departure, Lebolo made claims of some of Belzoni's discoveries. The description of Lebolo's discovery fits perfectly those made by Belzoni. We must assume that the hundreds of mummies found in the burial chamber "discovered" by Lebolo, was of a religious group associated with the Akhenaten (Moses) religion discussed later in this book.

universal method,[4] which is identified in *The Book of Mormon,* The Book of Moroni 10:4-5, shows that *The Book of Mormon* is an accurate record, translated accurately, of the ancestors of some of the Native American peoples of North America and South America. It is presumed that *The Book of Jasher* is, like *The Holy Bible*, correct to a degree, as are other Pseudepigrapha or apocalyptic literature. Where these add to the genealogies or history as found in *The Holy Bible*, or other sacred literature, and where no additional secular sources are available to the contrary, and where the formula noted has been used, these genealogies have been incorporated and referenced, as have some of the key historical facts contained in them. It is also presumed that oral genealogies found in the various cultures of the world are basically accurate because of the care with which they were memorized, transmitted, and later recorded. However, some of them have dramatic errors that have been identified and will be duly noted in the process of compiling this work.

Another premise that must be entertained by this conservative approach to history, if we are to accept to the extent possible some of the findings of the archeologists, is that even though all land life was destroyed by the Flood,[5] and the face of the world was dramatically changed in many places, in others there was little cataclysmic activity by comparison. Much of the life of the sea continued to exist despite the destruction of billions of fish and other sea creatures, as will be shown hereafter. Some artifacts and archeological discoveries undoubtedly pertain to civilizations that antedate the Flood, having withstood it because of the nature of their construction, and because of the minimal cataclysmic activity in that particular area of the world. For example, Flood deposits and

---

[4]"And when ye shall receive these things, I would exhort you that ye would ask God, the Eternal Father, in the name of Christ, if these things are not true; and if ye shall ask with a sincere heart, with real intent, having faith in Christ, he will manifest the truth of it unto you, by the power of the Holy Ghost. And by the power of the Holy Ghost ye may know the truth of all things."

[5]Genesis 8:21-22 says: "And all flesh died that moved upon the earth, both of fowl, and of cattle, and of beast, and of every creeping thing that creepeth upon the earth, and every man: all *in whose nostrils was the breath of life, of all that was in the dry land, died*. (emphasis added)

damage exist in Egypt which prove that the ancient pyramids and the Giza sphinx antedate the Flood. This is possible because there was less turmoil in Egypt when compared to other areas, such as off the coast of India where some sedimentary deposits are 60,000 feet thick. Civilizations, particularly Ebla, Sumer, Northwest India (Harappa/Mohenjo Daro) and Egypt appear to have been in existence prior to the Flood and were reinstituted within less than a generation on their original sites. Mankind quickly picked up its old ways and traditions. Many records and much knowledge was undoubtedly preserved by Noah and his family on the ark, and possibly - knowing the Flood was imminent - in buried vaults and tombs on earth. It is also obvious from the discoveries that have been made that not all pre-Flood artifacts were totally destroyed even if not purposefully preserved.

Although great civilizations like Atlantis were lost except in myth, and much of the history of the development of mankind relegated to tribal memories, great similarities and truths are emerging to piece together what happened. Whether Atlantis was on the Minoan islands in the Mediterranean (Crete and surrounding islands), or whether it was the City of Enoch, or the City of Zion, that was taken into heaven, or whether it was a city-state on an island in the Atlantic that became so corrupt that it was destroyed in the Flood, may not be known for some time. There will be no attempt to try and reconstruct what happened to Atlantis in this study except for appropriate references under the Minoan civilization.[6] Civilizations such as Pison, Havilah, Gihon, Ethiopia, Hiddekel, Assyria, Euphrates, Nod, Shulon,

---

[6]Possibly Atlantis is that land referred to in *The Pearl of Great Price*, The Book of Moses 7:12-15 where it talks of the battles Enoch and the righteous had against the wicked. Because of the faith of Enoch he was able to cause the earth to tremble, mountains to flee, rivers to be turned out of their courses. "There also came up a land out of the depth of the sea, and so great was the fear of the enemies of the people of God, that they fled and stood afar off and went upon the land which came up out of the depth of the sea. And the giants of the land, also, stood afar off; and there went forth a curse upon all people that fought against God." For this reference in the writings of Enoch to refer to the Minoan islands, it would need to be proved that the archeological remains now being uncovered, do not date prior to 3300 B.C. For it to refer to any other discoveries they must fit the same criteria.

Mahujah, Simeon, Sharon, Omner, Heni, Haner, and Hanannihah[7] have passed from history. Several of these may be renamed as Ebla, Sumer, Harappa/Mohenjo Daro, and Egypt, but this may never be known.

Where no other primary documentation, or circumstantial evidence, is available, religious records and tribal traditions will stand as guides against which later discoveries, decipherments, and translations can be measured. For example, it is obvious to the author that the breakthroughs in the 1980's in reading Mayan glyphs only substantiate what has been known all along by those who have studied the naming structures in *The Book of Mormon*: the Maya are a mixture of Jaredite/Nephite/Lamanite ancestries, these being names of tribes found within *The Book of Mormon*. They have common roots, with a similar writing system, to the Egyptians. Proof of these similarities will be forthcoming in this study. It is also obvious that the world at the time of the Tower of Babel was filled with millions of people, and that they had dispersed by that time from the Mesopotamian Valley, taking with them their languages, which with modern linguistic studies, are proving to have a common origin in most cases. These commonalities and differences will be used to show the way in which some of these early divisions of mankind came about.

There has been no attempt to record all individuals of ancient civilizations in this initial volume, clearly an impossibility - but rather to begin to compile a core of data for each century of the history of the world. In this core data, only a historical overview of the period will be attempted, briefly mentioning the principals involved in that era. Subsequent volumes will include biographical and genealogical information on all of the individuals that have been identified.

A systematic study of the families of the world shows that most lineages do not perpetuate themselves. It is, undoubtedly, for this reason that the blessing given by Jehovah to Abraham was such a great one. His posterity would continue to the ends of the earth. In any given generation there will be those recorded for whom there are no living descendants, however, as certain branches of their lineage

---

[7]*The Pearl of Great Price*, The Book of Moses 3:7,11; 5:41; 6:17; 7:2, 9.

die out. For others there will be millions of descendants. Each individual, however, is considered equally for purposes of documenting their existence. The desired result of this study is to compile a reference that can be used with a fair degree of certainty as a standard, the documentation for any given pedigree being as accurate and complete as exists. The concern here is not that a pedigree is only one generation long (a misnomer), but that an individual is able to be placed in an accurate spot in history, where they can be found when further information is available; where they can be linked to parents; and to descendants if they had any. For the period prior to the birth of Jesus Christ, which will be the focus of the first volumes of this work, there is great uncertainty in which century some individuals lived. What is known will be documented, what is supposed will be theorized, and what is not known will be obvious. Every effort will be made to correlate the information so that the proper time frames are maintained.

Place names, and individual names have been translated, and their various language spellings recorded, where known, and where appropriate. No attempt has been made to push all of the world's history into a modern interpretation of places and dates. Most records have been documented using the standard practice of the time, if possible, or an acceptable conversion of the same when necessary, or a combination of both. Where a known location has no known past jurisdictions, modern equivalents have been placed in brackets; where both are known, both are included. For example, The Garden of Eden's full description is The Garden of Eden, [Jackson County], Land of Shulon [Missouri], The United States of America.[8] These type of notations will be made primarily in volumes

---

[8]There are several references of importance to this fact. James E. Talmage in *A Study of the Articles of Faith* (Salt Lake City: Deseret Book Co., 1984), page 427 says: "Though there is no uniform belief among Christian scholars as to the geographical location of Eden, the majority claim that it was in Persia. The Latter-day Saints have more exact knowledge on the matter, a revelation having been given through Joseph Smith, at Spring Hill, Missouri, May 19, 1838, in which that place is named by the Lord 'Adam-ondi-Ahman, because, said he, it is the place where Adam shall come to visit his people, or the Ancient of Days shall sit, as spoken of by Daniel the prophet.' (D&C [*The Doctrine and Covenants*, hereafter sometimes called D&C], Section 116). From another revelation we learn (D&C 107:52-53) that three years

two and beyond.

Historical events and settings, descriptions of kingdoms and principalities, man's development and spread throughout the world, the rising and ebbing of generations and peoples, is what this collection is about. It has been compiled within the limitations of modern knowledge. If errors exist, it is expected that further studies and probing of the past will uncover things as they really were in the genealogy of mankind.

---

before his death, Adam called together in the valley of Adam-ondi-Ahman those of his sons who had been made high priests, together with the rest of his righteous posterity, and there bestowed upon them his patriarchal blessings." In the book by Alvin R. Dyer entitled *The Refiner's Fire* (Salt Lake City: Deseret Book Co., 1976), page 115, he quotes from the *Historical Record* of Andrew Jensen, Church Historian, referencing an article that appeared in volume 27 of the *Juvenile Instructor* which says: "From the Lord, Joseph learned that Adam dwelt on the land of America, and that the Garden of Eden was located where Jackson County now is." Quoting further from *Life of John D. Lee,* page 91, Dyer records: "Adam-ondi-Ahman was at the point where Adam came and settled and blessed his posterity after being driven from the Garden of Eden. This was revealed through Joseph Smith the Prophet. The Temple Block in Jackson County, Missouri, stands on the identical spot where once stood the Garden of Eden. When Adam and Eve were driven from the Garden they traveled in a northeasterly course until they came to a valley on the east side of the Grand River [about ninety miles from where they began].

THE DEVELOPMENT OF WORLD CULTURES

ESTABLISHING AN ACCURATE VIEW OF WORLD HISTORY

There has been a great deal of research done in the last fifty years regarding the true age of the earth and many proofs have come forth through archeological finds, written records, and tribal traditions showing that the theoretical basis of evolution and the aeons of natural history simply are dramatic miscalculations. In the following pages, the author feels it necessary to show sufficient proof of the earth's real history so that the basis for developing a history of the world's cultures can be founded on a solid footing, and so that the people identified in history can be accurately placed within their generations. Much can be gained from the archeological profession. Archeologists are tireless, exacting analyzers of minute pieces of information, the smallest shard, and they are trained in proper scientific methods for documentation. However, because most of them accept the theory of the evolutionary development of mankind, in direct opposition to the scientific approach to which they are supposed to adhere, their concept of time cannot be taken seriously, and it tends to distort many of their conclusions. The evolutionary theory as it pertains to time will necessarily be disproved within the context of this study.

Because of the errors that are contained in *The Holy Bible* regarding some of the generations recorded there and their uncertain connections to previous generations, an outline as contained in *The Holy Bible,* Genesis (Gn.), and a parallel outline as contained in *The Pearl of Great Price,* The Book of Moses (PG) are given here for reference. The first universal, empirical premise upon which the study contained herein is built is that this earth, since the Fall of Adam, has passed through nearly 6,000 years of temporal existence. According to the divine plan, the earth will have a mortal or temporal existence of seven millennia, or of 7,000 years.[9] In 1998 supposedly will have arrived at the completion of the first 6,000-year period.

---

[9]Bruce R. McConkie, *Mormon Doctrine* 2nd ed. (Salt Lake City, Utah: Bookcraft, 1966), page 492.

This will be documented and further explained in the sections "Establishing the Birth Year of Jesus Christ," and "Summary."

It is theorized, therefore, based on religious history, that Adam was driven from the Garden of Eden in 4002 B.C. How long he was in the Garden prior to that time is irrelevant to this study. No children were born during that time and no death existed on the earth. The expulsion from the Garden brought about the temporal world as we know it, with death, decay, procreation and the multiplication of the species.

An additional reference as to the age at which each of the patriarchs was ordained to the holy priesthood is important as historical proof of their existence, given that some do not believe that they were even real people. This will also establish that these patriarchs were fathers and sons and that there are no missing generations in this patriarchal succession between Adam and Noah. This information is found in *The Doctrine & Covenants*, Section 107 and constitutes knowledge revealed to the Prophet Joseph Smith about these patriarchs between the years of 1831 and 1835. The verse is given after the age of each, thereby saving space and confusion in the Reference section for the other pieces of information. The abbreviation B/D represents Birth/Death; those used in the Ordination Age column are: **y** for year; **mo** for month; and **d** for day.

THE PATRIARCHS FROM ADAM TO ABRAHAM

Patriarch	Bible B/D	Death Age	PGP B/D	Ord. Age	Death Age	Reference
Adam	4002-3072	930	4002-3072	not given	930	Gn. 5:2-5 PG 6:10-11
Seth	3872-2960	912	3872-2960	69 y (v. 42)	912	Gn. 4:3-8 PG 6:10-16
Enos	3767-2862	905	3767-2862	134 y 4 mo (v. 44)	905	Gn. 5:6-11 PG 6:13-18
Cainan	3677-2767	910	3677-2767	87 y (v. 45)	910	Gn. 5:9-14 PG 6:17-19
Mahalaleel	3607-2712	895	3607-2712	496 y 7 d (v. 46)	895	Gn. 5:12-17 PG 6:19-20
Jared	3542-2580	962	3562-2580	200 y (v. 47)	962	Gn. 5:15-20 PG 6:20-24
Enoch	3380-3015[10]	365	3380-2950	25 y (v. 48)	430	Gn. 5:19-24 PG 6:21; 7
Methuselah	3315-2346	969	3315-2346	100 y (v. 50)	969	Gn. 5:21-27 PG 6:25; 8:5-7

[10]This is not a death date, but rather the year in which Enoch was translated according to *The Holy Bible*: "And all the days of Enoch were three hundred sixty and five years: And Enoch walked with God: and he was not; for God took him." (Genesis 5:23-24). The record in *The Pearl of Great Price*, The Book of Moses, differs in this regard: "And all the days of Zion, in the days of Enoch, were three hundred and sixty-five years. And Enoch and all his people walked with God, and he dwelt in the midst of Zion; and it came to pass that Zion was not, for God received it up into his own bosom; and from thence went forth the saying, Zion is Fled. And all the days of Enoch were four hundred and thirty years." (Moses 7:68-69; 8:1) This is confirmed in another way in *The Doctrine and Covenants*, section 107, verse 49: "And he saw the Lord, and he walked with him, and was before his face continually; and he walked with God three hundred and sixty-five years, making him four hundred and thirty years old when he was translated."

Patriarch	Bible B/D	Death Age	PGP B/D	Ord. Age	Death Age	Reference
Lamech	3128-2351	777	3128-2351	32 y (v.51)	777	Gn. 5:25-31 PG 8:5-11
Noah	2946-1996	950	2946-	10 y (v. 52)	not given	Gn. 5:28-32; 9:28-29; PG 8:8-12
Shem	2454-1844	610	not given	not given	not given	Gn. 5:32[11]; 11:10-11; PG 8:12
Arphaxad	2344-1906	438	not given	not given	not given	Gn. 11:10-13
Salah	2309-1876	433	not given	not given	not given	Gn. 11:13-15
Eber	2279-1815	464	not given	not given	not given	Gn. 11:14-17
Peleg	2245-2006	239	not given	not given	not given	Gn. 11:16-19
Reu	2215-1976	239	not given	not given	not given	Gn. 11:18-21
Serug	2183-1953	230	not given	not given	not given	Gn. 11:20-23

[11]The statement in Genesis 5:32 "And Noah was five hundred years old; and Noah begat Shem, Ham, and Japheth" is not to be taken literally, except that Noah was 500 years old at the time that his son Ham was born, Ham being the youngest of the three. The Book of Moses 8:12 states: "And Noah was four hundred and fifty years old, and begat Japheth; and forty-two years afterward began Shem of her who was the mother of Japheth, and when he was five hundred years old he began Ham." [Silence on the matter supposes that Ham had another mother.] Also, the statement in Genesis 11:10 that Shem was 100 when he became the father of Arphaxad is incorrect. The same relationship exists between this statement and the one just clarified. Shem was actually 110 when he had Arphaxad in the year 2344, two years after the beginning of the Flood, or in the year after the Flood abated and they left the ark.

Patriarch	Bible B/D	Death Age	PGP B/D	Ord. Age	Death Age	Reference
Nahor	2153-2005[12]	148	not given	not given	not given	Gn. 11:22-25
Terah	2124-1910[13]	205	not given	not given	not given	Ge. 11:24-32
Abraham	2061-1886[14]	175	not given	not given	not given	Gn 11:26; Gn 25:7

In the *Book of Jasher* 13:9, it says: "At that time, at the end of three years of Abram's dwelling in the land of Canaan, in that year Noah died, which was the fifty-eighth year of the life of Abram; and all the

---

[12]We might assume, given the proximity of Nahor's death to the time of the Tower of Babel, that he may have died as a result of the drought and famine that was present in Mesopotamia at that time. By all accounts he was a wicked man. His death, within a year of that of Peleg, and the death of Noah within ten years of their deaths may point to the natural disasters of that era.

[13]According to the Samaritan Pentateuch, Terah died at age 145 (1979 B.C. according to our chronology). In the Acts of the Apostles 7:4 it says: "Then came he [Abraham] out of the land of the Chaldæans, and dwelt in Charran: and from thence, when his father was dead, he removed him into this land, wherein ye now dwell." If Terah died in Haran at the age of 145 and Abraham left Haran at age 62 (Book of Abraham 2:12 in his own words) or in 1999 by our chronology, then Terah was still alive. He lived even longer, to age 205, if *The Holy Bible* is correct. The only reference to Terah in *The Pearl of Great Price*, The Book of Abraham 2:5-6 says: "And the famine abated; and my father tarried in Haran and dwelt there, as there were many flocks in Haran; and my father turned again unto his idolatry, there he continue in Haran. But, I, Abraham, and Lot, my brother's son, prayed unto the Lord, and the Lord appeared unto me, and said unto me: Arise, and take Lot with thee; for I have purposed to take thee away out of Haran, and to make of thee a minister to bear my name in a strange land which I will give unto thy seed after thee for an everlasting possession, when they harken to my voice." Thus whether Terah died in 1979 or in 1910, in either case Abraham had already left Haran. Of interest in Abraham's quote is the fact that the famine had apparently been the cause of their leaving Ur, and was apparently sent by the Lord prior to the destruction of the Tower of Babel, in an attempt to get them to repent.

[14]The approximate birth year of Abraham is given as 2061 B.C., using the same criteria as in Footnote 11. His father was about 63 years of age when Abraham was born, rather than the 70 given in Genesis.

days that Noah lived were nine hundred and fifty years and he died." Noah died in the year 1996 B.C. according to the chronology calculated from the dates given in Genesis 9:29, or in 1998 according to the Bible Dictionary found in the L.D.S. version of the King James edition, page 636. If Abraham was in his fifty-eighth year when Noah died, then Abraham was born in 2053 B.C. This fact taken from the *Book of Jasher* appears incorrect or his father would have been seventy-one, which goes against the statement that he was seventy, and had by then had three sons. If Abraham was sixty-five three years after residing in Canaan when Noah died, then Abraham was born in 2061. This appears correct. He says he was sixty-two when he left Haran (in 1999). Jewish sources claim that Abraham was forty-eight when he left Ur.[15] This would have been in the year 2013 B.C., seventeen years prior to the destruction of the Tower of Babel, if it is correct. It would confirm the longevity and severity of the famine of that period which is consistent with all other facts known of the period.

It should be noted that Shem, Salah and Eber lived to a later time than did Abraham. This is highly significant insofar as the effect that they had on the growing population of the world. It is also likely that Japheth and Ham were long-lived, and would have had significant effect on their descendants, which by the time of Abraham, collectively could have totalled 33,554,432 individuals based on normal birth patterns as indicated in a later part of this study.

For the purposes of chronology in this section, the Flood year is determined from the following statements in Genesis 11:10, and in The Book of Moses 8:12. First from Genesis: "These are the generations of Shem: Shem was an hundred years old [110: see Footnote 11], and begat Arphaxad two years after the flood." Given the information from modern revelation cited above (Footnote 11) that Shem was born forty-two years after Japheth, Noah would have been 492 years old at the time, or in other words, Shem was born in the year 2454 B.C. As Arphaxad was born two years after the Flood began, when Shem was 110 years old, the Flood occurred in the

---

[15]Lisa Aaronson, *The Care & Feeding of Revision Hypotheses* (Jerusalem: Internet, 1995), page 6.

months of two successive years: 2346 and 2345 B.C., the end of the Flood coming in the year 2345 B.C. Another way the year of the Flood was determined was to add up the ages of each of the patriarchs at the time they had their successor in the patriarchal order: Adam was 130 when Seth was born, Seth was 105 when Enos was born, Enos was 90 when Cainan was born, Cainan was 70 when Mahalaleel was born, Mahalaleel was 65 when Jared was born, Methuselah was 187 when Lamech was born, Lamech was 182 when Noah was born and Noah was 600 when the Flood came. This totals 1656 years, which if subtracted from 4002 equals 2346 B.C. as the year in which the Flood began.

One final proof of when the Flood occurred is in the name "Methuselah," which, according to one source means "at his death the sending forth of waters." He died in the year of the Flood, according to the prophecy of his father Lamech as inspired by Jehovah. Another source gives the meaning of the name as "sending forth of death."[16]

[16]Unity School of Christianity, *Metaphysical Bible Dictionary* 2nd ed. (Kansas City, Missouri: Unity School of Christianity, 1942), page 446.

DISPELLING THE THEORY OF EVOLUTIONARY TIME

"For more than a century, orthodox archaeologists and evolutionists essentially have dealt with a single body of facts - facts that meet the requirements of their preconceived hypothetical framework, telling them that man of today is the result of an evolutionary process that has brought us upward both intellectually and physically from a lower order of beings. Millions of years are involved in this hypothetical view of history, and even though they cannot draw the curtain of recorded history back further than 6,000 years, they steadfastly stick to their theories, for their minds simply will not accept any other explanation for man's technological and cultural development.... [In fact, they have arrived at some of their most important conclusions using circular reasoning: the deposits in which Lucy is found are very old because Lucy is there. Lucy is old because she is found in the sedimentary deposits which have been proven to be very old.]

"For the past thirty years [written in about 1969], there has been a steadily increasing number of historical and archaeological discoveries made at various sites around the world, which, because of their mysterious and highly controversial nature, have been classified as 'out-of-place' artifacts.... They emerge from among the remains of the treasured past sans evidence of any preceding period of cultural or technological growth. In many cases, the technical sophistication of these [discoveries] extends far beyond the [supposed] inventive capabilities of the ancient peoples among whose remains they were discovered.

"There is little doubt that these artifacts are also out of place in *theory*, for in no way do they conform to what is accepted [by archaeologists, evolutionists, etc.] as a part of the development of the human race. There is simply no time slot to accommodate them.... A closer look at the strange artifacts ... suggests that [they] originated in a man-made civilization - one that antedated known [written] history - one that attained an elevated degree of development, but was destroyed to such an extent by a devastating catastrophe in the distant past that only a few remnants of its science and technology survived among the inferior cultures that succeeded it in history....

"Orthodox historians of course often disregard the significance of the historical books of the Old Testament and with them the story of the Flood and the antediluvian civilization. Yet the Genesis account of the Deluge may be the only answer to the enigma [of the recent discoveries]....

"According to the Genesis account, the antediluvian people were highly knowledgeable, being the first to develop agriculture, animal husbandry, construction, architecture, political organization, metalworking, the abstract arts, mathematics, chronology and astronomy. What's more, while the Genesis record tells us that there were altogether only ten generations of antediluvians, they developed the majority, if not all, of the basic elements of civilization by the sixth generation. Now if the antediluvians, beginning with the raw earth, were able to master the arts of civilization in the first six generations of their existence, we may well wonder to what degree they further developed and refined those arts in the remaining four prior to the Deluge....

"Over the years approximately 80,000 books pertaining to the Deluge have been written, in no less than seventy-two languages - and these are only the ones that are traceable through the card indexes of the great libraries of the world.   Many more have undoubtedly been written but never cataloged.... The famed German researcher Dr. Johannes Riem stated in the introduction to his impressive work on Flood legends, *Die Sintflut in Sage und Wissenschaft*: 'Among all traditions there is none so general, so widespread on earth, and so apt to show what may develop from the same material according to the varying spiritual character of a people as the Flood traditions. Lengthy and thorough discussions with Dr. Kunnike have convinced me of the evident correctness of his position that the fact of the Deluge is granted, because at the basis of all myths, particularly nature myths, there is a real fact, but during a subsequent period the material was given its present mythical character and form.'

"His position is one that is echoed by many other researchers. The noted nineteenth-century Scottish geologist Hugh Miller, an ardent collector of the world's most haunting traditions, writes: 'There is, however, one special tradition which seems to be more deeply impressed and more widely spread than any of the others. The destruction of well-nigh the whole human race, in an early age of the world's history, by a great deluge, appears to have impressed the minds of the few survivors, and seems to have been handed down to their children, in consequence, with such terror-struck impressiveness that their remote descendants of the present day have not even yet forgotten it. It appears in almost every mythology, and lives in the most distant countries and among the most barbarous tribes....' Yet among even these forgotten races of the human family [Indians of the Orinoco] he found the tradition of the Deluge still fresh and distinct; not confined to a single tribe, but general among the scattered nations of that great region, and intertwined with curious additions, suggestive of the inventions of classic mythology of the Old World....

"Are the common denominators in these traditions significant enough that we can regard them as different versions of the same event?

"Asia, particularly China, harbors some of the most striking Deluge traditions. For example, it is told that a tremendous flood of devastating force occurred there in approximately 2300 B.C. According to this story the flood, caused by an overflow of the great rivers, was stopped by the eventual swelling of the sea. The Chinese hero escaped the destruction, together with his wife, three sons and three daughters. But that isn't all: additional legends found on the mainland of China contend that all Chinese are direct descendants of an ancient ancestor called Nu-wah, who was known for having overcome a great flood.

"A fascinating aspect in connection with this Chinese flood story is that ancient Chinese writing contains words that can be traced *only* to 'Nu-wah' and the Flood. The Chinese word for 'righteousness,' for example, is a combination of the pictorial symbol for 'lamb' placed over the ideogram for 'myself.' Theologians tell me that this is apparently related to Noah's desire to justify himself in the eyes of his God, as shown by the burnt offering he made after disembarking from the ark.

"Dr. E. W. Thwing, a researcher who has spent many years in China investigating the Noah account, comments: 'The Chinese have records and traditions of a great flood. And it is a curious fact that the word used for *ship* as printed in Chinese books and papers today is the very ancient character, made up of the picture of a *boat* and *eight mouths*, showing that the first ship was a boat carrying eight persons.

"'In looking over some old books of ancient stories and traditions,' he continues, 'I found a story about the ancestor *Nu-wah*. Interestingly enough, *Nu* means *woman* and *wah* is *flowery*.' It seemed that the ancient one was considered to be a female ancestor. Further examination of the symbols, however, revealed two small *mouth* pictures placed *beside* the name, indicating that *not* the meaning but the *sound* of the characters was important, pointing toward a male ancestor named Nu-wah. Three legendary men then succeeded Nu-wah, and even though at various times they are referred to as heroes, sovereigns or monarchs, they bridge the gap between the Ancient One and the first three Chinese dynasties, the Hsia, the Shang and the Chou....

"The name Noah has survived for thousands of years, through a multiplicity of stories, even though ofttimes it evolved into a ... different spelling, depending on the letter symbols used. Such is the case with the Hawaiian legend of Nu-u, the Righteous Man. The island people believe that long after the creation of the world, the first man had become so wicked that his god, Kane, decided to destroy him and the earth on which he lived; but, being weary of creating, he decided to allow the one righteous man Nu-u and his family to escape his anger by building a great canoe with a house on it. Kane then instructed Nu-u to take his wife Lili Nu-u, their children and all the animals he wanted on the boat to await the great flood.

"When the rains came and the waters rose and the oceans merged, the Waa-Halau drifted for days on end, and while it drifted, all of mankind was destroyed. Finally, after leaving the rainbow as a token of his eternal forgiveness, Kane made the waters subside and told Nu-u and his three sons to repopulate the earth.

"More than thirty Flood legends have been discovered in the Orient, and the Indonesians can lay claim to possessing some of the most interesting.

"The Battaks of Sumatra say that when the earth grew old and dirty, the Creator - whom they call Debata - sent a flood to destroy every living thing. Debata was angry. The last human pair had taken refuge, not in an ark, but on the top of the highest mountain, and the waters of the deluge had already reached their knees when Debata, the Lord of all, repented of his resolution to make an end of all mankind....

"An almost limitless number and variety of universal Flood legends can be found in nearly every corner of the globe, but most significant is the fact that they all describe basically the same event.... There is almost complete agreement among them all on the three main features: 1) There was a universal destruction of the human race and all other living things by water; 2) An ark, or boat, was provided as the means of escape; 3) A seed of mankind was preserved to perpetuate the human race. To these might be added a fourth, which, though not occurring in all the traditions, occurs very frequently, namely that the wickedness of man in given as the cause of the Flood.

"Other information that is equally as important as the Flood legends and traditions is concealed in the genealogies of the antediluvian patriarchs as listed in the book of Genesis. Critics have ridiculed this list of pre-Flood giants, for the Bible ascribed fantastic lifespans to these men....

"Critics are prepared to discredit this entire section of Genesis, for they say these lifespans do not belong to the realm of possibility, but for now we are more interested in the names and the number of patriarchs than in their longevity. It seems reasonable that if the Bible story is accurate, Noah and his sons would have carried with them a fundamental knowledge of both the history and the technology that existed in the year[s] prior to the Flood, and this history would undoubtedly include the number of antediluvian 'kings' - the leaders who ruled from the beginning of their time until the moment of destruction. It is also obvious that these names, much like the history of the Deluge itself, will have experienced linguistic modifications as they passed into the different languages that developed in various parts of the world. Another point to be considered is that, depending on the value these developing nations placed on their religion, politics or social status, these early patriarchs may have been given the rank of king or god. If this is an acceptable hypothesis, history must have other lists of ten patriarchs - perhaps under other designations.

"We don't have to look far for such a list, for both the Egyptians and the Babylonians had lists of ten antediluvian kings:

BIBLICAL PATRIARCHS	EGYPTIAN GODS	CHALDEAN KINGS
Adam	Ptah	Alorus
Seth	Ra	Aloparus
Enos	Su	Almelon
Cainan	Seb	Ammenon
Mahalaleel	Osirus	Amegalarus
Jared	Set	Daonus
Enoch	Hor	Aedorachus
Methuselah	Tut	Amempsinus
Lamech	Ma	Otiartes
Noah	Hor	Xisuthros

"Whereas Noah is the hero of the Biblical Flood story, Xisuthros is the celebrated survivor of the similar Chaldean [Babylonian] account. Upon comparing the list of the prehistoric Chaldean kings with the pre-Flood patriarchs, we find a fascinating parallel that again supports our basic premise. The name of the third king, Almelon, means 'a man;' the name of the third patriarch is Enos, which means 'moral, weak mankind.' The fourth name on the Chaldean list, Ammenon, means 'craftsman;' Cainan, the name of the fourth Sethite patriarch, also means 'a craftsman.' Aedorachus, the seventh Babylonian king listed, has the connotation 'bearer of divine revelations, he to whom the secrets of heaven and earth are revealed;' Enoch, his Biblical counterpart, has a name meaning almost the same thing. The eighth king Amempsinus, is given in the original Sumerian listing as Sukarlam, a name which in part bears a resemblance to that of

Lamech, the ninth patriarch. Lastly, the tenth name, Xisuthros, according to Berosus, the high priest of the Babylonian temple Bel-Marduk, was the name of the hero who saved mankind from the terrible destruction. In the Sumerian royal lists, Xisuthros is called Utnapishtim, and following his name is written, 'After this, the Flood overwhelmed the land.' The famed Gilgamesh epic tells basically the same story, but since it was written on clay tablets several thousand years before Moses wrote the Noachian account in the book of Genesis, skeptics have often raised the question of whether Moses borrowed the facts from the Babylonians, thereby making his story a new version of the same tragedy....[This list will be treated in further detail later in this discussion.]

"The accumulated Flood legends and traditions tell a tale of a terrifying disaster, with sudden torrential rains, devastating waterspouts, and the agonized cries of drowning men and animals piercing the air. The story speaks of horrendous storms, cataclysmic earthquakes, and that terror-driven dash by man and beast to reach the safety of the ark, only to be dragged under by the relentless force of the onrushing waters.

"Outside of the great ship, man ceased to exist. Flying reptiles, towering dinosaurs and the enticing beauty of the antediluvian world perished from the face of the earth. The destruction was complete - and sudden. Today paleontologists are still puzzling over the fact that myriads of early life remains are embedded in the sprawling rock formations of the post-diluvian earth, and there simply is no way to account for them other than with the Flood story.

"The unprecedented disappearance of entire civilizations and multitudes of diverse plants and animals must have left traces which awaited their discovery by an investigative mind. But where are these traces? Combining the pertinent facts, we conclude that the Flood was undoubtedly accompanied by violent winds that first swept the turbulent waters to the lower levels of the land masses, then continued swirling upward until the peaks of the highest mountains were completely covered. It was a catastrophe that made the earth tremble and shake; never before or since has a calamity of such proportions and magnitude touched the globe on which we live. The upheaval was so terrific that today the greatest mountains on earth - the Rockies, the Andes, the Himalayas, the Alps - still bear the telltale signs of seashells and other evidence of ocean life that existed thousands of years ago. Their silent voice predates the records of... [Ebla, Egypt, and Babylon] by many years, but precisely how many years is a subject of scientific debate. Evolutionists believe there was a gap of millions of years; Deluge geologists claim it is only a matter of thousands. In any case, a global flood of this proportion unquestionably deposited vast amounts of sediment on the bottom of the newly formed water masses, and since this flood has been considered universal, it should be possible to discover remnants of such deposits at a variety of locations. *And this is exactly what's happened!* It has been scientifically estimated that over 75 per cent of the earth's surface is sedimentary in nature, with some areas having more and others less sediment. Testing has shown that while the United States has prodigious sedimentary deposits, centering in California and the Colorado plateau, India has the deepest sedimentary deposits found thus far: 60,000 feet deep!

"The evolutionist theory that slow erosion was followed by gradual accumulation over a period of millions of years hardly seems reasonable. Geologist Dr. H. G. Coffin, of the Geoscience Research Institute in Berrien Springs, Michigan, writes in his book *Creation:* 'Such processes as gradual submergence and the slow accumulation of sediments by erosion seem inadequate to account for the great quantities of water-and wind-deposited materials. Adjacent areas do not provide sufficient material for decomposition on such a scale. But a flood of sufficient extent to cover all land, and a storm of great violence that stirred roiled water or soft mud is sufficient to account for the transport of vast amounts of sedimentary material over great distances, and the filling in of depressions irrespective of the height or extent of adjacent landscapes.'

"Faced with such criticism, scientists are willing to admit - though reluctantly - that perhaps there are exceptions to their 'gradual deposit theory.' The Rockies, for example, certainly do not fit the scientists' often preposterous claims. There, well-preserved water ripple marks and a countless number of trilobite, together with other delicate fossils without signs of disintegration, are among the startling features that strongly suggest that they were laid down not in a slow and gentle manner but rather abruptly and suddenly, as if by a great and terrible catastrophe.

"Forget the mistaken idea that silence has no voice. It does. The ancient bones speak with clear voices, and prehistoric animals tell their tales from the glass enclosures of the museums; even the voices of tiny fossil shells and small vertebrates found imbedded in the rocks are forceful.

"Researcher Immanuel Velikovsky, who is highly controversial because of his unorthodox views, has examined the presence of fish in sedimentary rock, and his conclusions fully support the catastrophe theory: 'When a fish dies, its body floats on the surface or sinks to the bottom and is devoured rather quickly, actually in a matter of hours, by other fish. However, the fossil fish found in sedimentary rock is very often preserved with all its bones intact. Entire shoals of fish over large areas, numbering billions of specimens, are found in a state of agony, but with no mark of a scavenger's attack.'

"Many discoveries bear this out. It is estimated that eight hundred thousand million fish skeletons have been uncovered in the Karroo formation in South Africa.

"Geologist Hugh Miller, writing about the Devonian [a time period in the Paleozoic Era] rocks which cover most of the British Isles, comments that 'at this period in our history, some terrible catastrophe involved in sudden destruction the fish of an area at least a hundred miles from boundary to boundary, perhaps much more. The same platform in Orkney as at Cromarty is strewed thick with remains, which exhibit unequivocally the marks of violent death. The figures are contorted, contracted, curved; the tail in many instances bent around the head; the spines stick out; the fins are spread to the full as in fish that die in convulsions.' The area described by Miller is not small; it covers at least ten thousand square mile of territory bearing all the evidence of having been exposed to major destruction. Describing a spot closer to home, Harry S. Ladd of the United States Geological Survey says that 'more than a billion fish, averaging six to eight inches in length, died on four square miles of bay bottom.'

"In speaking of the disappearance of the dinosaurs, Edwin H. Colbert once remarked, 'The great extinction that wiped out all of the dinosaurs, large and small, in all parts of the world, and at the same time brought to an end various lines of reptilian evolution, was one of the outstanding events in the history of life and in the history of the earth....It was an event that has defied all attempts at a satisfactory explanation.'

"'It is as if the curtain were rung down suddenly on a stage where all the leading roles were taken by reptiles' says George Gaylord Simpson, one of the most respected men in paleontology, 'especially dinosaurs, in great number and in bewildering variety, and rose again immediately to reveal the same setting but an entirely new cast, in which the dinosaurs do not appear at all, other reptiles are mere supernumeraries and the leading parts are all played by mammals.'

"Having researched the Flood story for many years, I have files on the subject that are bulging with information about this unexplainable event. For instance, a fascinating find was made in the Geisental lignite deposits of Germany, where a mixture of plants, insects and other animals from all climatic areas of the world were found buried together in one common grave. In some cases leaves have been deposited and preserved in a fresh condition, the chlorophyll being still green, so that the 'green layer' is used as a marker during excavations. Among the insects are beautifully colored tropical beetles, with soft parts of the body, including the contents of the intestines, preserved intact. Under normal conditions such materials decay or change in color within a few hours of death, so that preservation by inclusion in an anaerobic and aseptic medium must have been sudden and complete. The same terrifying event that destroyed these inoffensive life forms also disposed of the plesiosaurs, the mesosaurs, and the other great marine reptiles. The turbulent seas were too wild, too hostile, for them to survive. Unable to escape, they joined the fate of their terrestrial brothers. Also caught in this death trap were the gigantic winged reptiles, the pterosaurs, with their 20-foot wingspans; the sky, too, made its sacrificial contribution. Only a worldwide, all-encompassing catastrophe can account for this phenomenon. There is simply no other way to explain the death of these individual species. Death took all of them

- and buried them in the deep recesses of nearly every continent on the earth....

"But there is more to the fossil world than the bones of the giants and the delicate structures of the fish. Fascinating discoveries have emerged through conscientious study of the coal deposits that lie under much of the world's visible surface. In attempting to evaluate the various factors that led to the formation of the coal beds, Dr. Coffin has uncovered some interesting facts. Limiting his comments to minable coal seams, he points out that 'the thickness of peat needed to produce one foot of coal depends on a number of factors, such as the type of peat, the amount of water in the vegetable matter, and the type of coal. The scientific literature on coal gives figures ranging from a few feet to as many as twenty. Let us assume that ten feet would be near the average figure. On this basis, a coal seam thirty feet thick would require the compression of 300 feet of peat. A 400-foot seam of coal would be the result of a fantastic 4,000 feet of peat....

"'There are few peat bogs, marshes, or swamps anywhere in the world today that reach 100 feet. Most of them are less than 50 feet. A much more reasonable alternative theory is that the vegetable matter has been concentrated and collected into an area by some force, undoubtedly water....

"'The concept of a global deluge that eroded out the forests and plant cover of the pre-Flood world, collected it in great mats of drifting debris, and eventually dropped it on the emerging land or on the sea bottom is the most reasonable answer to this problem of the great extent and uniform thickness of coal beds.'

"The big question is, *When* did this happen? The geological age theory, based on slow accumulation, obviously does not have the answer. But if we cannot account for the various phenomena as part of the geological age theory, which estimates its time periods in the millions of years, then there must be other signposts that will direct us to a time slot that is more logical and more realistic. Archaeology may have the answer - or at least credible indications leading to an acceptable answer.

"It is certain that we will never be able to determine an exact date for the great destruction, since no records have been found thus far to substantiate a historical date earlier than 3500 B.C. All other datings - some claiming that remnants of civilizations centered around Jericho should be set at approximately 5000 B.C. - become rather nebulous when exposed to scientific critique, for as yet there is no foolproof dating method. Perhaps the answer lies in ascertaining the dates for the rise of the world's great ancient cultures. The Sumerians have given us the oldest known historical texts, but even though these inscriptions take us back to 3000-3500 B.C., the origin of the authors remains a mystery. They came from somewhere, but that's all the archaeologists will agree on. Dr. Samuel Noah Kramer, research professor of Assyriology at the University of Pennsylvania says: 'The dates of Sumer's early history have always been surrounded with uncertainty, and they have not been satisfactorily settled by tests with the new method of radiocarbon dating. Be that as it may be, it seems that the people called the Sumerians did not arrive in the region until nearly 3000 B.C.'

"Egyptian history doesn't have the answer, either: 'We think that the first dynasty began not before 3400 and not much later than 3200 B.C.' says H. R. Hall, famed Egyptologist. 'A. Scharff, however, would bring the date down to about 3000 B.C., and it must be admitted that his arguments are good and that at any rate it is more probable that the date of the First Dynasty is later than 3400 B.C. than earlier.' [The author agrees that there were pre-Flood dynasties among the Egyptians, thereby placing their history earlier than any other nation. The reason for this is noted below (page 46): Egyptus, the discoverer of Egypt after the Flood found what she was seeking.]

"The Chinese have set 2250 B.C. as the beginning date for their history, while traditional Bible chronology estimates 2448 B.C. as the year for the Flood occurrence [not according to the author's basic mathematical calculations - see the chronology above, which shows 2346-2345 B.C.; the Chinese may be exactly right as to when their civilization started]. All dates are approximate, as they have been derived by archaeologists with varying backgrounds. True, the modern carbon-dating methods have been a notable help when probing into the dust of the ages, but all the so-called final dates are still the result of assumptions and assertions, especially when we approach the 3500-3000 B.C. mark. [Part of the problem with the carbon-dating method is the minimum variable of 10-20% error with even the simplest, modern materials. It is highly inaccurate the older the materials get.] The civilizations we encounter prior to those years present considerable mystery as to their origin. I recall from my studies in Egyptology that even the origin of the Egyptian *Book of the Dead* remains obscure. E. A. Wallis Budge comments in *The Book of the Dead: Papyrus of Ani:* 'The evidence derived from the enormous mass of new material which we owe to the all-important discoveries of the mastabah tombs and pyramids by M. Maspero, and to his publications of the early religious texts, proves beyond all doubt that all the essential texts comprised in the *Book of the Dead* are, in one form or another, far older than the period of Mena (Menes), the first historical king of Egypt. Certain sections, indeed, appear to belong to the pre-dynastic period.

'"The earliest texts bear within themselves proof not only of having been composed, but also of having been revised, or edited, long before the copies known to us were made, and, judging from many passages in the copies inscribed in hieroglyphics upon the pyramids of Unas (the last king of the Fifth Dynasty...), and Teta, Pepi I, Mehti-em-sa-t, and Pepi II (kings of the Sixth Dynasty...), it would seem even at that remote date, the scribes were perplexed and hardly understood the texts which they had before them.... To fix a chronological limit for the arts and civilization of Egypt,' he concludes, 'is absolutely impossible....' [Modern discoveries prove overlapping dynasties where it has previously been thought they were consecutive. The most dramatic case at the time is found in the burial chambers at Tanis of Psusennes of the 21st Dynasty and Osorkon of the 22nd Dynasty. The tomb of Psusennes has large stones cut to fit into the structure of the tomb of Osorkon, showing it post-dated Osorkon's death. Thus Psusennes of the 21st Dynasty died after Osorkon of the 22nd Dynasty, thereby altering the chronology of these and all previous dynasties by up to 200 years.]

"On returning to the United States from my second Noah's Ark Expedition in late 1960, one of our team members, Professor Arthur J. Brandenberger, professor of photogrammetry at Ohio State

University, received a curious letter from George F. Dodwell, retired government astronomer and director of the Adelaide Observatory in South Australia. Fascinated by our expedition into eastern Turkey to find the remains of the legendary ark on Mount Ararat, he shared with us an intriguing bit of information. He wrote: 'I am especially interested in such a remarkable result, because I have been making during the last 26 years an extensive investigation of what we know in astronomy as the secular variation of the obliquity of the ecliptic, and from a story of the available ancient observations of the position of the sun at the solstices during the last three thousand years, I find a curve which, after allowing for all known changes, shows a typical exponential curve of recovery of the earth's axis after a sudden change from a former nearly vertical position to an inclination of 26½ degrees, from which it was returned to an equilibrium at the present inclination of 23½ degrees, during the interval of the succeeding 3,194 years to A.D. 1850.

"'The date of the change in the earth's axis, 2345 B.C.,' he continued, 'is none other than that of the flood recorded in the Bible, and the resulting conclusion is the Biblical account of the flood as a universal one, together with its story of Noah's Ark, is historically true'"[17] If Mr. Dodwell has found an astronomical truth coinciding with the year of the Flood (2346-2345 B.C.) he may also have found the explanation for the ice age, for the physical cause of the Flood (something pulling the earth off its normal axis) and the reason why the post-Flood family was so anxious to understand what had happened, sending exploring parties to the ends of the earth, as proved by the pre-ice cap mapping of Antartica and other places in ways impossible except recently with sophisticated technology. These maps have survived and provide interesting proof of Noah's and his son's great knowledge in many areas of learning.

"Even with the chronological information available...it may come as a surprise to realize that it is extremely difficult to fix true or absolute dates in Egyptian chronology. Most of the information given in the

---

[17]Rene Noorbergen and Joey R. Jochmans, *Secrets of the Lost Races: New Discoveries of Advanced Technology in Ancient Civilizations* (New York: Barnes & Noble Books, 1969), selected quotations from pages 1-21.

inscriptions mentioned is relative, in that it shows a sequence of kings relative to each other with sometimes a length of time between each reign, but to fix them in an absolute framework is a different matter altogether. Absolute dates from ancient Egypt rely on astronomical dating. This is done by reference to the civil and astronomical calendars in a complicated calculation involving the Sothic cycle of 1460 years, based on the heliacal rising of Sirius, or Sothis, the 'dog star'. The ancient Egyptians knew that the year consisted of 365 days, but they made no adjustment for the additional quarter of a day each year - as we do with Leap Year every four years at the end of February. Hence their civil and astronomical calendars were gradually moving out of synchronization and could bring about extremes of dating between the two. Eventually, every 1460 years, the two calendars coincided and were correct for a short time, until they gradually became out of step again until the end of the next cycle.

"The heliacal rising of Sirius was, ideally, supposed to coincide with New Year's Day in the civil calendar, but did so only every 1460 years. The 3rd-century AD grammarian Censorinus records that in AD 139 the first day of the Egyptian civil year and the heliacal rising of Sirius did actually coincide - this being the end of a Sothic cycle."[18]

Chaim Bermant and Michael Weitzman state, regarding the problem faced by all of us as pertains to chronology: "Only a few absolute dates exist for Mesopotamia and Egypt and these, on closer examination, are not all that absolute. All of them are derived from astronomical data. In the case of Mesopotamia, for example, we have lists of Assyrian state officials who gave their names to the years in the first half of the first millennium B.C. In one such list there is a reference to a solar eclipse which we know took place about 763 B.C., during the year of one Bur-Sagale, from which it is possible to calculate with fair precision when the other officials and their contemporaries lived. Similarly we have Egyptian lists giving the names of various kings and how long they reigned, and we also have a text which records that on a particular date during the seventh year

---

[18]Peter A. Clayton, *Chronicle of the Pharaohs: The Reign-by-Reign Record of the Rulers and Dynasties of Ancient Egypt* (London: Thames and Hudson Ltd., 1994), pages 12-13.

of the reign of Sesostris III (of the twelfth Egyptian dynasty) the star Sirius rose at the same time as the sun.

"Now the Egyptian civil year consisted invariably of three hundred and sixty-five days, and, as there were no leap years, it steadily fell behind the progress of the seasons. Because of this lag, the occurrence of that astronomical event on the given date is rare, but the year in which it took place has been identified by calculation as (most probably) 1872 B.C. Hence it is possible to date the reign of Sesotris, as well, of course, as his successors and predecessors. These dates also provide fixed points to which other data are tethered and which in turn are used to calculate the chronology of other data still, so that anyone writing on the ancient Near East is like an Alpinist tethered to a whole line of climbers at the head of which (he hopes) there is one with his pick firmly anchored in rock. Unhappily the fixed points provided even by astronomers are not all that firm and from time to time whole chains of carefully calculated data slither into oblivion.

"Another difficulty is that in the absence of corroborative evidence from external sources one cannot always separate history from myth. In the case of Mesopotamia, for example, much speculation which was built on a list of kings which purported to have been drawn up in order of succession, had to be drastically revised when many of the kings were found to be contemporaries. All facts are tentative, but none are quite as tentative as those divulged by archaeology, and the further one goes back the more tentative they become."[19]

Returning to the archeological point of view for a few paragraphs, there is within their own arguments some possible proof against their arguments. From the book just quoted by Chaim Bermant and Michael Weitzman, same notation: "The Flood is placed by the biblical chronology in the late third millennium BC, but excavations at many sites outside Mesopotamia have reached down to a much earlier age (estimated, for example, as 8000 BC at Jericho or 6000 BC at Mersin in southern Turkey) without finding any trace of a universal

---

[19]Chaim Bermant and Michael Weitzman, *Ebla: A Revelation in Archaeology* (New York City: Times Books, 1979), 59-63.

deluge." [Does this, perhaps, indicate that their dating is off, and that the lack of sediment is proof that these civilizations are post-Flood only? Or was all the sediment of this area washed into the deeper areas of the proximate oceans, as in the case of the huge deposits in India?] At Ur in 1929, Sir Leonard Woolley made his famous discovery of a stratum of mud some ten feet thick at a level dating to the Ubiad period (usually dated to the last centuries of the fifth millennium...), and many saw this as proof of Noah's Flood. Excavations elsewhere, however, have offered little confirmation. At Ur itself Woolley apparently dug five pits down through the early levels of occupation and found 'flood deposits' in only two, though a level of mud and river sand some six feet thick found at Nineveh may belong to the same period. But at other sites, though 'flood layers' have occasionally been found, these prove to belong to a different age and most sites (including Ubaid, only four miles from Ur, and excavated down to the level of the Ur 'flood layer' by Woolley himself) have yielded none at all. All these 'floods' must have been more or less localized, requiring no more dramatic explanation than that the Euphrates had burst its banks.

Immanuel Velikovsky documented mythological and geophysical evidence of a worldwide flood occurring 3,500 years ago.[20] He also spoke of earlier catastrophes that produced immense global floods; such floods would have left distinctive evidence. The basic uniformitarian argument is that the great floods were unique events caused by ice-dammed lakes unleashed when the ice dams broke. This theory is impossible to prove because if localized floods occurred repeatedly during the last Ice Age, they would have washed away the whale fossils found on or near the earth surface. However, whale bones and other marine fossils have been found far inland, without having been either destroyed or eroded down to tiny fragments. This strongly supports the global flood hypothesis and contradicts the local flood theory. This evidence fully supports Velikovsky's hypothesis.

A global flood would have dramatic effects on the world, the

---

[20]Immanuel Velikovsky, *Worlds in Collision* (Garden City, New York: Doubleday, 1950), pages 148-152; *Earth in Upheaval* (Garden City, New York: Doubleday, 1955), pages 46-49.

continents, and on all life. For example, if the earth's axis tilted or the crust suddenly, violently, moved over the mantle, then the oceans would move en masse, as immense tidal waves, away from the equator and toward the poles. On the rotating earth, due to the coriolis force, these tide waves would move not only north and south but also counterclockwise in the northern hemisphere and clockwise in the southern hemisphere. Since the Pacific Ocean lies between the continents of North America and Asia in the northern hemisphere, and the continental coastlines form an inverted V (/ \) with its apex at the Bering Strait, the tidewater would veer east, over Alaska and Canada, and west, over Asia. In the Atlantic Ocean, the tidewater would flow more easily near the poles, covering a larger area; this would create smaller continental floods. Any icecaps in these regions would be swept away from their landlocked moorings out into the northern Atlantic Ocean and would break up, depositing large amounts of detritus on the sea bed. Since neither eastern Siberia nor Alaska were covered by such a continental ice sheet, minute amounts of glacial detritus should have been deposited in the Pacific Ocean compared to that laid down in the Atlantic Ocean.

The tidal waves flowing over the northern ice sheets would flow south and, in a return flood, where they swept back onto the continental surfaces, would produce stunning evidence of their rampage over the land: signs of violent flood erosion. Wherever mountains formed basins, these regions would fill up, forming immense lakes that would discharge their water, through passes, into rivers which would carve deep channels and leave ghost shorelines at higher elevations.[21]

This has already been confirmed by geological observation. According to Reginald Daly: "Beaches, all over the world, have been raised by forces shoving up from below. At each place the receding waters left an abandoned beach line, the raised beach theory postulates a local uplift. This theory requires uplifts, not only around all the world's oceans, but around all the world's lakes, and also along the banks of all (or almost all) the world's rivers; for there are raised terraces along the banks of all major rivers and abandoned shorelines

---

[21]Charles Ginenthal, *The Flood* (manuscript: Internet, 16 March 1995), pages 1-2.

around the world's lakes....Often the highest terraces of such rivers as the Seine or [the] Elbe, when followed down to the mouth, are seen to blend with old shorelines which border the oceans at levels considerably higher than [those of] the present beaches. This blending of river terraces with ocean shorelines established the fact that the general recession of water levels is a worldwide phenomenon common to both rivers and oceans, which cannot be reasonably attributed to a multiplicity of local uplifts."[22]

This evidence indicates that nearly all the lakes, drainage basins and rivers had greater reservoirs of water which flowed back to the ocean recently, leaving a worldwide system of relic beaches as evidence of this flood. If these flood beaches were ancient, they would have been eroded away. Most of the ocean would have flowed over the icecaps and back to the sea. The icecap would have been swept southward to lower latitudes and would have melted within a few years. The remaining ocean water would drain away as the melting glaciers produced immense runoff in the wake. Sea water would only be kept in extremely large collecting regions without outlets, such as the Caspian Sea in Asia or the former Lake Bonneville/Lake Lahontan in the Great Basin of the Western United States. Small lakes would then be diluted by the freshwater that melted from the residual icecaps.

Most of the detritus carried by the water would have been left as a ring in, near and around the polar regions as a heavy silt or mulch, containing material such as trees or animals that were swept off the continents. The flowback material would have contained mostly the lightest silts, which would form a second ring-like or annulus-like deposit containing additional animals and trees. Forests would be swept away and buried. The water would then flow into and down river valleys, leaving masses of this secondary silt in its wake. In regions where mountain ranges obstructed the return flow of water, the secondary silt would build up as the water slowed and dropped its load.

---

[22]Reginald A. Daly, "Rise and Fall of Floodwaters-Historical Record," *Earth's Most Challenging Mysteries* (1975): page 117.

All of this rampaging flood violence would have occurred in a very short time. To the human survivors of this deluge, it would have appeared as if the ground had opened up to a subsurface ocean pouring out of the Earth and inundating the land. If the continents were flooded, then the remaining water filling up all basins would have to be discharged. The ground water level would have risen. A stunning example of this flood-ground water relationship is found in Egypt. The evidence for such a flood is clear. If such an oceanic flood poured onto the African continent, it would have left clear traces and would have raised the ground water level immediately. Over hundreds of years, the ground water level would fall. This has been documented. In 1988, Joseph Davidovits and Margie Morris reported the following:

"Geological studies of the Sphinx have kindled more than debate over [its] attribution and age. The established history of the evolution of civilization has been challenged."[23]   The facts cannot be lightly disregarded although they are certainly subject to misinterpretation.

A study of the severe body erosion of the Sphinx and the hollow in which it is situated indicates that the damaging agent was water. A slow erosion occurs in limestone when water is absorbed and reacts with salts in the stone. The controversy arises over the source of the vast amount of water responsible.

Two theories are popular. One is that ground water slowly rose into the body of the Sphinx. This theory produces irreconcilable problems: A recent survey carried out by the American Research Center in Egypt (ARCE) determined that three distinctly separate repair operations were completed on the Sphinx between the New Kingdom and Ptolemaic rule, that is, during a period of roughly 700 to 1,000 years. The study also indicates that the Sphinx was already in its current state of erosion when these early repairs where made. No appreciable erosion has occurred since the original damage, nor is there further damage on the bedrock of the surrounding hollow, an area that never underwent repair.

---

[23]Joseph Davidovits and Margie Morris, *The Pyramids: An Enigma Solved* (New York: Hippocrene Books, 1988), pages 21-22.

Knowing this, one must consider that the inundating Nile slowly built up levels of silt over the millennia, and this was accompanied by a gradual rise in the water table. During Khafra's time, the water table was about [30] feet lower than it is today. For the rising ground water theory to hold, an unbelievable geological scenario would have to have taken place. It would mean that from [30] feet lower than today's water table, water rose to about two feet into the body of the Sphinx and the surrounding hollow, where it caused erosion for roughly 600 years, and then stopped its damaging effects.

Historians find the second theory offered more unthinkable. It suggests that the source of water stemmed from the wet phases of the last Ice Age, which they estimate at about 15000 to 10000 B.C. - when Egypt underwent periods of severe flooding. This hypothesis advocates that the Sphinx necessarily existed before the flood. The world's most mysterious sculpture dates to a time when historians place humanity in a Neolithic setting, living in open camps and depending largely on hunting and foraging.[24]

There is further evidence of the Sphinx and the Flood that has been preserved as an old Egyptian story about young prince Tuthmosis IV, who was hunting in his chariot near the pyramids. "At noon, when the sun was at its highest, he rested in the shadow of the Sphinx and fell asleep. The gigantic Sphinx was at that time more than **half buried**, with only its head visible above the sand. In his sleep, the prince had a vision in which he was addressed by Harmakhis, the sun-god with whom the Sphinx was identified, who said: 'Behold me, gaze on me, O my son Tuthmosis, for I, thy father Harmakhis-Khopri-Tumu, grant thee sovereignty over the Two Lands, in the South and the North, and thou shalt wear both the white and the red crowns of the throne of Sibu, the sovereign possessing the earth in its length and breadth. The flashing eye of the lord of all shall cause to rain on thee the possessions of Egypt. Vast tribute from all foreign countries, and a long life for many years as one chosen by the Sun, for my countenance is thine, my heart is thine, no other than thyself is mine. Now I am covered by the sand of the mountain on which I rest, and have given thee this prize that thou mayest do for me what my heart

---

[24]*Ibid.*

desires, for I know thou art my son, my defender; draw nigh, I am with thee, I am thy well-beloved father.' The prince took this encounter as a covenant between him and the god: he will inherit the kingdom if he clears the sand from the Sphinx. Immediately upon his accession to the throne, Tuthmosis IV hastened to fulfil his part of the covenant and, in order to preserve the memory of his action, recorded its details on a stele that is still to be found against the breast of the Sphinx between its forelegs."[25]

Richard C. Hoagland has discussed the Sphinx and John A. West's analysis of the evidence for its geological age in his recent book: "On researching a book in the mid-seventies about the philosophies and cosmologies of Ancient Egypt, West came upon a comment from another scholar, R. A. Schwaller de Lubicz: 'The Great Sphinx shows evidence of severe water erosion...' To which West internally responded with the obvious question: 'In a desert?!'

"West's curiosity, prompted by de Lubicz' casual reference to the 'anomalous erosion' of the Sphinx, was based on the following hard facts: To create 'severe water erosion' on the Sphinx, the Sahara Desert must at one time **not** have been a desert. Readily available climatological data for Ancient Egypt make it abundantly clear that the Sahara has been in place from [7 to 10,000 years]...since the end of the last Ice Age. Meaning that both the carving of the Sphinx and its 'severe water erosion' had to have taken place sometime before....

"Such an age, if established, would, of course, automatically preclude an Egyptian Pharaoh by the name of Chephren from ordering the carving of the Sphinx only 4,500 years ago--if the Sphinx's current state of weathering could a) be traced unambiguously, geologically to a period of massive rainfall on the Gizeh Plateau (as opposed to wind or sand erosion), and b) that period could be independently dated by geological (as opposed to 'Egyptological') techniques, to before Chephren's reign during Egypt's so-called 'Old Kingdom.'

---

[25] Ahmed Osman, *Stranger in the Valley of the Kings: The Identification of Yuya as the Patriarch Joseph* (London: Souvenir Press Ltd., 1987), pages 62-63.

"In 1991, both of these results came together for West's privately-funded Sphinx Project Team--resulting in the Team's highly significant, radical conclusions:

"Based on this chain of reasoning...we can estimate that the initial carving of the Great Sphinx (i.e., the carving of the main portion of the body and the front) may have been carried out c. 7000 to 5000 BC. This tentative estimate is probably a minimum date; given that weathering rates may proceed non-linearly...the possibility remains open that the initial carving of the Great Sphinx may be even older than 9,000 years ago.... Privately, West's geologists suspect an even greater age for this remarkable Egyptian effigy....

"This is required to produce the 'advanced state of water weathering' they detect (in part, via seismological techniques) - not merely on the Sphinx - but in the walls, and under the floor, of the carved ditch which separates the Sphinx from the limestone of the Gizeh Plateau proper. This pronounced state of deep erosion is also readily visible in the Sphinx Temple - the massive construction...a few hundred yards from the Sphinx, composed of 100-ton limestone blocks. It has long been presumed that these were excavated from the ditch at the time of the carving of the Sphinx itself.

"All these features...show evidence of such severe water weathering that eroded fissures twelve feet in depth are visible inside the ditch; similar manmade excavations (to the ditch), in similarly hard limestone on other parts of the Plateau (for Old Kingdom tombs, dated by other methods to 5,000 years), show literally no erosion....The remarkable conclusion?

"According to John [A.] West: If the Sphinx predates dynastic Egypt,...we would have to rewrite the history of when advanced civilization began....[26]

It is a well-established fact that, during the Ice Age, the amount of rainfall was much greater than at present. Historians believed and

---

[26]Richard C. Hoagland, *The Monuments of Mars: A City on the Edge of Forever* (Berkeley, California: North Atlantic Book, 1992), pages 361-362.

accepted that the Egyptian civilization emerged long after the Ice Age ended. Under these circumstances, it is clear that, after the Ice Age ended (supposedly 10,000 years ago), the amount of rainfall over Africa decreased and, therefore, the ground water level would have also decreased. However, the damage to the Sphinx indicates that the water table rose more than 30 feet and remained high for about 600 years. Geologically, an immense amount of water would have had to flood Africa after the Sphinx was constructed. Water tables simply do not rise over 30 feet and remain at a high level under the present gradualistic or uniformitarian conditions. This clearly indicates that a flood of extraordinary magnitude inundated Africa during the time of Egyptian civilization.

A temple was uncovered at Abydos, over 250 miles south of Gizeh, in the nineteenth century. The main temple complex, built of red granite, is located in a swamp thirty feet beneath the surface. According to David H. Childress, "[its] foundations are cut many feet below the current level of the water table, which has risen some [twenty] feet since the temple was built."[27]

When the Egyptians built this temple in the desert and laid its foundation, it seems obvious that the water table was at least twenty feet lower. The water table would not have risen twenty feet since then unless an enormous amount of water had, somehow, been added to the desert region and had, thus far, not subsided fully. Whale bones discovered in the Sahara Desert offer even more evidence of a flood in Egypt. Derek Ager argued against Velikovsky's concept of a flood by saying, "The idiocy of some of [Velikovsky's] dogmatic pronouncements is illustrated, for example, in the transport of vast numbers of large vertebrates from the tropics to the Arctic by a great wave that did not, apparently, carry with it a single marine organism."[28]

---

[27]David H. Childress, *Lost Cities and Ancient Mysteries of Africa and Arabia* (Stelle, Illinois: Adventures Unlimited Press, 1989), page 128.

[28]Derek V. Ager, *The New Catastrophism: The Importance of the Rare Event in Geological History* (New York and Cambridge: Cambridge University Press, 1993), pages 179-180.

The following descriptions about marine organisms found under Egyptian sand dunes and all over the Earth answer Ager's dogmatic pronouncement. According to James Trifil, some 243 fossilized whale skeletons and loose bones were discovered in a large valley 150 miles southwest of Cairo (100 miles inland from the Mediterranean Sea and more than 200 miles from the Red Sea). These skeletons are of Zeuglodon whales, like those found all over the southeastern United States. The Egyptian whale bones were scattered among the sand dunes; when the wind exposed them, the paleontologists rapidly dug out as much of the fossilized whale as possible because windborne sand erodes exposed bones.[29]

It is generally accepted that the Sahara Desert was created only after the Ice Age ended and the climate became arid. Therefore, whales had to have embedded themselves into the desert sand after the Ice Age ended and sand formed to cover them. The whales must have been left there recently. If Zeuglodons were lying on or near the surface for about forty million years, as some paleontologists submit, their bones would have eroded away. If they were encased in rock, over time, and the rock became sand, their bones would have become sand.

Thus, two pieces of information point to a recent oceanic flood in Egypt: water damage on the Sphinx, its surrounding niche and temple, and the presence of whale bones both 100 miles inland from the Mediterranean Sea and 200 miles inland from the Red Sea. Whale bones were also found in other regions of North Africa. Allan O. Kelly and Frank Dachille have stated that "there are a number of salt lakes, some of them below sea level, which show elevated shorelines of Pleistocene age. The University of California's expedition of 1947 [to] 1948 found the bones of whales along with those of present-day mammals in these old lake beds."[30]

Presently, whales are not found in landlocked inland lakes in Africa.

---

[29]James Trifil, "Whale Feet," *Discover* (May, 1991): 45-48.

[30]Allan O. Kelly and Frank Dachille, "Tunisia and Algeria," *Target Earth* (1953): page 168.

If Zeuglodons lived 50 million years ago and became extinct soon thereafter, they would never be found in strata containing present-day mammals. The implication is that Zeuglodon whales were deposited into these lakes, along with mammals, by an enormous flood. The trapped whales died alongside the mammals that were swept into the salt lakes with them.

Thus the case for dynasties in Egypt prior to the Flood, and Egyptus "finding" what she had been seeking - the land of her forefathers - has a much more solid foundation in fact. The water erosion of the Sphinx is a reality, and whales don't walk.

"Where does all this leave the historicity of the biblical Flood? That it is pure myth is certainly one conclusion which the archaeological evidence admits (though, incidentally, it does little to explain the remarkably widespread currency of flood stories). Others have posited a cataclysm far back in the Stone Age, without venturing, in view of the lack of archaeological data, to speculate as to its precise nature and scope, but this sacrifices the biblical chronology if nothing else. Another view is that the Flood was purely local and that one or more of the Mesopotamian mud-layers might even relate to it. The biblical text, however, cannot be so construed. Perhaps one way of accepting the literal truth of all that the Bible has to say about the time and scope of the Flood is to dwell on the statements (Genesis 8:13f.) that the earth dried out, and argue that there is no knowing *a priori* what sort of archaeological traces (if any) the Flood might have left, though of course, if one is bent on defending the literal truth of the Flood, the lack of archaeological support is the least of one's problems."[31]

There are, in fact, many archeological discoveries made around the world that have been conveniently forgotten by those who make claims such as the one just noted. Given this challenge, the following few examples, from among many that could have been used, will show that these theorists, among others of their peers, continue to overlook that which does not prove their position. It is, in fact, very easy to defend the literal truth of the Flood. This will be done before

---

[31]Bermant, *op. cit.*

analyzing the settlement of the newly cleansed earth because it is important to note that just because all land life had been destroyed, and just because there had been devastating cataclysmic activities, these facts do not mean that every evidence of the former civilizations was destroyed. In fact, much of what happened might lead the evolutionary scientists of our day to see the historical record, in its revolutionized mess, as having taken place over great aeons of time. Let's dispel their theory once and for all insofar as this treatise is concerned.

An interesting item appeared in many of the nation's newspapers on April 10, 1967, reporting the discovery of an artifact and human remains at the Rocky Point Mine in Gilman, Colorado. At a depth of 400 feet below the surface, according to an account in the Saturday *Herald* of Iowa City, the excavators found human bone embedded in a silver vein. By geological standards, the find was estimated to be several million years old. But in addition to the bones, they uncovered a well-tempered copper arrowhead four inches long. Neither bone nor arrowhead belonged there, because, as noted above the copper age began supposedly sometime around 5000 B.C., not several million years ago. And mankind was not claimed by this camp to be this old either. Yet there they were - unexplainable and certainly unexpected. The historians and geologists were unable to fit these remains into their theoretical frameworks of evolution; therefore, partly because of this, this find has been conveniently forgotten by them.

But this strange discovery is not an isolated one. In the June 1851 issue of *Scientific American* (Volume 7, page 298) a report concerning a metallic vase that had been dynamited out of solid rock on Meeting House Hill in Dorchester, Massachusetts, was reprinted from the *Boston Transcript*. The story read: "On putting the two parts together it formed a bell-shaped vessel, 4½ inches high, 6½ inches at the base, 2½ at the top and about an eighth of an inch in thickness. The body of this vessel resembles zinc in color, or a composition metal in which there is a considerable portion of silver. On the sides there are six figures of a flower, a bouquet, beautifully inlaid with pure silver, and around the lower part of the vessel, a vine, or wreath, inlaid also with silver. The chasing, carving and inlaying are exquisitely done by the art of some cunning craftsman. This curious and unknown vessel was blown out of a solid pudding stone, fifteen feet below the surface." Where did it come from? Neither the geologists nor the archaeologists knew, but the rock from which the man-made art object was taken was estimated by them to be at least several million years old. As is the case with many puzzling discoveries, the vase was circulated from museum to museum, and then disappeared.

Precisely forty years later, on June 9, 1891, a somewhat similar find was made by Mrs. S. W. Culp of Morrisonville, Illinois. While she was shoveling coal into her kitchen stove, her attention was drawn to one lump of coal which had broken in two, revealing a gold chain of intricate workmanship. The *Morrisonville Times* of June 11 reported, "Mrs. Culp thought the chain had been dropped accidentally in the coal, but as she undertook to lift the chain up, the idea of its having been recently dropped was shown to be fallacious, for as the lump of coal broke, it separated almost in the middle, and the circular position of the chain placed the two ends near to each other; and as the lump separated, the middle of the chain became loosened while each end remained fastened to the coal....This is a study for the students of archaeology who love to puzzle their brains out over the geological construction of the Earth from whose ancient depth the curious are always dropping out."

The paper editor really didn't know how to handle this bizarre discovery, but neither did the geologists, for the coal sample was supposedly from the Carboniferous period and so was thought to be several million years old.

The Morrisonville chain was in no way unique, for another gold artifact of unknown origin was discovered in 1844 in a quarry near Rutherford Mills, England. On June 22 of that year, workmen blasting granite out of the pit suddenly came upon a gold thread eight feet below the surface, embedded in rock judged by geologists to be sixty million years old. Investigators sent by the London *Times* reported that in their opinion the thread had indeed been of artificial manufacture.

Artifacts of precious metal have not been the only objects unearthed from solid rock. The *Springfield Republican* (Illinois) stated in 1851 that a businessman named Hiram de Witt had brought back with him from a trip to California a piece of auriferous quartz about the size of a man's fist, and while de Witt was showing the rock to a friend, it slipped from his hand and split upon striking the floor. In the center of the quartz, they discovered a cut-iron six-penny nail, slightly corroded but entirely straight, with a perfect head. The age of the quartz, you wonder? Scientists concluded that it was in excess of a million years old! The facts are so overwhelming as they continue to mount, that one must conclude that only because these things are ignored or suppressed, and the other theory perpetrated, does the truth not received wider acceptance.

But this wasn't the first nail discovered. Six years before this find, Sir David Brewster made a report to the British Association of the Advancement of Science which created quite a stir. A nail obviously of human manufacture had been found half-embedded in a granite block excavated from the Kindgoodie Quarry in northern Britain. It was badly corroded, but identifiable, nonetheless. Once again, the granite was determined to be at least sixty million years old.

Still another out-of-place artifact, a two-inch metal screw, was discovered in a piece of feldspar unearthed in 1865 from the Abbey Mine in Treasure City, Nevada. The screw had long since oxidized, but its form, particularly the shape of its threads, could easily be seen within the feldspar. Here too this discovery played havoc with accepted scientific theories, for how the impression of a two-inch metal screw could be found in something thought to be several million years old clearly perplexed the examiners.

"In 1885, in the foundry of the Austrian Isador Braun of Vocklabruck, a block of coal dating from the Tertiary period was broken open. Inside was discovered a small metal cube. Fascinated by this sudden find, Braun's son took the mysterious cube to the Salzburg Museum, where it was subjected to meticulous examination by the Austrian physicist Karl Gurls.

"Tests indicated the cube was composed of a steel-and-nickel alloy. It measured 2.64 by 1.85 inches, weighed 1.73 pounds, and had a specific gravity of 7.75 The edges of this strange cube were perfectly straight and sharp; four of its sides were flat, while the two remaining sides, opposite each other, were convex. A rather deep groove had been cut all the way around the cube about midway up its height. There was no doubt that the cube was machine-made, and it seemed to be part of a larger mechanism.

"Unfortunately the cube disappeared from the Salzburg Museum in 1910, and during the bombings of the Second World War the museum's inventory files relating to the time period when the cube was on exhibit (1886-1910) were completely destroyed. However, there is still sufficient evidence to support the authenticity of the find, for an account of its discovery was published in the scientific journals *Nature* (London, 1886) and *L'Astronomie* (Paris, 1887).

"Another equally controversial find was made more recently. On February 13, 1961, three rock hunters, Mike Mikesell, Wallace Lane and Virginia Maxey, were collecting geodes about six miles northeast of Olancha, California. On this particular day, while searching in the Coso Mountains, they found a stone located near the top of a peak approximately 4,300 feet above sea level and about 340 feet above the dry bed of Owens Lake. The rockhounds mistakenly identified it as a geode, a round stone with a hollow interior lined with crystals, though it bore traces of fossil shells. The following day, when Mikesell cut the stone in half, ruining a ten-inch diamond saw in the process, he saw that it contained not crystals but rather something totally unfamiliar. Inside were the remains of some form of mechanical device. Beneath the outer layer of hardened clay, pebbles, and fossil inclusions was a hexagonal layer of an unknown substance softer than agate or jasper. The layer surrounded a three-quarter-inch-wide cylinder made of solid porcelain or ceramic, and in the center of the cylinder the finders discovered a two-millimeter shaft of bright metal. This shaft, the rock enthusiasts discovered, was magnetic and showed no signs of oxidation. Circling the ceramic cylinder were rings of copper, and these also had not corroded.

"Not knowing what to do with their unusual find, they sent the object to the Charles Ford Society, an organization specializing in examining extraordinary things. X-rays taken of the fossil-encrusted rock revealed further evidence that the content of the 'geode' was indeed some form of mechanical apparatus. The photographs indicated that the metallic shaft was corroded at one end, but the other end was affixed to a spring or helix of metal. The Coso artifact, as it is now known, is believed to be more than just a piece of machinery. The finely shaped ceramic and metallic shaft and copper components hint at some form of electrical instrument. It bears a close resemblance to a spark plug, but there are certain features - particularly the spring or helix terminal - that do not correspond to any spark plug known today. To complicate the mystery surrounding this strange little instrument, the geologists tell us that the rock in which it was found has to be at least half a million years old.[32]

These out-of-place objects found in the various rock strata not only reveal evidence of simple metal production, but also indicate that the antediluvians had the ability to shape metal by machines.

POPULATION STATISTICS

Pre-flood statistics are not available. However, one author has made an approximation based on several theoretical assumptions. The longer lifespans of the antediluvians could have meant that the reproductive capacity of the pre-Flood mother was half her age - as it is for women today. "If so, we come to the sobering conclusion that 400 years of childbearing per woman could have been the norm. Allowing the average antediluvian mother this reproductive capability, we must conclude that a family of eighteen or twenty children was not unreasonable. Using the genealogy mentioned in the book of Genesis and accepting that there were ten generations from Adam to Noah, the development of the antediluvian population could easily have been on the following scale for the 1656 years prior to the flood." This can also be deduced from the notations made above regarding Noah, who was having children at age 500. His wife would likely have been of a similar age. Only Japheth, Shem and Ham are mentioned by name as having been born during the years of 450-500 of Noah's life. Daughters are also mentioned as having been born earlier, thereby assuming that other male children were also born, all

---

[32]Noorbergen, *op. cit.*, pages 43-45.

of whom became unrighteous, along with all of the daughters.

First generation	2
Second generation	18
Third generation	162
Fourth generation	1,458
Fifth generation	13,122
Sixth generation	118,098
Seventh generation	1,062,882
Eighth generation	9,565,938
Ninth generation	86,093,442
Tenth generation	774,840,978

Add to the last figure an estimate for the surviving members of previous generations, and the number 900,000,000 doesn't seem so unrealistic. It could easily have been much greater. "In *Medical Science and the Bible*, William R. Vis prepared a graph indicating the contrast between the ages of the patriarchs before and after the Flood and points out that 'a study of this chart shows in a striking way that something extremely significant happened to the earth and to man at the time of the Flood. It would seem that whatever this was, it probably removed the dominant factor for the long life of the patriarchs.... Could some antediluvian climatic or other condition have been extremely favorable for long life in man? Perhaps future scientific research will cast some light on this.'

"After having examined all possible angles of population increase before the great catastrophe, John C. Whitcomb comments, 'We are confident, therefore, that our estimate of a population of one billion people on the earth at the time of the Deluge is very conservative; it could well have been far more than this. A population of this order of magnitude would certainly have spread far beyond the Mesopotamian plains.'"[33]

Man began to populate the earth anew in the year 2345 B.C. The Lord Jehovah commanded Noah and his people to spread out upon

---

[33]Noorbergen, *op. cit.*, page. 24.

the face of the earth from their landing place atop Mt. Ararat in modern-day Turkey. The family of eight souls became the ancestors of all living human life thereafter.

Changes in population are caused by births and deaths, and, as far as studying any particular area of the world, by movements in and out of that area. An attempt is being made in this study to reconstruct the development of civilization from the year 2345 B.C. Some initial statistics and long-term development of civilization are necessary to have an overview of the scope of this project.

Dan Rottenberg states: "...most demographers maintain that any attempt to arrive at practical population figures for any group prior to 1800 are little more than exercises in fantasy."[34] Given that warning, a general fantastic overview is still desired.

Abba Eban says: "Between 2000 and 1000 BCE - roughly from the time of Abraham to the reign of David - the earth's population nearly doubled, from about 27,000,000 to 50,000,000. Of this increase, Asia and Europe accounted for a disproportionate share, with the bulk of European growth concentrated in the Mediterranean region."[35]

Probably no more than 8,000,000 people were alive at any one time on the earth during the B.C. era, according to *The New Book of Knowledge*. This, at face value, is a bold statement based on normal population trends and birthrates in basically agrarian and nomadic societies. However, this same source gives a total population of 250,000,000 in 1 A.D., thereby contradicting itself. Other sources estimate 240,000,000 people were living on the earth in 1 A.D.

The *Encyclopedia Americana* shows a world population of 508,000,000 in 1650, 711,000,000 in 1750; 912,000,000 in 1800; 1,131,000,000 in 1850; and 1,590,000,000 in 1900. By 1930 the population had reached

---

[34]Dan Rottenberg, *Finding our Fathers: A Guidebook to Jewish Genealogy* (Baltimore, Maryland: Genealogical Publishing Co., Inc., 1986), page 42.

[35]Abba Eban, *Heritage: Civilization and the Jews* (New York City: Summit Books, 1984), page 36.

2,000,000,000. In 1975 the total had reached 3,967,000,000. It is expected to reach 6,214,000,000 by the year 2000 and eight billion by 2010 if the 1975 birth rate remains constant, which it is not. In many third world countries, birthrates have already declined from six to four children per family within the last ten years, and in the United States the growth rate is below a status quo. The population is not reproducing itself at the same rate it is dying.

The *Encyclopedia Americana* breaks its statistics into regions of the world as well. A few of these are important for this study. Europe and USSR: 103,000,000 in 1650; 144,000,000 in 1750; 192,000,000 in 1800; and 274,000,000 in 1850; North America: 1,000,000 in 1650; 1,000,000 in 1750; 6,000,000 in 1800; and 26,000,000 in 1850; Oceania: 2,000,000 in 1650; 2,000,000 in 1750; 2,000,000 in 1800; and 2,000,000 in 1850; Asia: 292,000,000 in 1650; 456,000,000 in 1750; 596,000,000 in 1800; and 698,000,000 in 1850; Latin America 10,000,000 in 1650; 10,000,000 in 1750; 21,000,000 in 1800; and 33,000,000 in 1850; Africa: 100,000,000 in 1650; 98,000,000 in 1750; 95,000,000 in 1800; and 98,000,000 in 1850.

In 1650 - the beginning of the scientific revolution - it is established that the world population was about 500,000,000 persons. Of this total, a little less than 60% was in Asia, about 20% in Europe, about 20% in Africa, and perhaps 2% in the Americas.

CHRONOLOGY

The scientific world claims that the Neolithic Age began about 8,000 years ago, or roughly 6000 B.C. in the areas of the Mediterranean and the Fertile Crescent. They claim that during the fifth millennium before Christ, the Age of Metals began in the valleys of the Nile and the Tigris-Euphrates. They maintain that the earliest part of this period was the Chalcolithic (copper and stone) Age, which developed into the Copper Age, this in turn developing into the Historic Age (also called the Bronze Age) around 3000 B.C. Finally, they give the Iron Age as beginning around 1500 B.C. All of these dates have serious flaws as noted above, as artifacts in complex metal structures and mechanically created parts have been found for the pre-Flood period in various part of the world. Because of this it is necessary to develop a more realistic chronology of human development.

The information concerning birth years, death years, ordination years, ages, and other miscellaneous information regarding the patriarchs before the Flood is taken from *The Holy Bible*, Genesis, Chapter 5, and *The Doctrine & Covenants*, Section 107. The dates for the kings of Egypt are approximate dates based on the latest chronological revisions as recorded by Peter A. Clayton in his well documented study *Chronicle of the Pharaohs* referenced where appropriate.

4002 B.C.	Beginning of physical world; [birth] of Adam, possibly October 24th (see pages 65, 121-122).
3872 B.C.	Birth of Seth, son of Adam.
3803 B.C.	Seth, son of Adam, ordained a high priest at age 69 by Adam.
3767 B.C.	Birth of Enos, son of Seth.
3677 B.C.	Birth of Cainan, son of Enos.
3677 B.C.	The people of God, led by Enos, son of Seth, leave the land of Shulon and settle in the land of Cainan; this due to the wickedness of Adam's other descendants.
3337 B.C.	Cainan, son of Enos, called by God at age 40.
3633 B.C.	Enos, son of Seth, ordained a high priest at age 134 years four months by Adam.

3607 B.C.	Birth of Mahalaleel, son of Cainan.
3590 B.C.	Cainan, son of Enos, ordained a high priest at age 87 by Adam as he journeyed to the place Shedolamak.
3542 B.C.	Birth of Jared, son of Mahalaleel.
3517 B.C.	Enoch, son of Jared, ordained a high priest at age 25 by Adam
3380 B.C.	Birth of Enoch, son of Jared.
3315 B.C.	Birth of Methuselah, son of Enoch.
3315 B.C.	Enoch, son of Jared, was blessed at age sixty-five by Adam.
3175 B.C.	Scorpion, of unknown ancestry, first king of Upper Egypt.[36]
3150 B.C.	Narmer, possibly the son of Scorpion, first king to wear the crowns of both Upper and Lower Egypt.[37]

---

[36]Clayton, *op. cit.*, pages 16-18. Scorpion is identified on the fragmented so-called "Scorpion" Macehead, where he is seen in full ritual dress with the ritual bull's tail hanging from the back of his belt, wearing the tall White Crown (*hedjet*) of Upper Egypt and performing a ceremony using a hoe or mattock. Before the king's face, and therefore presumably signifying his name, is a scorpion with a seven-petalled flower above it. This discovery was made at Hierakonpolis in Upper Egypt in 1897-1898. Hierakonpolis was the ancient city of Nekhen on the west bank of the Nile north of Aswan and dedicated to the falcon-headed god Horus. Excavations here produced some remarkable finds, including a gold-headed hawk representing the town deity Horus, and an almost life-size, hollow-cast copper statue of Pepi I and his son Merenre of the 6th Dynasty. The Scorpion and Narmer objects also discovered here were obviously deposits made by the later dynastic rulers. Does this show a lineal descent, or pre-Flood relationship between Scorpion and the descendants of Egyptus? This will probably never be known. However, the circumstantial evidence would point to it.

[37]Clayton, *op. cit.*, pages 17-19. Two major discoveries at Hierakonpolis (see previous footnote) were the Narmer Palette and the Narmer Macehead. The Palatte, a monumental piece of dark green slate, is the earliest historical record from Egypt. It shows a victorious king whose name appears within a *serekh* - the early form of presenting royal names - at the head of both sides between facing heads of the cow-faced goddess Hathor. The hieroglyphs of the royal name are a mud fish depicted horizontally above a vertical chisel, read as the name of Narmer. Narmer is shown in two aspects, wearing respectively the White Crown of Upper Egypt (the *hedjet*) and the Red Crown of Lower Egypt (*deshret*), implying that he is king of both lands. The Narmer Macehead shows him celebrating the King's Jubilee, probably celebrated

3128 B.C.	Birth of Lamech, son of Methuselah.
3115 B.C.	Methuselah, son of Enoch, ordained a high priest at age 100 by Adam.
3114 B.C.	Beginning of the Mayan Calendar date wise, August 13. Does this indicate its Egyptian origins? Certainly Mayan history has never claimed that early of a beginning despite their calendar's early origin. Is 3114 the calendrical beginning of Egyptian history?
3114 B.C.	Hor-Aha, probably son of Narmer and possibly Queen Nithotep, his successor, as King of Upper and Lower Egypt.[38] It is possible that Hor-Aha was the same as Menes, also known as the first king of both Upper and Lower Egypt? Ruled for 62 years.
3111 B.C.	Mahalaleel, son of Cainan, ordained a high priest and blessed at age 496 years seven days by Adam.
3080 B.C.	Djer (probably Manetho's Athothis) succeeded Hor-Aha and is said to have reigned for 57 years.

---

after thirty years of rule.

[38]Clayton, *op. cit.*, pages 19-22. Hor-Aha (The Fighting Hawk), also known by the *nebti* name (the second royal name) of Men, which means "established," possibly indicating the origin of the later record of the first king as being called Menes. Hor-Aha is considered by Egyptologists as the first king of the first dynasty. His names appear side by side on a small broken ivory label in the tomb of Queen Nithotep at Naqada. During his reign he fought campaigns against rebels in Nubia. He founded a temple to the goddess Neith at Sais in the Delta. His greatest achievement was the founding of the capital city at Memphis. He reigned, according to Manetho, for sixty-two years. After Memphis was founded the early Egyptian kings began to construct their tombs at the sacred site of Abydos in middle Egypt and the nobles theirs on the edge of the desert plateau at Saqqara, overlooking Memphis. At Abydos, in October 1991, a fleet of 12 boats dating from about 3000 B.C. were found buried side by side. The boats - the oldest surviving large-scale vessels in the world - were up to 100 feet in length and their superstructures had been protected by mudbrick structures protruding slightly above the desert surface.

His queen was Merneith.[39]

3075 B.C.   Last blessing by Adam on his righteous posterity at Adam-ondi-Ahman, including Seth, Enos, Cainan, Mahalaleel, Jared, Enoch, and Methuselah, all high priests. Adam was called Michael, the prince, the archangel.

3072 B.C.   Death of Adam, the first man, age 930 years.

3040 B.C.   Birth of Djet (probably Manetho's Uadji), probably son of Djer and Merneith. See footnote 39. His royal *serekh* contains a snake hieroglyph and is surmounted by the Horus falcon.

3050 B.C.   Birth of Den (probably Manetho's Udimu), probably son of Djer and Merneith. His throne name was Semti.[40] He may have reigned for 20 years.

3030 B.C.   Birth of Anedjib (Safe is His Heart), king of the 1st Dynasty of Egypt who followed Den. He reigned for 26 years. He is recorded as a Thinite king.

3015 B.C.   Translation of Enoch and all of the inhabitants of the City of Enoch.

3000 B.C.   Birth of Semerkhet (Thoughtful Friend), king of the 1st Dynasty of Egypt who followed Anedjib. He reigned for 9 or 18 years. He was apparently a usurper as he erased his predecessor and was erased by his successor from the Saqquara King

---

[39]Clayton, *op. cit.*, pages 22-23. Merneith's name was recently found at Abydos on a clay seal impression that gives the names of the early kings in order from Narmer to Den, confirming her status and giving her the title of "King's Mother," presumably of Den (Horus who Strikes) for whom she may have acted as regent during his minority. This would likely indicate that Djet (Horus Cobra) was also her son. The meaning of Djer is Horus who Succors.

[40]Clayton, *op. cit.*, page 23-24. With Den the historical record becomes stronger. There are many labels and inscriptions on stone vases which cite this king and events in his reign. There is also an interesting correlation across to the Palermo Stone (which dates from the 5th Dynasty and lists kings from 3150 B.C. to Neferirkare in the mid-5th Dynasty). We can identify Den (Udimu) via his throne name, Semti, as king of the Two Lands, with a king in the Abydos King List (this royal list is still *in situ* on the walls of the corridor in the Hall of Ancestors in the magnificent temple of Seti I), called Hesepti.

List. He was a Thinite King.

2996 B.C. Lamech, son of Methuselah, ordained a high priest at age 32 by Seth.

2980 B.C. Birth of Qa'a (His Arm is Raised), possibly Manetho's Bieneches, both called the last king of the 1st Dynasty. He rules for 26 years. He was a Thinite King.

2960 B.C. Death of Seth, son of Adam, age 912 years.

2940 B.C. Birth of Hotepsekhemwy (Pleasing in Powers) first king of the 2nd Dynasty of Egypt. He ruled for 38 years according to Manetho, but his king list for the 2nd Dynasty are probably off by 100 years.

2946 B.C. Birth of Noah, son of Lamech.

2936 B.C. Noah, son of Lamech, ordained a high priest at age 10 by Methuselah.

2870 B.C. Birth of Raneb (Re is the Lord), 2nd king of the 2nd Dynasty of Egypt. Ruled for 39 years according to Manetho.

2862 B.C. Death of Enos, son of Seth, age 905 years.

2830 B.C. Birth of Nynetjer (Godlike), 3rd king of the 2nd Dynasty of Egypt. Ruled for 47 years according to Manetho.[41]

2767 B.C. Death of Cainan, son of Enos, age 910 years.

2733 B.C. Rule of Skehemib (Powerful in Heart), later called Seth-Peribsen (Hope of All Hearts). 4th king of the 2nd Dynasty of Egypt. He reigned for 17 years.[42]

2716 B.C. Rule of Khasekhemwy 5th and last king of the 2nd

---

[41]Clayton, *op. cit.*, pages 26-27. The Palermo Stone records events between Years 6 and 26 of his reign, including various feats of gods; a "running of the Apis bull" in year 9; a military campaign in Year 13 when there occurred the "hacking up of the city of Shem-Re" and the "House of the North"; and in Year 15 the birth of Khasekhemwy, second king to follow him.

[42]Between Peribsen and Khasekhemwy, Manetho lists three additional kings: Sethenes (Sendji); Chaires (Neterka); and Nephercheres (Neferkara) reigning respectively for 41, 17, and 25 years. The evidence for these kings is slight and archeological remains are non-existent to date.

Dynasty of Egypt. He ruled for 30 years.[43]

2712 B.C.   Death of Mahalaleel, son of Cainan, age 895 years.

2686 B.C.   Rule of Sanakhte (Strong Protection), also known as Nebka, 1st king of the 3rd Dynasty of Egypt. He ruled for 18 years. He may have married the female heir of the 2nd Dynasty, the matrilineal nature of ancient Egyptian society being evident from very early times. He was likely the brother of his successor Djoser.

2668 B.C.   Rule of Djoser whose Horus name was Netjeri-khet (Divine of the Body). Also known as Zoser or Tosorthos [Greek]. He was the 2nd king of the 3rd Dynasty of Egypt. To him is credited the building of the Step Pyramid at Saqqara, the first fully stone building in the world, erected by his vizier Imhotep. Djoser reigned for about 19 years, dying about 2649 B.C.

2649 B.C.   Rule of Sekhemkhet (Powerful in Body) 3rd king of the 3rd Dynasty of Egypt.[44] In 1951 an unfinished step pyramid attributed to Sekhemkhet was found. The name of the owner was revealed when five small clay jar sealings were found, impressed by a cylinder seal with his name. He ruled for six years.

2643 B.C.   Rule of Khaba (The Soul Appears), 4th king of the 3rd Dynasty of Egypt. He ruled for 6 years.

2637 B.C.   Rule of Huni (The Smiter), 5th and last king of the 3rd Dynasty of Egypt. He built the Meydum pyramid fifty miles south of Cairo. It was finished

---

[43]Khasekhemwy was the last king of the dynasty, although some authorities suggest that he had an immediate predecessor with a very similar name, Khasekhem. Others are of the opinion that they are one and the same person. who reigned for 30 years. His queen was a northern princess named Nemathap, her title "The King-bearing Mother." She may be the ancestress of the kings of the 3rd Dynasty. Her husband Khasekhemwy died about 2686 B.C.

[44]Clayton, *op. cit.*, page 38. According to Manetho, there were six more kings of the 3rd Dynasty. It is now generally accepted that there were only three and that they ruled for a span of about 36 years.

by his son-in-law and successor Snefru. Huni died about 2613 B.C. One of his wives was Meresankh I. He had a son Rahotep whose wife was Nofret.

2613 B.C.   Rule of Snefru (He of Beauty) also known as Sneferu, Snofru and Soris, 1st king of the 4th Dynasty of Egypt. His wife was Hetep-heres I, daughter of Huni. He was a son of Meresankh I. His wife was his half-sister. He ruled until about 2589 when he died.

2589 B.C.   Rule of Khufu (Protected by Khnum), also known as Cheops, Kheops [Greek] and Suphis I [Manetho], 2nd king of the 4th Dynasty of Egypt. He was the son of Snefru and Hetep-heres I. Two of his wives were Meritates and Henutsen. His sons were Djedefre, Kawab, Khafre (Chephren), Djedefhor, Banefre, and Khufukaef. His daughters were Hetep-heres II, Meresankh II, and Khamerermebty I. He died about 2566. He was the builder of the Great Pyramid.[45]

2580 B.C.   Death of Jared, son of Mahalaleel, age 962 years.

2566 B.C.   Rule of Djedefre (Enduring like Re) also known as Djedefra, Redjedef, and Radjedef, 3rd king of the 4th Dynasty of Egypt, son of Khufu. He ruled for 8 years. One of his wives was Hetepheres II. He had a son Setka and a daughter Neferhetepes. He was the first king to use the name "son of Re."

2558 B.C.   Rule of Khafre (Appearing like Re) also known as Khafra, Rakhaef, Chephren, Khephren [Greek] and Suphis II [Manetho], 4th king of the 4th Dynasty of Egypt, son of Khufu and Henutsen. His wives were Meresankh III and Khameremebty I. His sons were Nekure, and Menkaure. His daughter was Khameremebty II. Builder of the Second Pyramid and Great Sphinx at Giza. He

---

[45]Clayton, *op. cit.*, pages 46-47. There are about 2,300,000 separate blocks in the Great Pyramid, each weighing about 2.5 tons with a maximum weight of 15 tons. It is the only one of the Seven Wonders of the Ancient World that still stands. Its chief architect was probably Khufu's cousin Hemon.

	died about 2532 B.C.

2532 B.C.   Rule of Menkaure (Eternal like the Souls of Re) also known as Menkaura, Mycerinus/Mykerinus [Greek] and Mencheres, [as per Manetho], 5th king of the 4th Dynasty of Egypt, son of Khafre and Khamerernebty I.   One of his wives was Khameremebty II.   His sons were Khuenre and Shepseskaf. He had a daughter Khentkawes.   He died about 2504 B.C.

2504 B.C.   Rule of Shepseskaf (His Soul is Noble), 6th king of the 4th Dynasty of Egypt, son of Menkaure. His wife was Bunefer. His daughter was Khamaat. He died about 2500 B.C.   He had a half sister Khentkawes, who married Userkaf, 1st king of the 5th Dynasty.

2498 B.C.   Rule of Userkaf (His Soul is Powerful), also known as Weserkaf, son of his mother Neferhotep, daughter of Djedefre (3rd king of the 4th Dynasty), 1st king of the 5th Dynasty of Egypt. His wife was Khentkawes, just noted.   One of Khentkawes' pseudonyms may have been Reweddjedet and if this is so, her husband was the High Priest of Re at Heliopolis. Userkaf ruled for 7 years.

2496 B.C.   Birth of Japheth, son of Noah.

2491 B.C.   Rule of Sahure (He who is Close to Re), 2nd king of the 5th Dynasty of Egypt, probably a brother of Userkaf and son of Neferhotep.   He ruled for 14 years.

2477 B.C.   Rule of Neferirkare (Beautiful is the Soul of Re), whose birth name was Kakai, 3rd king of the 5th Dynasty of Egypt, probably a brother of Userkaf and son of Neferhotep. He ruled for 10 years.

2467 B.C.   Rule of Shepseskare (Noble is the Soul of Re), 4th king of the 5th Dynasty of Egypt. He ruled for 6 years.

2460 B.C.   Rule of Neferefre (Beautiful is Re), 5th king of the 5th Dynasty of Egypt. He was also known as Raneferef. He ruled for 7 years.

2454 B.C.   Birth of Shem, son of Noah.

2453 B.C.	Rule of Niuserre (Possessed of Re's Power), born as Ini, 6th king of the 5th Dynasty of Egypt. He rule for 31 years.
2446 B.C.	Birth of Ham, son of Noah.
2422 B.C.	Rule of Menkauhor (Eternal are the Souls of Re), born as Kaiu, 7th king of the 5th Dynasty of Egypt. He ruled for 8 years.
2414 B.C.	Rule of Djedkare (The Soul of Re Endureth), born at Isesi, 8th king of the 5th Dynasty of Egypt. He ruled for 39 years.
2375 B.C.	Rule of Unas, also known as Wenis and Unis, 9th and last king of the 5th Dynasty of Egypt. He ruled for 29 years and perished in the Flood in 2346 B.C.
2351 B.C.	Death of Lamech, son of Methuselah, age 777 years.
2346 B.C.	Death of Methuselah, son of Enoch, age 969 years.
2346 B.C.	Flood begins.
2345 B.C.	Man leaves the ark and begins to spread forth upon the land.
2344 B.C.	Birth of Arphaxad, son of Shem.
2344 B.C.	Approximate birth of Cush, son of Ham and Egyptus.
2342 B.C.	Approximate birth of Mizraim, son of Ham and Egyptus.
2340 B.C.	Approximate birth of Egyptus, daughter of Ham and Egyptus.
2320 B.C.	Approximate birth of Pharaoh, eldest son of Egyptus [daughter of Ham] and Mizraim [son of Ham]. Given this, it is supposed that Anom (titled Teti), who began Egypt's sixth dynasty, was this eldest son of Egyptus and Mizraim. Baines and Málex[46] give Teti's rule as 2323-2291 B.C. They are probably off a few years based on the internal chronology of this study, but not significantly. Clayton gives Teti's rule as beginning in 2345

---

[46]John Baines and Jaromir Málek, *Atlas of Ancient Egypt* (New York: Facts on File Publications, 1983), page 36.

which we know is impossible based on the chronology given herein.[47]   It is also possible that this Pharaoh was Anom's brother Lud.

2320 B.C.	Approx. birth of Nimrod, son of Cush and one of his sisters.
2309 B.C.	Birth of Selah, son of Arphaxad.
2300 B.C.	Approximate departure of Egyptus into Egypt from Sumer, or Ebla, together with her son Anom (pharaoh Teti) and probably others of her family; establishment of the sixth dynasty of Egypt.
2279 B.C.	Birth of Eber, son of Selah.
2056 B.C.	Approximate birth of Jared and Mahonri Moriancumer, brothers.
2250 B.C.	Chinese claim their history began in this year.
2245 B.C.	Birth of Peleg, son of Eber.
2006 B.C.	Death of Peleg, son of Eber.
2005 B.C.	Death of Nahor, grandfather of Abraham.
1996 B.C.	Approximate departure of Jaredites from Tower of Babel.
1996 B.C.	Confusion of tongues; dispersion at the Tower of Babel.
1996 B.C.	Death of Noah.

---

[47]Clayton, *op. cit.*, page 64.

THE LIMITED RECORD OF CIVILIZATION
PRIOR TO THE FLOOD
4002-2345 B.C.

First Generation: 1) Adam (4002-3072 B.C.); 2) Eve (born 4002 B.C.). Jewish traditions have the beginning of the world starting on October 24th.

Second Generation: "And Adam knew his wife and she bare unto him sons and daughters, and they began to multiply and to replenish the earth. And from that time forth, the sons and daughters of Adam began to divide two and two in the land..." [*The Pearl of Great Price*, The Book of Moses 5:2-3]; Moses 6:11 says that Adam "begat many sons and daughters." 1) Cain son of Adam and Eve [Genesis 4:1]; 2) Abel son of Adam and Eve [Genesis 4:2]; 3) Seth (3872-2960 B.C.), son of Adam and Eve [Genesis 4:25; 5:6-7]; 4) Lebuda, supposed daughter of Adam and Eve.[48]

Third Generation: [And the sons and daughters of Adam and Eve] "they also begat sons and daughters." [The Book of Moses 5:3]; 1) Enoch son of Cain [Genesis 4:17]; 2) Enos (3767-2862 B.C.) son of Seth [Genesis 4:26; 5:6-11]

"And Seth lived, after he begat Enos, eight hundred and seven years, and begat many sons and daughters. And the children of men were numerous upon all the face of the land And in those days Satan had great dominion among men, and raged in their hearts; and from thenceforth came wars and bloodshed; and a man's hand was against his own brother, in administering death, because of secret works, seeking for power." [The Book of Moses 6:14-15]

Thus, by the third generation there was a sufficient population in the world, which had spread throughout the land, for there to be armies, war, and great numbers of casualties. This also supposes the use of

---

[48]James H. Charlesworth, editor, *The Old Testament Pseudepigrapha*, volume 1 (New York City: Doubleday, 1983), page 994, Testament of Adam.

weapons of war.

"And Cain knew his wife, and she conceived and bare Enoch, and he also begat many sons and daughters. And he builded a city, and he called the name of the city after the name of his son, Enoch." [The Book of Moses 5:42]

Fourth Generation: 1) Irad son of Enoch the Canaanite [Genesis 4:18]. Irad was killed by Lamech because Irad revealed the secrets given by Satan to Cain, unto the children of Adam [The Book of Moses 5:49-50]; 2) Cainan (3677-2767 B.C.) son of Enos [Genesis 5:9-14]

"And unto Enoch was born Irad and other sons and daughters." [The Book of Moses 5:43]

"And Enos lived ninety years, and begat Cainan. And Enos and the residue of the people of God came out from the land, which was called Shulon, and dwelt in a land of promise, which he called after his own son, whom he had named Cainan. And Enos lived, after he begat Cainan, eight hundred and fifteen years, and begat many sons and daughters." [The Book of Moses 6:17-18]

Fifth Generation: 1) Mehujael son of Irad [Genesis 4:18]; 2) Mahalaleel (3607-2712 B.C.) son of Cainan [Genesis 5:12-17]

"And Irad begat Mehujael and other sons and daughters." [The Book of Moses 5:43]

Sixth Generation: 1) Methusael son of Mehujael [Genesis 4:18]; 2) Jared (3542-2580 B.C.) son of Mahalaleel [Genesis 5:15-20]

"And Mahujael begat Methusael, and other sons and daughters." [The Book of Moses 5:43]

Seventh Generation: 1) Lamech son of Methusael [Genesis 4:18]; 2) Adah wife of Lamech [Genesis 4:19]; 3) Zillah wife of Lamech [Genesis 4:19]; 4) Enoch (3517-2950 [translation]) son of Jared [Genesis 5:18-24]; 5) Mahijah [The Book of Moses 6:40]

Eighth Generation: 1) Jabal son of Lamech and Adah [Genesis 4:20];
2) Jubal son of Lamech and Adah [Genesis 4:21]; 3) Tubal-cain son
of Lamech and Zillah [Genesis 4:22]; 4) Naamah daughter of Lamech
and Zillah [Genesis 4:22]; 5) Methuselah (3315-2346) son of Enoch
[Genesis 5:21-27]; 6) Naamah, wife of Noah and the daughter of
Enoch [*The Book of Jasher* 5:15]

Ninth Generation: 1) Lamech (3128-2351) son of Methuselah
[Genesis 5:25-31]; 2) Elishaa son of Enoch [*The Book of Jasher* 4:11];
3) Eliakim, son of Methuselah [*The Book of Jasher* 5:35] These *Jasher*
entries are not likely real people. Too many errors can be proven. 4)
Scorpion, of unknown ancestry, 1st King of Upper Egypt (see page
49).

Tenth Generation: 1) Noah (2946-1996) son of Lamech [Genesis 5:28-
29]; 2) Ashmua, wife of Lamech, mother of Noah, and daughter of
Elishaa [*The Book of Jasher* 4:11-13]; 3) a daughter of Eliakim,
supposedly the wife of Japheth [*The Book of Jasher* 5:35]; 4) a
daughter of Eliakim, supposedly the wife of Shem [*The Book of Jasher*
5:35]. Additionally is says in this same reference that Ham's wife was
also a daughter of Eliakim, the son of Methuselah, but modern
revelation shows that Ham's wife was 5) Egyptus, a descendant of
Cain: "The land of Egypt being first discovered by a woman, who was
the daughter of Ham, and the daughter of Egyptus, which in the
Chaldean signifies Egypt, which signifies that which is forbidden. [*The
Pearl of Great Price,* The Book of Abraham 1:23] 6) Narmer, son of
Scorpion (see page 46).

The names listed above are all the names recorded in *The Holy Bible*,
in *The Book of Jasher*, and in *The Pearl of Great Price* in the time
period prior to the Flood. Besides these given names, there are place
names that may also refer to individuals that lived prior to the Flood.
From The Book of Moses: Pison, Havilah (3:11); Gihon, Ethiopia,
Hiddekel, Assyria, Euphrates (3:7); Nod (5:41); Shulon (6:17);
Mahujah, Simeon (7:2); Sharon, Omner, Heni, Haner, Hanannihah
(7:9); and Shedolamak (D&C 107).

Also of note is the reference in The Book of Moses regarding the
people of Shum, who lived in the valley of Shum, in tents, who were

all destroyed by the people of Canaan, who also lived in tents. Because the wording is prophetic, it is not certain whether the people of Shum were pre-Flood, or post-Flood. It is believed they were pre-Flood. (7:5-7) This was a land that became barren and unfruitful, where only the people of Canaan dwelt from that day forward. It was a land cursed with much heat, "and the barrenness thereof shall go forth forever; and there was a blackness came upon all the children of Canaan, that they were despised among all people." (7:8) It would appear from this description, that Enoch was seeing a land which is now on the continent of Africa. And he was seeing the descendants of Cain, or the Canaanites, the Negroes: "for the seed of Cain were black, and had not place among them." (7:22) The context of his prophecy is given below.

Finally, there is the record of Enoch found in The Book of Moses, which gives us a further glimpse of the pre-Flood generations. As Enoch traveled from the land of Cainan by the "sea east" he came across a man named Mahijah, living in a place called Mahujah near the mount called Simeon. He told Mahijah and his people who had lost all contact with god and the righteous patriarchal lineage about his own vision. He says in part: "And I saw the Lord; and he stood before my face, and he talked with me, even as a man talketh one with another, face to face; and he said unto me: Look, and I will show unto thee the world for the space of many generations. And it came to pass that I beheld in the valley of Shum, and lo, a great people which dwelt in tents, which were the people of Shum. And again the Lord said unto me: Look; and I looked towards the north, and I beheld the people of Canaan, which dwelt in tents.

"And the Lord said unto me: Prophesy; and I prophesied, saying: Behold the people of Canaan, which are numerous, shall go forth in battle array against the people of Shum, and shall slay them that they shall utterly be destroyed; and the people of Canaan shall divide themselves in the land, and the land shall be barren and unfruitful, and none other people shall dwell there but the people of Canaan;

"For behold, the Lord shall curse the land with much heat, and the barrenness thereof shall go forth forever; and there was a blackness came upon all the children of Canaan, that they were despised among all people.

"And it came to pass that the Lord said unto me: Look; and I looked and I beheld the land of Sharon, and the land of Enoch, and the land of Omner, and the land of Heni, and the land of Shem, and the land of Haner, and the land of Hanannihah, and all the inhabitants thereof; and the Lord said unto me: Go to this people, and say unto them - Repent, lest I come out and smite men with a curse, and they die. And he gave unto me a commandment that I should baptize in the name of the Father, and of the Son, which is full of grace and truth, and of the Holy Ghost, which beareth record of the Father and the Son. And it came to pass that Enoch continued to call upon all the people, save it were the people of Canaan, to repent;

"And so great was the faith of Enoch that he led the people of God, and their enemies came to battle against them; and he spake the word of the Lord, and the earth trembled, and the mountains fled, even according to his command; and the rivers of water were turned out of their course; and the roar of the lions was heard out of the wilderness; and all nations feared greatly, so powerful was the word of Enoch, and so great was the power of the language which God had given him.

"There also came up a land out of the depth of the sea, and so great was the fear of the enemies of the people of God, that they fled and stood afar off and went upon the land which came up out of the depth of the sea.

"And the giants of the land, also stood afar off; and there went forth a curse upon all people that fought against God; and from that time forth there were wars and bloodshed among them; but the Lord came and dwelt with his people, and they dwelt in righteousness. The fear of the Lord was upon all nations, so great was the glory of the Lord, which was upon his people. And the Lord blessed the land, and they were blessed upon the mountains, and upon the high places, and did flourish. And the Lord called his people Zion, because they were of one heart and one mind, and dwelt in righteousness; and there was no poor among them.

"And Enoch continued his preaching in righteousness unto the people of God. And it came to pass in his days, that he built a city that was called the City of Holiness, even Zion. And it came to pass that Enoch talked with the Lord; and he said unto the Lord: Surely Zion shall dwell in safety forever. But the Lord said unto Enoch: Zion have I blessed, but the residue of the people have I cursed. And it came to pass that the Lord showed unto Enoch all the inhabitants of the earth; and he beheld, and lo, Zion, in process of time, was taken up into heaven. And the Lord said unto Enoch: Behold mine abode forever.

"And Enoch also beheld the residue of the people which were the sons of Adam; and they were a mixture of all the seed of Adam save it was the seed of Cain, for the seed of Cain was black, and had not place among them.

"And after that Zion was taken up into heaven, Enoch beheld, and lo, all the nations of the earth were before him; and there came generation upon generation; and Enoch was high and lifted up, even in the bosom of the Father, and of the Son of Man; and behold, the power of Satan was upon all the face of the earth. And he saw angels descending out of heaven; and he heard a loud voice saying: Wo, wo be unto the inhabitants of the earth.

"And he beheld Satan; and he had a great chain in his hand, and it veiled the whole face of the earth with darkness; and he looked up and laughed, and his angels rejoiced. And Enoch beheld angels descending out of heaven, bearing testimony of the Father and Son; and the Holy Ghost fell on many, and they were caught up by the powers of heaven into Zion. And it came to pass that the God of heaven looked upon the residue of the people, and he wept; and Enoch bore record of it, saying: How is it that the heavens weep, and shed forth their tears as the rain upon the mountains? (*The Pearl of Great Price*, The Book of Moses 7:4-28)

Thus we see that the basic divisions of mankind prior to the Flood were thirteen major nations: Canaan (the Negro race, descendants of Cain, who dwelt in a barren, desert land, and who later inhabited the island that came up out of the sea - Atlantis? - together with the giants and other enemies of the people of God); the land of Shulon (where Adam dwelt, the land of the Garden of Eden, the land of modern Missouri); the land of Havilah (Genesis 2:11); the land of Ethiopia (Genesis 2:13); the land of Assyria (Genesis 2:14) the land of Sharon; the land of Cainan where Enos went with the righteous of the Lord, the land of Enoch's birth; the land of Nod (Genesis 4:16) which land was where Cain first dwelt; the land of Enoch, the land of Omner, the land of Heni, the land of Shem, the land of Haner, and the land of Hanannihah. These were the thirteen great nations of the world prior to the Flood. To these may also be added a fourteenth, Shedolamak, although it was probably in Shulon or Cainan.

It is theorized by this author that the land of Canaan was in the land which includes what is now called Egypt, a land of barrenness, surrounded everywhere by desert. It is the land which Egyptus sought after the Flood, and "found" indicating it was the land she was seeking, the land of her forefathers, as she was of the race of Cain. It was apparently the land of the Pharaohs prior to the Flood, and became their land again after the Flood.

One other notation from the pre-Flood period says that in the days of Methuselah "...there came forth a great famine into the land, and the Lord cursed the earth with a sore curse, and many of the inhabitants thereof died." (The Book of Moses 8:4) This is further expanded in *The Book of Jasher* 4:2-7: "And when Enoch had ascended into heaven, all the kings of the earth rose and took Methuselah his son and anointed him, and they caused him to reign over them in the place of his father. And Methuselah acted uprightly in the sight of God, as his father Enoch had taught him, and he likewise during the whole of his life taught the sons of men wisdom, knowledge and the fear of God, and he did not turn from the good way either to the right or to the left. But in the latter days of Methuselah, the sons of men turned from the Lord, they corrupted the earth, they robbed and plundered each other, and they rebelled against God and they transgressed, and they corrupted their ways, and would not hearken to the voice of Methuselah, but rebelled against him. And the Lord was exceedingly wroth against them, and the Lord continued to destroy the seed in those days, so that there was neither sowing nor reaping in the earth. For when they sowed the ground in order that they might obtain food for their support, behold, thorns and thistles were produced which they did not sow. And still the sons of men did not turn from their evil ways, and their hands were still extended to do evil in the sight of God, and they provoked the Lord with their evil ways, and the Lord was very wroth, and repented that he had made man." This latter should read that it repented Methuselah and Noah that the Lord had made man.

Prior to the Flood Noah bore many sons and daughters. Among them were Japheth, Shem, and Ham. These also bore children prior to the Flood. "And Noah and his sons hearkened unto the Lord, and gave heed and they were called the sons of God. And when these men began to multiply on the face of the earth, and daughters were born unto them, the sons of men saw that those daughters were fair, and they took them wives, even as they chose. And the Lord said unto Noah: The daughters of thy sons have sold themselves; for behold mine anger is kindled against the sons of men, for they will not hearken to my voice." (Moses 8:13-14) Thus even many of the family members of the righteous patriarchs turned from the Lord. Those that were righteous were caught up with Enoch and the City of Zion, or died prior to the Flood, except for Noah, Naamah (supposed wife of Noah, also called Lili Nu-u by the Hawaiians), Japheth, his wife, Shem, his wife, Ham and Egyptus, his wife.

MANKIND SPREADS ACROSS THE EARTH AFTER THE FLOOD, 2345 B.C.

Noah was born in the year 2946 B.C. (Genesis 5:28-29), "and Noah was six hundred years old when the flood of waters was upon the earth." (Genesis 7:6) "In the six hundredth year of Noah's life, in the second month, the seventeenth day of the month, the same day were all the fountains of the great deep broken up, and the windows of heaven were opened. And the rain was upon the earth forty days and forty nights. In the selfsame day entered Noah, and Shem, and Ham, and Japheth, the sons of Noah, and Noah's wife, and the three wives of his sons with them, into the ark." (Genesis 7:11-13) "And the water prevailed exceedingly upon the earth; and all the high hills, that were under the whole heaven, were covered. And all flesh died that moved upon the earth, both of fowl, and of cattle, and of beast, and of every creeping thing that creepeth upon the earth, and every man: All in whose nostrils was the breath of life, of all that was in the dry land, died....And the waters prevailed upon the earth an hundred and fifty days." (Genesis 7:19-22, 24) "And God remembered Noah, and every living thing, and all the cattle that was with him in the ark: and God made a wind to pass over the earth, and the waters assuaged; the fountains also of the deep and the windows of heaven were stopped, and the rain from heaven was restrained; and the waters returned from off the earth continually: and after the end of the hundred and fifty days the waters were abated." (Genesis 8:1-3)

This does not mean that all the waters that had fallen were dried up, but that they receded sufficiently for the mountain tops to begin to be exposed. "And the ark rested in the seventh month, on the seventeenth day of the month, upon the mountains of Ararat. And the waters decreased continually until the tenth month: in the tenth month, on the first day of the month, were the tops of the mountains seen." (Genesis 8:4-5)

The waters continued to decrease upon the earth for another five months. "And it came to pass in the six hundredth and first year, in the first month, the first day of the month, the waters were dried up from off the earth: and Noah removed the covering of the ark, and looked, and, behold, the face of the ground was dry. And in the second month, on the seven and twentieth day of the month, was the earth dried." (Genesis 8:13-14) This repetition of the earth being dried shows a continuing process, in the mountain tops. It was not something that happened quickly. And all the lowlands were still under water. However, there was sufficient dry land to go forth in the second month, on the seven and twentieth day. This would have been in the warm time of the year and crops were badly needed. Thus, man began to multiply and replenish the earth again in the year 2345 B.C. Children began to be born immediately thereafter.

"And the sons of Noah, that went forth of the ark, were Shem, and

Ham, and Japheth: and Ham is the father of Canaan. These are the three sons of Noah: and of them was the whole earth overspread." (Genesis 9:18-19)

As Noah and his family looked out over a world of receding waters, of a world crushed by massive plate movements, upthrusts, worldwide tidal waves changing the whole surface of the earth beneath the united oceans, of barrenness everywhere, of a lifeless planet (albeit the dove brought back a live olive leaf), certainly, the position from atop Ararat was bleak and foreboding. Where to begin? They were well prepared with supplies, animals, knowledge, and prophetic vision; thus, the new beginning was better than the first after Eden. A casual view of any map with Mt. Ararat in the middle would show the Mesopotamian Valley, the Fertile Crescent, as the most logical place to begin civilization anew. Undoubtedly much of the lower valley was under water for many years, but the upthrusted regions at the head of the Tigris and the Euphrates would have been ideal places of settlement.

A proposed scenario of the next few years might be appropriate, although speculative; however, it is based to a certain extent on facts. As one looks at the side of Mt. Ararat on which the ark supposedly landed (if the modern sightings are of the actual ark, a fact not proven, but generally accepted both by local long-standing traditions, and to the extent possible to date, by physical evidence), the natural descent of Noah's family would have been towards the headwaters of either the Euphrates or the Tigris, most likely the Euphrates, as it is closer. It would have been natural for them to have followed its course to the upper Mesopotamian Valley. As a strategic first site for colonization, the place called Ebla, located at the upper end of what would become the fertile crescent, resting between the Mediterranean and the Euphrates, would have been an ideal location from which to begin colonies throughout the region. It was centrally located insofar as trade routes would be concerned between the settlements which followed thereafter in Egypt, Sumer, Crete, and other regions bordering the Mediterranean.

Following shortly after the initial civilization in the upper Mesopotamian was that of the lower, at whatever point the water receded, probably several years. As it states in Genesis 11:2 "And it came to pass, as they journeyed east that they found a plain in the land of Shinar and they dwelt there." There are those who hold that they came from the country east of Babel. Most scholars, however, translate *miqqedem* "eastward" or "toward the east," because of Genesis 13:11 "Then Lot chose him all the plain of Jordan; and Lot journeyed east:..." A recently discovered fragment of the Egyptian Sinuhe legend shows that the country east of Byblos (on the coast north of Beruit, Lebanon), was called Qedem; and it is likely that this region is meant as the quarter whence the Hamites referred to came, who moved into Shinar.[49]

Returning to the archeological evidence and its viewpoint, some confirmation of this position is seen. It should be remembered, as noted above, that what is being quoted below was before Ebla was discovered.

Whatever has been said about the history of mankind prior to the flood, the ages assigned to the life of man on the earth, (Australopithecines in East Africa some 1.5 million years ago, modern humans appearing 10,000 years ago), most researchers are basically in agreement about the ages being studied since the flood. In *The Concise Encyclopedia of Ancient Civilizations* edited by Janet Serlin Garber[50] it says: "Northern Mesopotamia, inhabited since the Mousterian period (about 50,000 B.C.) was later one of the regions in which settlement in permanent villages with a food-producing economy began. This transition is shown at the Neolithic site of Jarmo (about 5000 B.C.). The earliest pottery is found at Tell Hassuna near Mosul [upper Tigris in modern Iraq], which also yields evidence of domesticated animals and cultivated plants, though no trace of metals. This phase is found at sites extending from the Tigris

---

[49]Albert T. Clay, *The Empire of the Amorites* (New Haven, Connecticut: Yale University Press, 1919), page 79. It should be remembered that Mr. Clay wrote prior to the discovery of Ebla. He also called the migrators Semites, but they were, in fact, of the lineage of Ham, Semite referring to the language only.

[50]Janet Serlin Garber, editor. *The Concise Encyclopedia of Ancient Civilizations* (New York City, London: Franklin Watts, 1978), page 188.

to the Mediterranean. Copper began to be employed about 4500 B.C., in a period known at Tell Halaf, from a site on the Khabur River [a tributary of the Euphrates]. Here occurred a wider range of cereals and domestic animals, while technical developments included wheeled vehicles, cobbled streets, mastery of the principle of the vault, and high-temperature kilns.

"Occupation of southern Mesopotamia began, contemporaneously with the Tell Halaf period, at Eridu [near Ur, both close to modern Basra, near the head of the Persian Gulf]. This was a fishing and farming community, employing primitive irrigation and drainage techniques. The subsequent Al-Ubaid culture, though apparently unacquainted with metals, was an efficient peasant economy. It endured several centuries and eventually spread over all Mesopotamia, a notable site of its northern extension being Tepe Gawra."

"Ebla (Tell Mardikh [in modern Syria]) is a fair distance to the West of the Euphrates River. The main epigraphic finds of Ebla, which are to be dated approximately to the mid-part of the third millennium B.C. (about 2500-2300 B.C. [more likely 2250-2100 B.C., as the Flood occurred in 2345 B.C.]), have caused scholars to reassess and to expand their concept of what constituted ancient Mesopotamia. Instead of viewing all the great cultural achievements in the earliest stages as coming from the south, from Sumer, in what is today southern Iraq, the Ebla finds have forced scholars to take a broader view of Mesopotamia, and to include northern Syria into the scope of that area which gave rise to the earliest recorded historical civilizations of mankind.[51]

"The Euphrates River, one of the most important waterways in the world throughout history, [arises in Turkey], bisects the country of Syria, then turns to the East and flows through Iraq. The Tigris River, farther to the East, also arises in Turkey and follows its way south. The Tigris and the Euphrates come very close together near

---

[51]John M. Lundquist, "Was Abraham at Ebla?" *Studies in Scripture, Volume 2: The Pearl of Great Price* (Salt Lake City, Utah: Randall Book Co., 1985), page 226. See Millet, Robert L. in Bibliography.

Baghdad, the capital of Iraq. They then separate and flow into the Persian Gulf. The area between the Tigris and Euphrates Rivers is commonly known as Mesopotamia, the land between the rivers. And it is this region which is commonly thought by scholars to have given rise to the earliest civilizations which have recorded texts."[52]

Returning to our chronology shortly after the Flood, if we assume that Ebla was the first site, or one of the first sites settled, other things begin to fall into place. Arabian traditions tell us that Haran and Nineveh were the first two places resettled after the Flood. However, Abraham states in his record (quoted below) that it was he who named Haran after leaving Ur of the Chaldees (about 2013 B.C.), thereby making Haran later in its development. (some 332 years after the Flood). Archeological studies just quoted show other sites were also settled early on in the same general area. It would appear that we can look to Ebla for many answers as the 17,000 tablets found there continue to be translated. To date over 5,000 places in the region have been identified, and Ebla itself has been shown to have held a population of some 260,000 people at its height, according to archeologists. Dr. Hugh Nibley, professor at Brigham Young University, says that the region held millions of people. Either figure shows a dense population compared to what has heretofore been believed regarding the Fertile Crescent.

"One aspect of special interest to Bible students is that a number of Old Testament cities are mentioned [in the tablets of Ebla]. There are cities that were previously known in the 1st and 2nd millennia B.C. records, but now they are referred to in these 3rd millennium B.C. tablets. There is Salim (possibly the city of Melchizedec), Hazor, Lachish, Megiddo, Gaza, Dor, Sinai, Ashtoroth, and Joppa. Of special interest is Urusalima (Jerusalem) this being the earliest known reference to this city.

"Although a city called Salim is referred to in the tablets, there is no indication as to its geographic location. It is referred to separately from Urusalima (Jerusalem), and this would indicate that the two cities are separate. [However, one interpretation of the word

---

[52]Lundquist, *op. cit.*, page 225.

"Jerusalem" is "the city of Salem" or Salim.]

"Two of the towns mentioned are Sodom and Gomorrah. Here we are transported back to about 2300 B.C., and we find that these towns were regularly visited, being on the route of the King's Highway that ran down from Damascus.

"That is not all. There are actually five "cities of the Plain" (to use the Biblical term at Genesis 14:2), and these were Sodom, Gomorrah, Admah, Zeboiim, and Zoar. We are told in that same verse that an earlier name for Zoar was Bela. These tablets from Ebla refer very precisely, by name, to those five cities of the plain, and at this point we quote from Professor Freedman's public address in November, 1976: 'This record precedes the great catastrophe which many scholars, especially of more recent vintage, have regarded as entirely fictional.'

"He goes on to say that many scholars had regarded the Biblical story of the destruction of Sodom and Gomorrah as an etiological [seeking to assign a cause] tale, set down to explain the collapse of those cities, but now from Ebla we are taken to the other side of the catastrophe. We find that these were real cities, cities that were flourishing at the time of these tablets.

"Damascus is mentioned a number of times. This is very interesting, for this means that this city has been in continuous existence from approximately 2,300 B.C. and perhaps even considerably [slightly] earlier."[53] The fact that Damascus is not more frequently mentioned in the inscriptions of the early period is not due to the fact that it did not possess much importance. Rather, the identification of the spelling of the name has been the problem. Such considerations prompted Albert T. Clay to look for Damascus among the earliest records of Babylon, which resulted in the identification of *Mash* or *Ki-Mash* in the inscriptions of Gudea and in date formulae of the Ur Dynasty, as the ancient name of the city; and also in asserting that it is highly probable that Mesheq in the Old Testament (Genesis 15:2),

---

[53]Dr. Clifford A. Wilson, *Ebla Tablets: Secret of a Forgotten City.* San Diego, California: Master Books, 1979, pages 36-37.

is the same, namely *Mash-qi.* If the identification of the mountain Mashu of the Gilgamesh epic with Hermon, and the city *Ki-Mash* with Mesheq (Damascus) is correct, then it seems highly probable that the early name of the country was Mash, which is to be identified with Mash, the son of Aram, the son of Shem (Genesis 10:23). The Joktanites (Joktan was a son of Eber, who was the son of Selah, son of Arphaxad, son of Shem) were Arabian tribes which dwelt in the land "from Mesha as thou goest towards Sephar, the mountain of the East." (Genesis 10:30) Sephar has not been located, but it seems that the direction in the description of the land, occupied by these descendants of Eber, was from north to the southeast; and that Mesha is probably the city referred to.[54]

Thus the identification of Damascus has shown several critical pieces of information regarding the offspring of Shem. We now can show that all of his sons originally settled in the northern Mesopotamian Valley, mostly living in the region between the rivers and the Mediterranean, spreading out from there into Assyria, Persia, Africa, the Mediterranean and Europe. This will be shown in more detail later.

In an article in *National Geographic*[55] additional light is shed on the discoveries at Ebla. The kings of Ebla signed treaties with Assur, on the Tigris River, and with Khamazi, far to the east. The names of cities thought to have been founded much later, such as Beirut and Byblos, leap from the tablets. Damascus, mentioned above, and Gaza are noted as is Iram, an obscure city referred to in Sura 89 of the Koran. Most intriguing of all are the personal names found on the Ebla tables. They include Ab-ra-mu (Abraham), E-sa-um (Esau), and Sa-u-lum (Saul). Present as well is a name never found before in ancient literature, save for the Old Testament: Da-u-dum (David). Further, the name of a king, Ebrium, who reigned about 2300 B.C., bears an uncanny resemblance to Eber of the Book of Genesis.

---

[54]Taylor, *op. cit.*, pages 122-123.

[55]Howard LaFay, "Ebla, Splendor of an Unknown Empire," *National Geographic* 154 (1978): 731-757.

The references to Ebla as to when it existed are that after "an intense period of formation" Ebla became, by about 2400 B.C., a thriving city. [The year 2340 is the date being allowed in this study for its beginning.] Prosperity and power burgeoned under the reigns of five successive kings. Indeed, so powerful did Ebla's kings become that they apparently contended with Sargon of Akkad. The struggle apparently ended when Sargon defeated the Eblaites sometime before 2300 B.C. [This date is LaFay's. It does not allow sufficient time according to the chronology noted herein. There is great controversy as to when Sargon of Akkad lived. It is estimated in this study that he lived between 2300-2125, the year 2300 being the earliest year he could have been born as a son of Nimrod. As will be demonstrated below, Akkad is likely the name with which Sargon was born, possibly being a son of Nimrod; regardless, clearly being of the lineage of Ham. It is estimated that he destroyed Ebla about 2240.] The economic considerations involved stand out clearly in Sargon's victory inscription: "He worshiped the god Dagan, who gave him from that time onwards the Upper Country, Mari, Yarmuti and Ebla, as far as the Forest of Cedars and the Mountain of Silver." Less than a century later Sargon's grandson Naram-Sin burned Ebla. It was destroyed by fire about 2250 [2180] B.C. However, it rose from the ashes. Royal records from Ur of the Chaldees mention two Eblaites by name - Ili-Dagan and Gura. Also mentioned is "Surim, the messenger, the man from Ebla." About 2000 B.C. Ebla was destroyed again. We know this because of the thick layers of ash found everywhere in this stratum. What happened? Well, Ur fell to the Elamites and the nomadic Amorites around 2000 B.C. Several texts show the presence of Amorites throughout northern Syria during this period. Doubtless they struck at Ebla too and wiped it out. This time the attack resulted in the collapse of early Syrian culture as well as the destruction of the city. In the aftermath we find a new people with a new culture. Ebla flourished briefly once again, but around 1800 B.C. the city began to decline, and within two hundred years finally disappeared from history. Dr. Pettinato disagrees with this chronology. For a number of reasons, he feels that some of the tablets from the royal archives date from at least 2500 B.C., making the city older than Dr. Matthiae's estimate.

A note must be interjected here regarding Egypt. Many ancient cities are named after persons, and in fact, these cities in a number of cases became the name of the country. Cases in point are Rome, Babylon, Misr, and Mexico, among others. It is agreed today that the great invasions of Egypt in early times came by way of the Wadi Hammamat. And what is the first place one would settle down on reaching the valley? It is the plain at Koptos, the very place where the Wadi Hammamat opens on the Nile valley. Many scholars have noted this fact. Koptos is not only traditionally but also logically the oldest settlement in Egypt; and just as it could have given its name to the whole land, it could have gotten that name from the person who led the enterprise. This person was Egyptus, daughter of Ham and Egyptus, as noted elsewhere in this work. However, for purposes of continuity, a brief quote from The Book of Abraham 1:23-24 will suffice: "The land of Egypt being first discovered by a woman, who was the daughter of Ham, and the daughter of Egyptus, which in the Chaldean signifies Egypt, which signifies that which is forbidden. When this woman discovered the land it was under water, who afterward settled her sons in it."

What have the Chaldeans got to do with Egypt one might ask? A few years ago scholars would have quickly discredited the whole passage, but not today. There are very reputable Egyptologists who now believe that in the early period of civilization after the Flood, Egypt and Mesopotamia were parts of one empire and ruled by one man. The ties between Egypt and Babylonia are better substantiated every day. The Semitic origin of much of what is Egypt has been a puzzle to man, however. Perhaps the quotation from The Book of Abraham 1:26 shows why these Semitic and Hamitic[56] cultures cross each

---

[56]The terms *Semitic* and *Hamitic* are actually linguistic terms, not ethnic designations. These terms refer to groups of people that spoke the same language. There are a lot of misunderstandings in the use of these terms, however; therefore, in this study it will always be distinguished that the reference is to the race or to the language.

The language of ancient Egypt stood geographically between the Semitic languages of the Middle East and the Hamitic languages of northern and eastern Africa. Traditionally, Egyptian has been termed a hamito-semitic language since it contained significant characteristics of Semitic languages, as well as elements of Berber and Chad, which are Hamitic. This was a result of the prehistoric migrations of both

other's paths so often: "Pharaoh, being a righteous man, established his kingdom and judged his people wisely and justly all his days, seeking earnestly *to imitate* (emphasis added) that order established by the fathers in the first generations, in the days of the first patriarchal reign, even in the reign of Adam, and also of Noah, his father, who blessed him with the blessings of the earth, and with the blessings of wisdom, but cursed him as pertaining to the Priesthood.[57] Perhaps Mesopotamia and Egypt all were the land of the pharaohs, and in the first generations after the Flood were ruled righteously from Mesopotamia, Egypt being settled only after the waters subsided sufficiently for the land to again be inhabited. And the ancient ruins of what had been, were built upon and around in memory of the past and in the hope of again becoming a great nation. The knowledge basis for this was taken from Noah and his three sons, but is called Semitic by modern scholars.

A PRELIMINARY LOOK AT THE PATRIARCH ABRAHAM

Leaving this early period for now, we turn to the time of Abraham. "Three great religions - Judaism, Christianity, and Islam - trace their historical origins to the Patriarch Abraham. The Book of Genesis introduces him as a native of Ur of the Chaldees, in southern Mesopotamia. Scholars have always taken this at face value. Most of them believe that about 1800 B.C. Abraham and his followers migrated through the Fertile Crescent - north from Ur, across Syria, and down into Palestine.

But we now encounter a Syrian capital, dating from five hundred years *before* the widely accepted date for Abraham - a place rich in patriarchal and Biblical names. Provocatively, the Ebla tablets mention a nearby Syrian city called Ur, while Deuteronomy refers to Jacob, Abraham's [traditional] grandson, as a Syrian. Furthermore,

---

language (and racial) groups into the Nile Valley. This will be discussed in more detail in the Linguistic History section of this study.

[57]LaFay, *op. cit.*, pages 741, 748; Hugh Nibley, *There Were Jaredites* (Salt Lake City: Deseret Book Company, 1988), pages 322-324.

Muslim scholars have long held that Abraham's epic journey occurred about 2300 B.C.

These discoveries at Ebla, combined with the Muslim scholastic position, point out the possibility that the time period that Abraham lived might have been much earlier than Biblical accounts would have us believe. They confirm the existence of Salim, and the cities of the plain, and may give us further evidence of when Abraham lived. All of this agrees with the theory presented herein that the fourteen generations from David to Abraham are figurative only, and have religious rather than genealogical importance. There are missing generations somewhere between Abraham and David, and based on the evidence they are likely between Abraham and Isaac, although it is possible they are between Isaac and Jacob. No primary nor circumstantial evidence exists to suggest the missing generations are earlier than Abraham. And as we will see, there is a great deal of evidence surrounding his time period.

Quoting from Genesis 14:1-24 and from "Joseph Smith Translation: Excerpts too Lengthy for Inclusion in Footnotes" found in the L.D.S. version of *The Holy Bible,* for Genesis 14:25-40, we have the following important information regarding Abraham, Melchizedek and some general flavor about this period:

"And it came to pass in the days of Amraphel [we will return to him momentarily] king of Shinar, Arioch king of Ellasar, Chedorlaomer king of Elam, and Tidal king of nations; that these made war with Bera king of Sodom, and with Birsha king of Gomorrah, Shinab king of Admah, and Shemeber king of Zeboiim, and the king of Bela, which is Zoar.

"All these were joined together in the vale of Siddim, which is the salt sea. Twelve years they served Chedorlaomer, and in the thirteenth year they rebelled. And in the fourteenth year came Chedorlaomer, and the kings that were with him, and smote the Rephaims in Ashteroth, Karnaim, and the Zuzims in Ham, and the Emims in Shaveh Kiriathaim. And the Horites in their mount Seir, unto Elparan, which is by the wilderness.

"And they returned, and came to Enmishpat, which is Kadesh, and smote all the country of the Amalekites, and also the Amorites, that dwelt in Hazezontamar.

"And there went out the king of Sodom, and the king of Gomorrah, and the king of Admah, and the king of Zeboiim, and the king of Bela (the same is Zoar); and they joined battle with them in the vale of Siddim; with Chedorlaomer the king of Elam, and with Tidal king of nations, and Amraphel king of Shinar, and Arioch king of Ellasar; four kings with five.

"And the vale of Siddim was full of slimepits; and the kings of Sodom and Gomorrah fled, and fell there; and they that remained fled to the mountain. And they took all the goods of Sodom and Gomorrah and all their victuals, and went their way. And they took Lot, Abram's brother's son, who dwelt in Sodom, and his goods, and departed.

"And there came one that had escaped, and told Abram the Hebrew; for he dwelt in the plain of Mamre the Amorite, brother of Eshcol, and brother of Aner: and these were confederate with Abram. And when Abram heard that his brother was taken captive, he armed his trained servants, born in his own house, three hundred and eighteen, and pursued them unto Dan. And he divided himself against them, he and his servants, by night, and smote them, and pursued them unto Hobah, which is on the left hand of Damascus. And he brought back all the goods, and also brought again his brother Lot, and his goods, and the women also, and the people.

"And the king of Sodom went out to meet him after his return from the slaughter of Chedorlaomer, and of the kings that were with him, at the valley of Shaveh, which is the king's dale.

"And Melchizedek, king of Salem brought forth bread and wine: and he was the priest of the most high God. And he blessed him, and said, Blessed be Abram of the most high God, possessor of heaven and earth: and blessed be the most high God, which hath delivered thine enemies into thy hand. And he gave him tithes of all.

"And the king of Sodom said unto Abram, Give me the persons, and take the goods to thyself. And Abram said to the king of Sodom, I have lift up mine hand unto the Lord, the most high God, the possessor of heaven and earth, that I will not take from a thread even to a shoelatchet, and that I will not take any thing that is thine, lest thou shouldst say, I have made Abram rich: save only that which the young men have eaten, and the portion of the men which went with me, Aner, Eshcol, and Mamre; let them take their portion.

"And Melchizedek lifted up his voice and blessed Abram. Now Melchizedek was a man of faith, who wrought righteousness; and when a child he feared God, and stopped the mouths of lions, and quenched the violence of fire. And thus, having been approved of God, he was ordained an high priest after the order of the covenant of God made with Enoch, it being after the order of the Son of God; which order came, not by man, nor the will of man; neither by father nor mother; neither by beginning of days nor end of years; but by God; and it was delivered unto men by the calling of his own voice, according to his own will, unto as many as believed on his name.

"For God having sworn unto Enoch and unto his seed with an oath by himself; that every one being ordained after this order and calling should have power, by faith, to break mountains, to divide the seas, to dry up waters, to turn them out of their course; to put at defiance the armies of nations, to divide the earth, to break every band, to stand in the presence of God; to do all things according to his will, according to his command, subdue principalities and powers; and this by the will of the Son of God which was from before the foundation of the world.

"And men having this faith, coming up unto this order of God, were translated and taken up into heaven.

"And now, Melchizedek was a priest of this order; therefore he obtained peace in Salem, and was called the Prince of peace. And his people wrought righteousness, and obtained heaven, and sought for the city of Enoch which God had before taken, separating it from the earth, having reserved it unto the latter days, or the end of the world; and hath said, and sworn with an oath, that the heavens and the earth should come together; and the sons of God should be tried so as by fire.

"And this Melchizedek, having thus established righteousness, was called the king of heaven by his people, or, in other words, the King of peace.

"And he lifted up his voice, and he blessed Abram, being the high priest, and the keeper of the storehouse of God; him whom God had appointed to receive tithes for the poor.

"Wherefore, Abram paid unto him tithes of all that he had, of all the riches which he possessed, which God had given him more than that which he had need.

"And it came to pass, that God blessed Abram, and gave unto him riches, and honor, and lands for an everlasting possession; according to the covenant which he had made, and according to the blessing wherewith Melchizedek had blessed him."

This battle took place ten years after Abraham left Haran, or in 1989 B.C. (Genesis 16:3)[58] From this extensive quotation we have placed Abraham within a historical context in conjunction with individuals who were his contemporaries. One of them provides another proof as to the time period in which Abraham lived. He is Amraphel, king of Shinar, also known as Hammurabi.

"Hammurabi is generally identified with Amraphel, king of Shinar, who with Arioch of Ellasar, Cheodorlaomar of Elam and Tidal, king

---

[58]The statement that Abram had dwelt ten years in the land of Canaan includes the period of time that he was also in Egypt. This can be determined because the biblical ages for Abraham do not agree with The Book of Abraham and therefore must be revised downward thirteen years. Genesis 12:4 says he was seventy-five when he departed Haran. He was sixty-two. Genesis 16:16 says he was eighty-six when Ishmael was born eleven years after residing in Canaan. He was seventy-three.

of Goiim, invaded Canaan in the days of Abraham.[59]   Since Hammurabi apparently enjoyed peaceful relations with the powerful Elamitic king, Rim-Sin of Ellasar, and his father, Kudur-mabug, *ad-da* of Emutbal and of Amurru, the biblical records appear to harmonize with these facts and the identification has never been successfully disproved....

"Hammurabi, 6th king of the Amoritic or West Semitic dynasty of Babylonia, reigned forty-three years, 2067-2025 [1990-1947 B.C. according to the chronology contained herein] and is one of the most illustrious figures of ancient history.   The so-called 1st Babylonian dynasty was founded by Sumuabi in 2169 [2090] B.C. at Babylon, which thus was raised from an unimportant town on the eastern bank of the Euphrates to the dignity of a capital, and a rival of the far more ancient and greater city, Kish, eight miles to the east.

"The invasion of Babylonia by the Canaanitic race of the west had already resulted in the founding of a West Semitic dynasty at Isin in ... [2090] B.C., a city in southern Sumer, which, until the rise of the Canaanitic kingdom of Babylon, shared with Ellasar the control of Sumer and Accad. At first, the kingdom founded at Babylon by this ancestor of the famous line of eleven kings at Babylon had control of only a small region north and south of the capital, and under the first two kings there was even a rival kingdom at Kish, only eight miles away.   During the reigns of Hammurabi's five predecessors the kingdoms of Isin and Ellasar successfully maintained control of the whole southern area of Babylonia; and Simmuballit, predecessor [and father] of Hammurabi, conquered and put an end to the kingdom of Isin with the aid of Rim-Sin of Ellasar, in ... [1999 B.C.], or only nine years before Hammurabi came to the throne, only to lose it again to Rim-Sin, the powerful king of Ellasar, seven years later, and

---

[59]The University of Chicago, editor, *Encyclopaedia Britannica: A New Survey of Universal Knowledge*, Volume 11 (Chicago, London, and Toronto: Encyclopaedia Britannica, Inc.), page 135. The derivation of Hammurabi's name is disputed; the element *hammu, 'ammu, ammu, ammi* is clearly the West Semitic word *'am*, "family, relative," or Arabic "uncle," and it is characteristic of West Semitic religion to describe a deity as "father, brother, uncle." The element *rabi* is usually explained as meaning "great," "the uncle is great."

Hammurabi himself did not gain control of the whole of Babylonia and put an end to the kingdom of Rim-Sin until his 30th year [1960 B.C.]."

Returning to the general time period following the Flood, the Sumerians have, up to recent times been thought to have founded the first civilization after the Flood (Genesis 10:8-12), but we have shown that they were not the first, even though they followed shortly thereafter. "And Cush begat Nimrod: he began to be a mighty one in the earth. He was a mighty hunter before the Lord: wherefore it is said, Even as Nimrod the mighty hunter before the Lord. And the beginning of his kingdom was Babel, and Erech, and Accad, and Calneh, in the land of Shinar." At Larsa - a few miles north of Ur - was the site where the Weld Prism was found. This prism contains a history written by a scribe named Nur-Ninsubur in approximately 2100 B.C. In his account he records the history of ten pre-Flood kings [this list is given above, page 26] and ends his writing with the sad words, "and the Flood overthrew the land."[60]

Although the following chart does not reflect exactly the chronology that has been developed in this presentation, it shows what is known and believed by scholars regarding the kingdoms of central and southern Mesopotamia.[61] The notations on Sargon reflect the traditional timing and the possible timing based on the fact given herein. If the possible timing is used, it obviously moves many of the other dates forward in time by seventy-five to a hundred years.

---

[60]Noorbergen, *op. cit.,* page 26.

[61]Giovanni Pettinato, *Ebla: A New Look at History,* translated by C. Faith Richardson (Baltimore and London: The Johns Hopkins University Press, 1991), page 188. [Originally published as *Ebla: Nuovi orizzonti della storia* (Milan, Italy: Rusconi Libri, S.p.A., 1986)] A few references in the chart are taken from elsewhere.

Date & Place	Ur	Lagash	Umma	Kish	Akkad
2700					
2675				Mebaragesi	
2650				Aka	
2625					
2600				(Mesalim)	
2575		Enkhengal			
2550					
2525					
2500		Ur-Nanše	Uš		
2475	Mesanepada	Akurgal	Enakale		
2450	Meskiagnuna	Eannatum			
2425	Balulu	Entemena	Urlumma		
2400		Enannatum II			
2375	Dungi	Lugalanda			
2350		Urukagina	Lugalzagesi		Sargon (trad.)
2325					
2300				Rimuš	Sargon (poss.)
2275				Maništusu	
2250				Naram-Sin	
2225				Šarkališarri	
2200					

Scholars disagree about the periods of reigns of the individual sovereigns and the synchronism of the dynasties of the various city-states. For a different chronological table, see H. Nissen, *Zur Datierung des Königsfriedhofs von Ur* (Bon, 1966), plate 37. Another table, found in the book by Chaim Bermant and Michael Weitzman entitled *Ebla: A Revelation in Archaeology* (New York City: Times Books, 1979), pages 200-202, gives a broader and slightly different interpretation. A caution placed at the beginning of the chart reads: "... the earliest dates are to be treated with particular caution. The chronology adopted in the *Cambridge Ancient History* (3rd ed.) is, in the main, followed here.

BC	EBLA	EGYPT	MESOPOTAMIA
3100	Acropolis and adjacent areas occupied	Foundation of 1st Dynasty	Development of Sumerian city-states
			Rulers of city-states include:
2700			Mebaragesi of Kish
2686		Old	
2680		Kingdom founded	Gilgamesh of Uruk
			Aka of Kish
2600			Shub-Ad also spelled Pu-Abi, Queen or Ur
2550		Pharaohs	
2540		include	Ur-Nanshe of Lagash
2500		Chephren	Eannatum of Lagash
2400	Range of dates proposed for Iblul-Il, King of Mari, vanquished by Ebla (2685-2400)		Urukagina of Lagash
2378-2371			Lugalzagesi of Umma
2371-2347			Dynasty of Agade: Sargon
2371-2316	Ebla destroyed by Sargon?		Rimush
2315-2307		Pepi I	Manishtushu (2306-2292)
2300			Naram-Sin
2291-2244	Ebla destroyed by Naram-Sin?		Shar-kali-sharri
2254-2230			Kaku of Lagash
2200		End of Old	
2181		Kingdom	Gudea of Lagash
2175		Middle	
2133		Kingdom Begins	Utuhengal of Uruk

As has been noted previously, but necessarily reiterated here, the dates given above and below are those of the historians, the archeologists, and others who follow the academic view of history. These are given for comparison and reference only. We will return to Abraham later in the book, after establishing a more solid footing from other historical sources, for the premises contained herein.

BC	EBLA	EGYPT	MESOPOTAMIA
2120-2114			Third Dynasty of Ur:
2113-2096			Ur-Nammu
2095-2048			Shulgi
2047-2039			Amar-Sin
2038-2030			Shu-Sin
2029-2006			Ibbi-Sin
2017-1985			Ishbi-Erra (Isin)
2000	Destruction by the Amorites? Beginning of range of dates proposed for Abraham (2000-1400)[62]		
1792-1750			Hammurapi of
1786		End of Middle Kingdom	Babylon[64]
1700			Rise of Kassite Dynasty
1684-1567		Hyksos Rulers[63]	
1650-1600	Destruction (by Hittites?)		
1590			Babylon destroyed by Hittites under Murshilis I
1567		New Kingdom begins. Pharaohs include:	
1503-1482		Hatshepsut	
1504-1450		Tuthmosis III in co-regency	
1379-1362		Akhenaten	

[62]This range of centuries shows that the historical and archeological evidence as compared to *The Holy Bible* has never been reconciled, and points out circumstantially that there is a problem with the time frame therein.

[63]The Hyksos rule may have begun as late as 1659 B.C.

[64]This time period does not agree with the revised chronology given above. It coincides with the traditional period in which Abraham was supposed to live, but as shown above is inaccurate.

THE INITIAL DIVISIONS OF THE GROWING POPULATION, 2345-2245 B.C.

THE BASIC DIVISIONS OF MANKIND BY ETHNIC DESIGNATIONS: INTRODUCTION

The three sons of Noah and their three wives had within them the entire genepool currently available on the earth. The diversity is incredible; nevertheless, it exists. Anyone who has done any studies in even simple genetics knows that the possible combinations are unlimited. The following general divisions must be considered as just that. There has been throughout the history of the world interracial combining from the earliest days. Most of these will never be identified in this life.

Also of note in the genetic make-up of humanity is that each individual has thousands of genes which, in other individuals, are absent or occur in different forms. Thus the particular combination likely to result from sexual pooling of the *genotypes* (genetic repertories) of any two individuals will be in some respects an unprecedented combination. Racial groupings larger than mated pairs may be identified at the level of family, tribes, ethnic groups, nations, regions, or continents. The time span involved may be a single generation, two generations, and so forth. And the number of possible combinations of genes for particular traits or their *alleles* (in other words, alternate forms of the same gene) may range from one to hundreds of thousands.[65]

---

[65]Marvin Harris, *Culture, Man, and Nature: An Introduction to General Anthropology* (New York City: Thomas & Crowell Company, 1971, page 88).

There seems little doubt that most of the allelic genes in the human *genome* (system of genes) have distributions that cut across the Caucasoid-Negroid-Mongoloid divisions as if these simply did not exist. (This is true, in part, because of the early infusions of genes from each of the major divisions into each other through intermarriage and miscegenation.) Of highest interest in this regard are the genes controlling the immunochemical reactions of the blood. These genes at one time were thought to be the best possible source of a genetic classification of the races. Unlike traits such as skin color or hair form, the precise genetic mechanism for the inheritance of the blood groups is well understood and thousands of controlled blood-group studies have been made throughout the world. The best-known series is the *ABO system*. Each human being has a genotype that puts him in either blood group A, B, AB, or O. (We shall ignore the complexities of the subtypes which in any event make the distribution even more erratic.) Type O has the widest distribution, occurring on all continents and crosscutting all racial divisions. For example, it occurs with a frequency of 60-69 percent in India, Central Africa, Southern China, Central Australia, and Western Europe. Type A is equally unmindful of what the raciologists think the major divisions of mankind ought to be. Africa, India, and China all have 1-9 percent frequencies, while Japan, Scotland, and much of aboriginal Australia are in the 20-29 percent bracket. Old World Mongoloids have frequencies of B ranging from 10-30 percent, yet the New World American Indians are in the 0-5 percent range, a frequency shared by the Australian aborigines. West Africa and Eastern Europe both show B frequencies of about 15-20 percent. Similar racially nonconforming distributions are characteristic of other blood systems. It should be emphasized that this distribution of blood groups could very well serve as the basis for a taxonomy of major geographical races. Of course, the resulting races would simply bear little resemblance to the races identified by the traditional criteria.[66]

It is obvious from the reading of names and the minimal notes pertaining to the dispersion found in the various editions of *The Holy Bible*, that Noah's children and grandchildren began to spread out rapidly from their initial landing site in the mountains of Ararat,

---

[66]Harris, *op. cit.*, pages 96-98.

even before the general dispersion at the time of the Tower of Babel, approximately 300 years after the Flood. It would appear that within the first 100 years after the Flood, many of the lands of Europe, the Middle East, Africa, and Asia had been staked out by the expanding families. This historical development will be treated as fully and with as much documentation as possible.

Calvin Kephart says: "About 2300 B.C. an intense and disastrous drought must have overspread central Asia, creating great disturbance and causing a dispersion..."[67] He then goes on to tell how the various cultures began to move throughout the earth, or move into lands already populated with other tribes. His timing is about right even if all the facts are not correct.

In the book by John Baines and Jaromir Málek[68], entitled *Atlas of Ancient Egypt,* there is a chronological table, the main point of which are as follows. This table shows the standard archeological theories as to time periods. As will be noted in the period prior to 3500 B.C. no substantive finds have been made that can be documented with certainty.

---

[67]Calvin Kephart, *Races of Mankind, their Origin and Migration* (New York City: Philosophical Library, Inc., 1960, page 248).

[68]John Baines and Jaromir Málek, *Atlas of Ancient Egypt* (New York City: Facts on File Publications, 1984), no page numbers indicated.

PLACE & YEAR	B.C. 6500	B.C. 4500	B.C. 4000	B.C. 3500
Egypt	Late Paleolithic	Badarian: Nile Valley; Merimda: Delta; Faiyum	Nagada I: Nile Valley Painted terracotta figure of a dancing woman.	Nagada II: Nile Valley; Ma'ada el-Omari: Memphite area
Lower Nubia (Upper Nubia)	Late Paleolithic	Neolithic Abkan Post-Shamarkian Khartum Variant	Early A Group	Early A Group Classic A Group
Syria (Palestine)	Neolithic Jericho 8500			Urban Society Habuba-el Kebira
Mesopotamia (Iran)	Neolithic 6500 Neolithic 6000 Irrigation farming 5500	Late Neolithic Ubaid 5000		Urban Society Uruk Invention of writing
Anatolia	Neolithic Catal Hüyük 6500			
Aegean	Neolithic 6500			

It is obvious that there is a general discrepancy between this train of thought and the chronology in the Bible. We must assume at this point, taking the conservative approach, that anything prior to 2345 was pre-Flood. However, we are basically only interested in the post-Flood period anyway. Let's analyze this time period in as much detail as possible, beginning with the children of Japheth, the eldest. Part of this information (Webster is noted below) is also taken from the book edited by Susa Young Gates.[69]

[69]Susa Young Gates, *Surname Book and Racial History* (Salt Lake City, Utah: General Board of the Relief Society, 1918).

PLACE & YEAR	B.C. 3000	B.C. 2500	B.C. 2000	B.C. 1500
Egypt	Foundation of the Egyptian state (late Naqada II) c. 3050; Early Dynastic Period (2920-2575) Dynasties: 1st 2920-2770 2nd 2770-2649 3rd 2649-2575 The Step Pyramid of Djoser at Saqqara, c.2630 Painting: geese tomb of Itet at Maidum c.2560	Old Kingdom 2575-2134 Dynasties: 4th 2575-2465 5th 2465-2323 6th 2323-2150 1st Intermediate Period 2134-2040 Dynasties: 9th-10th Herakleopolis 2134-2040 11th Thebes 2134-2040 The Step Pyramid of Djoser at Saqqara, c.2630 Painting: geese tomb of Itet at Maidum c.2560	Middle Kingdom 2040-1640 Dynasties: 11th all Egypt 2040-1991 12th 1991-1783 13th 1783-after 1640 2nd Intermediate Period 1640-1532 15th Hyksos 1640-1532 17th Thebes 1640-1550 Head of Ma'ya, relief in Theban tomb of Ra'-mose, c.1360 Inlaid gold mask of Tut'ankha-mun c.1325	New Kingdom 1550-1070 Dynasties: 18th 1550-1307 Amarna 1352-1333 19th 1307-1196 20th 1196-1070 3rd Intermediate Period 1070-712 21st 1070-945 Detail of façade of Great Temple of Abu Simbel c.1270 Inlaid gold mask of Tut'ank-hamun c.1325
Lower Nubia (Upper Nubia)	Classic A Group Terminal A Group: little settled populations	C Group Kerma culture	Egyptian occupation; Kerma conquest; Pangrave culture	Egyptian conquest: Upper & Lower Nubia
Syria (Palestine)	Early Bronze Ebla; Egyptian contact with Palestine	Egyptian contact with Byblos; Hittite incursions	Mitanni 1520-1330; Hittite domination	Late Bronze: city state; Egy. occ. c. 1530-1200; Mitanni 1520-1330; Hittite domination. Ind. of Assur c.1380; Elamite expansion;
Mesopotamia (Iran)	Early Dynastic Jamdat Nasr	Sargonid & 3rd dynasty of Ur	1st Dyn.of Babyl Old Elamite K.; Fall of Babylon Kassite Dynasty Hittite Old King	Hittite Empire
Anatolia Aegean	Early Bronze	Middle Bronze	Late Bronze	Cretan destr. Mycenaean destr Sub-Mycenaean

Professor William Albright's comment regarding the Table of Nations found in *The Holy Bible*, Book of Genesis, chapter 10 is significant:

"It stands absolutely alone in ancient literature without a remote parallel even among the Greeks....'The Table of Nations' remains an astonishingly accurate document.... [It] shows such remarkably 'modern' understanding of the ethnic and linguistic situation in the modern world, in spite of all its complexity, that scholars never fail to be impressed with the author's knowledge of the subject."

Archeology has given clear testimony to the accuracy of the chapter, for nearly all the names mentioned are now known. The Bible records have been substantiated in no uncertain manner, not only as regards the people who are in the center of Biblical history, but as regards many other peoples as well. The Assyrians, the Medes, the Greeks, the Egyptians, and numerous others are mentioned, and in many ways that are very precise and accurate. We even find reference to points that were long ago forgotten, but are now known to have been just as the Bible briefly states.

Only the Bible gives an acceptable history of a people from its actual development through individuals.[70]

Following is a study of the basic divisions of mankind as compiled by Hutton Webster.[71] He is wrong in some of his designations, based on *The Book of Mormon* and *The Pearl of Great Price* knowledge of some races. These errors have been corrected in the study noted below.

---

[70]Wilson, *op. cit.*, pages 80-81.

[71]Hutton Webster, *History of Civilization, Ancient & Medieval* (Boston, Massachusetts: D.C. Heath and Company, 1947).

THE DESCENDANTS OF JAPHETH
ELDEST SON OF NOAH

From the eldest son Japheth come the basic stock of the Mongoloid races proper as well as some of the Mediterranean, western Asiatic and European kingdoms. These are divided into stock language types.

Sinitic family: Chinese, Siamese, Burmese, and Tibetan

Japanese family: Japanese

Korean family: Koreans

Altaic family: Turkish, Mongolian, Manchu, and probably Siberian tribes. To Webster's list here should also be added the Getae (the Nordic, Aryan, or Scythian tribes), and the Medes.

He lists these latter two grouping as part of the Asiatic Family descended from Shem. However, the Scythians are from Gomer, son of Japheth; and Madai, son of Japheth was the father of the Medes. The Armenians, which he assigns to the Altaic family have been moved because Arphaxad, son of Shem was the father of Armenia. These facts are confirmed by Gates.[72] Webster also classifies the Hittites with the Asiatic Family of Shem, but they are neither from Shem, nor Japheth, but principally from Ham, through his son Canaan, and Canaan's son Heth. (Genesis 10:6, 15)

Finno-Ugrian family: Magyar, Estonian, Finnish, and Lapp

Malayo family: Malays (in Formosa, the Philippines, Malay Archipelago, and Madagascar); Indonesians (in Malay Archipelago). Webster had the Polynesians included as part of the Malayo-Polynesian group, but the Polynesians belong under Shem, as will be noted below.

Slavic Family: South Slav (Serb, Montenegrin, Croat, Slovene); West

---

[72]Gates, *op. cit.*, page 14.

Slav (Czech, Slovak, Pole); East Slav (Great Russian, Little Russian or Ruthenian, and White Russian). It is much more likely that all the Slavic nations are descendants of Japheth rather than of Shem as noted in Webster. They have been placed here because of their obvious relationship to the Altaic families noted above.

"Now these are the generations of the sons of Noah, Shem, Ham, and Japheth: and unto them were sons born after the flood. The sons of Japheth; Gomer, and Magog, and Madai, and Javan, and Tubal, and Meshech, and Tiras. And the sons of Gomer; Ashkenaz, and Riphath, and Togarmah. And the sons of Javan; Elishah, and Tarshish, Kittim, and Dodanim. By these were the isles of the Gentiles divided in their lands; every one after his tongue, after their families, in their nations." (Genesis 10:1-5)

When the sons of Noah with their descendants spread abroad after the Flood, the sons of Japheth went into the Mediterranean coasts, into Asia Minor to the "isles of the Gentiles," also across Armenia, into the Tigris and Euphrates valleys over Media and Persia, and eastward into India, embracing probably the peoples who spoke what is now called the great Indo-European languages. In Greek mythology the Titan Japetus is the progenitor of the human race. Ion, his son, in the Hebrew form is Javan.[73]

Japheth means "enlarged." The first generation born after the Flood, the male children of Japheth, consisted of Gomer, Magog, Madai, Javan, Tubal, Meshech, and Tiras. These nations of families are responsible for the clan development in India, Ireland, Scotland, and among the Slavs.

GOMER, SON OF JAPHETH

The second generation, the male children of Gomer, included Ashkenaz, Riphath, and Togarmah. (Genesis 10:1-5) Gomer is the father of the Teutons. Some Mormon authorities claim Semitic descent for the Teutons. It is quite certain that the seed of Israel is scattered through the Teuton peoples. However, we give the line

---

[73]Gates, *op. cit.*, page 29.

here as it is given in modern histories.[74]

Ashkenaz

Medieval Hebrew uses the word "Ashkenaz" as the name for the region of modern Germany. The Hebrew name Ashkênâz refers to Noah's grandson, and was the name used by the Hebrews referring to a neighboring but unidentified nation.

Undoubtedly, Ashkenaz, went north when his brothers, who settled in the regions of the Mediterranean, left the upper Mesopotamian Valley and travelled west. The descendants of Ashkenaz spread into the steppes of western and central Asia, becoming the ancestors of the Getae, or as they are commonly known, the Scythian, Nordic or Aryan tribes. Their northern homeland, Geté, lay in the foothills and lower mountains of Western Turkistan between Kashgaria and Lake Balkhash, partly in the Bolor range. Thereupon, the Nordic or Aryan tribes over the centuries moved throughout Asia and into Europe, being the ancestors of, or mixing with, dozens of nations.

As the land became drier with the passing of time, and the forests returned to these northern regions, the southerly edge of vast oak and beech forests extended across Siberia and Russia north of a line from the Altai Mountains to the middle course of the Obi River in central Siberia, thence southwestward to the southerly end of the Ural Mountains, and beyond to the upper reaches of the Dnieper River. South of this course, below the great east-and-west ridge, the lands were still largely marshy from the waters of melting glaciers in the mountains, and the residue of the Flood waters. This was particularly true around the northerly shores of the Caspian Sea, and Lake Aral still covered an immense area, much of which now is arid. In the extreme north, in both Siberia and Russia, vast tundras extended to the Artic Ocean.

With the passing of time the Nordic peoples expanded both westward and southward into the regions north, east, and southeast of Lake Aral, including the lower courses of the Jaxartes and Oxus Rivers.

---

[74]Gates, *ibid.*

Ultimately, they separated into five tribes, which became different nations. The first Nordic tribe to move farther west, as far as the Ural River, was the Suebian. This migration must have been accelerated by the movements of others on their east, and about 2100 B.C. the vanguard of the Suebians entered Europe around the north of the Caspian Sea. By 2000 B.C. they had conquered the rich lands of the Ukraine (western ancient Scythia), for it was soon after this time that their bands of adventurers poured over the Carpathian Mountains into Transylvania, Moravia, and Bohemia, and even across Hungary, Bosnia, Croatia, and Dalmatia as they explored the regions on the south and the west. They brought a complete civilization, far less advanced than that of the Turks but representative of the status of the Nordic nations at that time. They were largely hunters and herdsmen, whose leaders, upon the conquest of Danubian peasant lands, established themselves on hilltops. They brought new types of vases, corded ware, strange implements, and splendid stone and copper battle axes. They heaped a barrow over their dead. All over the region from the Caspian Sea to the Dnieper River, graves containing skeletons covered with red ochre and surmounted by a mound or kurgan have been found; also the bones of sheep, cattle, and horses, the last-named being the desert species used by the Turks of Turkistan, the steppe horse. They possessed wheeled vehicles, which they, like the Iranians, used as habitations. Grain found in kurgans shows that they practiced some agriculture, and that later they settled in villages. Their armory corresponded closely with that of the Iranians and their industry showed the imprint of Sumerian and Hittite culture, gained by long contact with Turkish tribes from Turkistan to Iran, but not that of the Minoan, Egyptian, or western European civilizations, as proved by the existence in the graves of female figurines like those of Mesopotamia.[75]

Riphath

"And the children of Rephath are the Bartonim, who dwell in the land of Bartonia by the river Ledah, which empties its waters in the

---

[75]Kephart, *op. cit.*, page 248-250. Kephart's dates have been changed by 200 years to reflect a later time period for the Nordic movements westward. This has been done to allow for the development of nations after the Flood.

great sea Gihon, that is, oceanus. (*The Book of Jasher* 10:10)

Togarmah

"And the children of Tugarma are ten families, and these are their names: Buzar, Parzunac, Balgar, Elicanum, Ragbib, Tarki, Bid, Zebuc, Ongal and Tilmaz; all these spread and rested in the north and built themselves cities. And they called their cities after their own names, those are they who abide by the rivers Hithlah and Italac unto this day. But the families of Angoli, Balgar, and Parzunac, they dwell by the great river Dubness; and the names of their cities are also according to their own names. (*The Book of Jasher* 10:10-12)

"One of the descendants of Japheth through Gomer wandered with some of his tribes into the valley of the Ganges as early as 1500 B.C. These fair-skinned invaders found some descendants of Ham, through Cush probably, already settled in this country. The two peoples gradually became one, but the Aryans or sons of Japheth were the dominant race and these became the nobles and warriors, the Brahmins or priests; while the native inhabitants were the Sudras, the Pariahs or outcasts, the lowest and most despised of the native races."[76]

It is not known which branch of Japheth's family is responsible for the establishment of China. There are two distinct races in China, the Mongols scattered through the nation, and the Tartars mostly living in the northern regions. Based on the racial tables given above, the Mongols have been credited as descendants of Madai, son of Japheth. If this is the case, the Chinese descend from Madai. One source supposes that Noah, "wearied with the growing depravity of his descendants, retired with a few select friends to the remotest part of Asia, and there began what has since been called the Chinese monarchy. Its early history is not connected with that of other nations, and is also very obscure and much mixed with fable."[77] Given that Noah lived until the year 1996 B.C. and Japheth to about the

---

[76]Gates, *op. cit.*, page 32.

[77]Gates, *ibid.*

year 1896 B.C. it is very possible that both or either of them were the founders of the ancient and noble kingdom of China. There are ample proofs in the Chinese language, that it is based on scriptural beginnings linked with a knowledge of the creation, the Fall, the Flood, and many other religious beliefs.[78]

The earliest account of religious worship, found in the *Shu Ching* (the *Book of History)* compiled by Confucius, records of Emperor Shun in 2230 B.C., "He sacrificed to Shang Ti." (the Heavenly [above] Emperor) The Chinese at this time were monotheistic. There are many examples of religious worship portrayed in the written symbols of the Chinese language showing early belief in the creation, the expulsion from a beautiful garden, the destruction of the world by a massive catastrophe, a flood, which covered the earth, wherein only eight souls were saved. Their word for "tower," shows a knowledge of the dispersion at the time of the Tower of Babel. It is comprised of the components clay, united, joined together, to undertake. The Chinese themselves built no towers or pagodas until the Buddhist era. Many other excellent examples are found in the work of Kang and Nelson just cited.

MAGOG, SON OF JAPHETH

The sons of Magog were Elichanaf and Lubal. The Bible Dictionary (page 728) says that Magog is a country or people near the Black Sea, and equivalent to Scythian. Inasmuch as Scythian is not a race but a general designation, this is proper. All of the northern tribes descended from Japheth were in this sense Scythians. In *The Holy Bible,* The Book of the Prophet Ezekiel, 38:2, it states that Magog was the chief prince of Meshech and Tubal, indicating significant intermarriage between the families of these three sons of Japheth.

MADAI, SON OF JAPHETH

"And the children of Madai are the Orelum that dwell in the land of

---

[78]C. H. Kang and Ethel R. Nelson, *The Discovery of Genesis: How the Truths of Genesis were found Hidden in the Chinese Language* (St. Louis, Missouri: Concordia Publishing House, 1979).

Curson." (*The Book of Jasher* 10:13); all these went and built themselves cities; those are the cities that are situate by the sea Jabus by the river Cura, which empties itself in the river Tragan." (*The Book of Jasher* 10:14)

Madai, son of Japheth is the father of the Medes.[79] His children were Achon, Zeelo, Chazoni and Lot. (*The Book of Jasher* 10:14) Madai is also the father of the Mongols.[80]

"Media, which was settled, we are told, by Madai, son of Japheth, was an important, very ancient Asiatic monarchy, lying south and west of the Caspian Sea and between that sea and Assyria. It was larger than Assyria and Chaldea combined, and the river Tigris watered its fields. In the mountain region the climate is severe, but on the plains the thermometer rarely registers ninety degrees in the shade.

"The Medes were a handsome race of men, noble and graceful, the women beautiful and cultured. Their love of luxury was their final destruction..... Media is first mentioned in the Bible as the part of Assyria to which the Ten Tribes were transplanted: at first, those beyond Jordan, by Tiglath-pileser (1 Chronicles 5:26); and afterwards, about 721 B.C., the remainder of Israel, by Sargon (II Kings 17:6)."[81]

Native American Family: Jaredite [Olmec]. This is a departure from Gates and others within the Mormon community, who have maintained that Jared and his brother and their friends were from Shem (see their genealogy below). It may be that descendants of Shem were mixed in with the main blood of Japheth, but it is clear from archeological discoveries throughout Mesoamerica, that the Jaredites (Olmecs) were of a Mongoloid extract, probably from the family of Madai.

---

[79]Gates, *op. cit.*, page 29.

[80]Gates, *op. cit.*, page 14.

[81]Gates, *op. cit.*, pages 30-31.

JAVAN, SON OF JAPHETH

The second generation, the male children of Javan, included Elishah, Tarshish, Kittim, and Dodanim. (Genesis 10:1-5)

"And the children of Javan are the Javanim who dwell in the land of Makdonia." (*The Book of Jasher* 10:13); all these went and built themselves cities; those are the cities that are situate by the sea Jabus by the river Cura, which empties itself in the river Tragan." (*The Book of Jasher* 10:14)

Tarshish, son of Javan, is father of southern Spain.[82] The children of Tarshish are the Almanim between the mountains of Job and Shibathmo. Of them are the people of Lumbardi who dwell opposite the mountains of Job and Shibathmo. (Jasher 10:14)

It would appear from these quotes that Javan's descendants principally settled in the coastal areas of the Mediterranean becoming the progenitors of some of the Turkish races, as well as Greeks, Lombards and Spanish. As was noted above, in Greek mythology the Titan Japetus is the progenitor of the human race. Ion, his son, in the Hebrew form is Javan.[83]

As pertains to the Greek descendants of Javan, it is possible that the mainland of Greece was once known as Ionea or its inhabitants as Ionians. According to Herodotus the original home of the Ionians was in the northeast Peloponnese in the region around Troezen. Hence they were expelled by the Achaeans and occupied Attica, from which they later spread to the Cyclades and to Asia Minor. This traditional history of the Ionians is feasible and need not be dogmatically contradicted. We may perhaps view the Ionians as pre-Achaean inhabitants of the Peloponnese. N. P. Nilsson regards the Ionians as the foremost wave of Greek-speaking peoples to reach Greece and as the originators of the Mycenaean culture. The name of the Ionian sea, for example, is pre-historical. No Ionians Greeks

---

[82]Gates, *op. cit.*, page 29.

[83]Gates, *ibid.*

lived in historical times on the shores of the Ionian sea. To the Hebrews the name represented the whole Greek race. It was finally the Italians and Illyrians who gave the name Graeci to the Greeks[84]

TUBAL, SON OF JAPHETH

"And the children of Tubal were Ariphi, Kesed, and Tuari; these are those that dwell in the land of Tuskanah by the river Pashiah; all these went and built themselves cities; those are the cities that are situate by the sea Jabus by the river Cura, which empties itself in the river Tragan." (*The Book of Jasher* 10:13-14)

As noted above, the chief prince of Meshech and Tubal was Magog, indicating significant intermarriage between the families of these three sons of Japheth. Magog was a country or people living near the Black Sea. They, along with other descendants of Japheth, were generally called Scythians. Gates states that Tubal's descendants settled in the Caucasus Mountains and Europe, being Uigurians (typical Turks).[85]

MESHECH, SON OF JAPHETH

"And the children of Meshech were Dedon, Zaron, and Shebashni; they are the Shibashnic; all these went and built themselves cities; those are the cities that are situate by the sea Jabus by the river Cura, which empties itself in the river Tragan." (*The Book of Jasher* 10:14)

As noted above, the chief prince of Meshech and Tubal was Magog, indicating significant intermarriage between the families of these three sons of Japheth. Magog was a country or people living near the Black Sea. They, along with other descendants of Japheth, were generally called Scythians. Meshech's descendants are spread throughout Russia and Europe. It is generally believed that Meshechites are Muscovites, and the progenitors of that population around Moscow, or the region from Scandinavia to the provinces east

---

[84]The University of Chicago, *op. cit.*, Volume 12, page 576.

[85]Gates, *op. cit.*, page 14.

of Moscow.

TIRAS, SON OF JAPHETH

"And the children of Tiras are Rushash, Cushni, and Ongolis; all these went and built themselves cities; those are the cities that are situate by the sea Jabus by the river Cura, which empties itself in the river Tragan." (*The Book of Jasher* 10:14)

This statement links the descendants of Tiras with those of Magog, Meshech and Tubal. However, Tiras is not mentioned in the ancient prophecies as belonging to that group. It is likely that his descendants settled in Thrace, south and west from the main group of Magog's kingdom, and that they became more associated with Javan's family and the Greeks, than they did with the descendants of the other brothers.

THE DESCENDANTS OF SHEM
SECOND SON OF NOAH

Semitic Family: Babylonian, Assyrian, Phoenician, Carthaginian, Canaanite, Hebrew, Aramaean, Arab (partially), Lydians, and Abyssinian. Webster is wrong in some of his assessments here. The Phoenicians were of Ham as were the Canaanites, and Abyssinians.

Asiatic Family: Indo-Aryans, Medes [according to Webster, but not likely; Madai was a son of Japheth, as noted above; he is the father of the Medes] and Persians, Hittites, Armenians, and Scythians. Webster is so wrong here that he is almost totally wrong. The Hittites descend from Heth, son of Canaan, son of Ham (Genesis 10: 6, 15). The Scythians have been noted above as being from Japheth. The Armenians are from Arphaxad, son of Shem. We have shown above (page 98) that Persia was also settled by Japheth. Thus, only the Armenians in this section by Webster, on the Asiatic Family, should be assigned to the descendants of Shem.

Greco-Latin Family: Albanian, Greek, Italian, Spaniard, Catalonian, Portuguese, French Provençal, Walloon, and Rumanian

Celtic Family: Breton, Welsh, Irish, and Highland Scot

Teutonic Family: German, Frisian, Dutch, Fleming, Dane, Norwegian, Swede, English, and Lowland Scot. These designations are very loose. Webster has not taken into account the influence of Japheth in the European incursions from Asia. Most, if not all of these races, are mixed with Japheth to a significant degree.

Lettic Family: Lett and Lithuanian

Slavic Family: South Slav (Serb, Montenegrin, Croat, Slovene); West Slav (Czech, Slovak, Pole); East Slav (Great Russian, Little Russian or Ruthenian, and White Russian). It is much more likely that all the Slavic nations are descendants of Japheth. They have been noted above in that regard.

Malayo-Polynesian Family: Maoris of New Zealand, Samoan,

Tahitian, Marquesan, and Hawaiian

Native American Family: Nephite [Maya]; and most other Central American tribes]; Uto-Aztecan (Siberian tribes mixed with Jaredite/Nephite and some European influences prior to 1492: includes Toltecs, Aztecs, Utes, Cherokee, most other North American tribes); Lamanite [Quechua, most other South American and Caribbean tribes at Conquest, although Caribbean has influences from both North American mixtures, Maya/Olmec, and possibly from European influences]. See Jaredites under Madai, son of Japheth for the Olmec culture.

"Unto Shem also, the father of all the children of Eber, the brother of Japheth the elder, even to him were children born. The children of Shem; Elam, and Asshur, and Arphaxad, and Lud, and Aram. And the children of Aram; Uz, and Hul, and Gether, and Mash. And Arphaxad begat Salah; and Salah begat Eber. And under Eber were born two sons; the name of one was Peleg; for in his days was the earth divided; and his brother's name was Joktan. And Joktan began Almodad, and Sheleph, and Hazarmaveth, and Jerah, and Hadoram, and Uzal, and Dilah, and Obal, and Abimael, and Sheba, and Ophir, and Havilah, and Jobab; all these were the sons of Joktan. And their dwelling was from Mesha, as thou goest unto Sephar a mount of the east. These are the sons of Shem, after their families, after their tongues, in their lands, after their nations." (Genesis 10:21-31) The first generation of male children of Shem were Elam, Asshur, Arphaxad, Lud, and Aram.

There are, according to native historians, two races of Arabs: those descended through Joktan, son of Eber, son of Salah, son of Arphaxad, son of Shem; and those who claim Ishmael as their ancestor. There were also in Arabia, descendants of Cush, son of Ham. Added to these tribes were some of the descendants of Lot through his two sons, Moab and Ammon.[86]

ELAM, SON OF SHEM

---

[86]Gates, *op. cit.*, page 18.

Descendants settled Assyria and are the Assyrians.[87] His sons were Shushan, Machul, and Harmon.

ASSHUR, SON OF SHEM

Descendants inhabited Syria and are the Syrians.[88] The children of Ashur built Nineveh, Resen, Calach, and Rehobother (*The Book of Jasher* 10:33). His sons were Miras and Mokil.

ARPHAXAD, SON OF SHEM

Descendants inhabited Persia and are the Armenians and Persians.[89] His sons were Shelach, Anar and Ashed. It is likely that Arphaxad's children were also some of the unrighteous of the city of Salim, ruled by Melchizedek, who caused them to repent and become a righteous people.

The Joktanites (Joktan was a son of Eber, who was the son of Selah, son of Arphaxad, son of Shem) were some of the Arabian tribes which dwelt in the land "from Mesha as thou goest towards Sephar, the mountain of the East." (Genesis 10:30) Sephar has not been located, but it seems that the direction in the description of the land, occupied by these descendants of Eber, was from north to the southeast; and that Mesha is probably Damascus, as noted earlier.

LUD, SON OF SHEM

Descendants scattered throughout Anatolia and the Mediter-ranean and are the Lydians and other nations.[90] His sons were Pethor and Bizayon.

---

[87]Gates, *op. cit.*, page 15.

[88]Ibid.

[89]Ibid.

[90]Gates, *op. cit.*, pages 5, 15.

ARAM, SON OF SHEM

Descendants scattered throughout Syria and Mesopotamia (the Greek and Roman name for Chaldea), from which the Chaldeans, including Israelites partially descend, the Chaldeans being a mixture of Semitic-Hamitic-Japhetic races.[91] His sons were Uz, Chul, Gather, and Mash.

Mash, son of Aram gave his name to the country of Mash, which became Damascus. This is discussed previously.

FROM UNKNOWN ORIGINS

The Australian aborigine

The Dravidian of southern India

The Basque of northern Spain

---

[91]Gates, *op. cit.*, page 5.

THE DESCENDANTS OF HAM, THIRD SON OF NOAH

Negro proper

Negrito: Negrito in equatorial Africa

Negrito: Negrito in Andaman Islands, Malay Peninsula, Philippines and New Guinea

Bantu family: Bantu

Hamitic: Libyan, Egyptian, Eastern Hamite; and Hittites

Hittites? See Japheth and Shem.

Hottentot and Bushmen

Papuan: Papuan in New Guinea and the Melanesian Islands

The story of Ham in Chapter 9 of Genesis is the story of the curse, of the black skin, and also of very successful nations and great dynasties. In *The Pearl of Great Price*, The Book of Abraham 1:20-23, it shows that the wife of Ham was a negress named Egyptus, descendant of Cain, on whom the curse was first placed. Ham and Egyptus had a daughter, also called Egyptus, who, with her children, were the first to settle the land of Egypt after the Flood. More on this later.

"And the sons of Ham; Cush, and Mizraim, and Phut, and Canaan. And the sons of Cush; Seba, and Havilah, and Sabtah, and Raamah, and Sabtecha; and the sons of Raamah; Sheba, and Dedan. And Cush begat Nimrod: he began to be a mighty one in the earth. He was a mighty hunter before the Lord: wherefore it is said, Even as Nimrod the mighty hunter before the Lord. And the beginning of his kingdom was Babel, and Erech, and Accad, and Calneh, in the land of Shinar. Out of that land went forth Asshur, and builded Nineveh, and the city Rehoboth, and Calah, and Resen between Nineveh and

Calah: the same is a great city. And Mizraim begat Ludim, and Anamim, and Lehabim, and Naphtuhim, and Pathrusim, and Caluhim (out of whom came Philistim,) and Caphtorim. And Canaan begat Sidon his firstborn, and Heth, and the Jebusite, and the Amorite, and the Girgasite, and the Hivite, and the Arkite, and the Sinite, and the Arvadite, and the Zemarite, and the Hamathite: and afterward were the families of the Canaanites spread abroad. And the border of the Canaanites was from Sidon, as thou comest to Gerar, unto Gaza; as thou goest, unto Sodom, and Gomorrah, and Admah, and Zeboim, even unto Lasha. These are the sons of Ham, after their families, after their tongues, in their countries, and in their nations." (Genesis 10: 6-20) It is obvious from this dialogue that the Hamitic families spread far and were very illustrious during this first one hundred year period currently being reviewed. In fact, they were at the heart of the great cities and dynasties of this period.

Referring to the first Pharaoh of Egypt, The Book of Abraham says: "Now this king of Egypt was a descendant from the loins of Ham, and was a partaker of the blood of the Canaanites by birth. From this descent sprang all the Egyptians, and thus the blood of the Canaanites was preserved in the land. The land of Egypt being first discovered by a woman, who was the daughter of Ham, and the daughter of Egyptus, which in the Chaldean signifies Egypt, which signifies that which is forbidden; when this woman discovered the land it was under water, who afterward settled her sons in it; and thus, from Ham, sprang that race which preserved the curse in the land. Now the first government of Egypt was established by Pharaoh, the eldest son of Egyptus, the daughter of Ham, and it was after the manner of the government of Ham, which was patriarchal. Pharaoh, being a righteous man, established his kingdom and judged his people wisely and justly all his days, seeking earnestly to imitate that order established by the fathers in the first generations, in the days of the first patriarchal reign, even in the reign of Adam, and also of Noah, his father, who blessed him with the blessings of the earth, and with the blessings of wisdom, but cursed him as pertaining to the Priesthood. Now, Pharaoh being of that lineage by which he could not have the right of Priesthood, notwithstanding the Pharaohs would fain claim it from Noah, through Ham, therefore my father was led away by their idolatry." (1:21-27)

The first generation of male children of Ham were Cush, Mizraim, Phut and Canaan. (See *The Book of Jasher* 10:21-22)

CUSH, SON OF HAM

The second generation, the male children of Cush, included Seba, Havilah, Sabtah, Raamah, Sabtecha, and Nimrod. The descendants of Cush settled on the continent of Africa and are the Ethiopians, and in the Mesopotamian Valley, being the fathers of the Sumerians and related families.

And the sons of Raamah were Sheba, and Dedan.

And Cush begat Nimrod: he began to be a mighty one in the earth. He was a mighty hunter before the Lord: wherefore it is said, Even as Nimrod the mighty hunter before the Lord. And the beginning of his kingdom was Babel, and Erech, and Accad, and Calneh, in the land of Shinar. Out of that land went forth Asshur, and builded Nineveh.

Nimrod was the father of Mardon. We have also postulated above that Nimrod may have been the father of Sargon who was possibly called Akkad as a youth.

MIZRAIM, SON OF HAM

The descendants of Mizraim settled on the continent of Africa and are the Egyptians, and the Libyans, among others.

"And the children of Mitzraim are Lud (the Ludim), Anom (the Anamin), Lehabim, Naphtuchim, Pathros (the Pathrusim), Chasloth (the Casluchim), and Chaphtor (the Caphturim), seven families. All these dwell by the river Sihor, that is the brook of Egypt, and they built themselves cities and called them after their own names.

Mizraim was the husband of Egyptus; they were the parents of Pharaoh, probably Anom (titled Teti), the first Pharaoh of the 6th Dynasty. Anom was a King of Egypt (*The Book of Jasher* 14:2), of whom descend the Anamin. His son was Oswiris (Osiris?).

Lud or Ludim

"Ludim was the traditional father of the Libyans. One of the eight sons of Egyptus and a grandson of Ham."[92]

Pathros

"And the children of Pathros (the Pathrusim) and Casloch (the Casluchim) intermarried together, and from them went forth the Pelishtim, the Azathim, and the Gerarim, the Githim, and the Ekronim, in all five families; these also built themselves cities, and they called their cities after the names of their fathers unto this day." (*The Book of Jasher* 10:23)

Casloch or Chasloth

"And the children of Pathros and Casloch intermarried, and from them went forth the Pelishtim, the Azathim, and the Gerarim, the Githim, and the Ekronim, in all five families; these also built themselves cities, and they called their cities after the names of their fathers unto this day." (*The Book of Jasher* 10:23)

PHUT, SON OF HAM

The descendants of Phut settled on the continent of Africa and intermarried with the children of Lud and are the Libyans. His children were Gebul, Hadan, Berah, and Adan.

CANAAN, SON OF HAM

The descendants of Canaan are one of the more prolific tribes of Ham. They settled in southern Arabia and Palestine and are the Canaanites and Phoenicians. His sons were Zidon, Heth, Amori,

---

[92]Ronald Brownrigg and Joan Comay, *Who's Who in the Bible: Two Volumes in One (Who's Who in the Old Testament together with the Apocrypha; Who's Who in the New Testament)*, New York City; Avenel, New Jersey: Wings Books, 1980, page 245.

Gergashi, Hivi, Arkee, Seni, Arodi, Zimodi, and Chamothi. From Hivi was Hur who had Seir (opposite Mt. Paran).

"And four men from the family of Ham went to the land of the plain; these are the names of the four men, Sodom, Gomorrah, Admah and Zeboyim. And these men built themselves four cities in the land of the plain, and they called the names of their cities after their own names. And they and their children and all belonging to them dwelt in those cities, and they were fruitful and multiplied and dwelt peaceably. (*The Book of Jasher* 10:25-27)

And Seir the son of Hur, son of Hivi, son of Canaan, went and found a valley opposite to Mount Paran, and he built a city there, and he and his seven sons and his household dwelt there, and he called the city which he built Seir, according to his name; that is the land of Seir unto this day. (Jasher 10: 28)

This, then, is the basic situation in which the world finds itself at the end of the first hundred years after the Flood. Mankind has spread from its beginnings at Ararat throughout the Fertile Crescent, into adjoining part of Africa, the Mediterranean, Anatolia, the steppes of Asia, and throughout the southern climes as far as China. Shortly after this they will spread to the American continent, into Europe, and then into the islands of the sea and the far reaches of the continents. Within another 100 years, the world will have been explored in most of its regions and settlements begun in all major areas of the world. The descendants of Noah quickly diversified even before the Tower of Babel. The intermarriage, new religious ideas, and technological developments were important to this diversification. Very few remained true to the doctrines as taught by Noah, Japheth, Shem and Ham. Many of their children, and most of their grandchildren strayed from these doctrines to worship their own gods.

A GENEALOGICAL HISTORY
OF
THE WORLD

There is little agreement among the scholars as to chronological events much prior to the reign of King David. Dates calculated from Adam to David and backward from David to Adam can be off by as much as 407 years. It appears obvious when engaging in this kind of a study that some dates are wrong and some generations have been omitted. There are a few accurate sign posts in between David and Adam which can be used to guide us, but as with all other chronologies, the one created herein will also be subject to error, particularly if any premise is incorrect.

The first premise noted in developing this chronology (see page 14) was that this earth, according to a divine plan, is passing through a mortal or temporal existence of seven millennia, 7,000 years. The first six of these millennia cover the period of time from the **fall** of Adam until the beginning of the Millennium, or the last period of time. It is widely accepted in many denominations of the Christian world, that there were 4,000 years from the **fall** of Adam to the birth of Jesus Christ. Commonly, it has been stated that these two events took place in 4000 B.C. and in 4 A.D.[93] or 1 A.D. according to the 1974 edition of *The Book of Mormon*, 3 Nephi 1:4). The following documentation will establish that the actual dates were 4002 B.C. and 2 B.C.

ESTABLISHING THE BIRTH YEAR OF JESUS CHRIST

Historical records bear out the fact that Jesus Christ was born in the fall of 2 B.C. Even within *The Book of Mormon* there is proof of this fact. For example 1 Nephi 1:4 and 2:4 give the departure of Lehi's family as in the commencement of the first year of the reign of

---

[93]*The Holy Bible*, King James Version (Salt Lake City: Deseret Book Co., 1959), Old Testament Chronology, page 54.

Zedekiah, which the new Bible Dictionary of the L.D.S. Church, and all known historical records, give as 598 B.C. (See footnote 93: Bible Dictionary, page 639). This would make Christ's birth 600 years later (1 Nephi 10:4) as being in 2 B.C. The internal dating of *The Book of Mormon* created by men in our time gives the dating of his birth as 2 A.D. This is an error created partially after the original record was written and also possibly a mistranslation occurred in 3 Nephi 1:1. Note Helaman 16: 13, 24, and 3 Nephi 1:1, 4. These quotations, when referenced to the footnotes indicating time, show that the ninetieth year of the reign of the judges was 2 B.C. (Helaman 16:13) The ninety and first year then was 1 B.C. and the ninety and second year was 1 A.D. There was no 0 year between 1 B.C. and 1 A.D., at least not among those who used the Julian and Gregorian calendars. There is historical evidence to show that the Nephites were the purveyors of the earlier Jaredite calendar. This can be assumed because the Mayan calendar, which begins on August 13, 3114 date wise, obviously pre-dates Mayan civilization. (Of course it also pre-dates Jaredite civilization as well, showing that they must have brought their calendar system with them from the Old World.) See page 57 for the possible event from which the calendar sprung.

The modern error is created in the following way. 3 Nephi 1:1 says: "Now it came to pass that the ninety and first year had passed away and it was six hundred years from the time that Lehi left Jerusalem." Lehi's family apparently left Jerusalem in 598 B.C., as they left in the first year of the reign of King Zedekiah, which historical records show began on August 8, 598 B.C. (2 Kings 25:3) and ended August 7, 597 B.C. Thus, the translation of 3 Nephi 1:1 might have read: "Now it was six hundred years from the time that Lehi left Jerusalem, and thus began the ninety and first year."

Further proofs of the timing of the birth of Christ are also found in biblical and secular history. *The Holy Bible* contains proof that Jesus Christ died in 33 A.D. It will be shown that he was thirty-three and one-half years old at the time of his death, which again would place his birth in 2 B.C. The prophecy of Daniel (9:25) which spans the time from the commission to Nehemiah to rebuild the walls of Jerusalem (in the first month [Nisan - April] of the 20th year of

Artaxerex [444 B.C.] - Nehemiah 2:1-8) to the death of Messiah, a period of sixty-nine weeks (seven weeks and threescore and two weeks). This prophetic cycle, as with all time prophecies, must be computed on the basis of prophetic time: 360 days per year, at 1 day = 1 year. See the last footnote in this book for a further explanation of prophetic time and how it is distinguished from earth time. Breaking the calculation above down into units of one day, one prophetic day is equal to .985609 of a solar day, derived by dividing 360 by 365.2564 = .985609. Thus, one prophetic week becomes 6.89936 days (7 x .985609 = 6.89936). The sixty-nine weeks of Daniel's prophecy becomes 476 prophetic years (69 x 6.89936 = 476). The precision with which this prophecy tells the death of Jesus Christ is accurate to the month. (Nisan 444 B.C. to Nisan 33 A.D. = 476 - 444 = 32 + 1 for year 0 which does not exist between 1 B.C. and 1 A.D. = 33 A.D.).

Tertullian, born about 140 A.D., an early Christian Father, stated that Augustus began to rule forty-one years before the birth of Jesus and died fifteen years after that event. He died August 19, 14 A.D. This would place the birth of Jesus at 2 B.C. One year is subtracted because there is no zero year between 1 B.C. and 1 A.D. In the same chapter Tertullian states that Jesus was born twenty-eight years after the death of Cleopatra. Her death is recorded in history as 30 B.C., again placing the Lord's birth at 2 B.C. Idrenaeus, born about 98 A.D., stated: "Our Lord was born about the forty-first year of the reign of Augustus," who began to rule in the autumn of 43 B.C. Eusebius, about 264-340 A.D., the Father of Church History, wrote concerning the birth of Jesus: "It was the forty-second year of the reign of Augustus and the twenty-eighth from the subjection of Egypt on the death of Anthony and Cleopatra." The forty-second year of Augustus began in the autumn of 2 B.C. and ended in the autumn of 1 B.C., requiring Jesus' birth to be between approximately September of 2 B.C. and September of 1 B.C. The subjugation of Egypt and its inclusion in the Roman Empire occurred in the autumn of 30 B.C.; therefore, the twenty-eighth year from that time extended from the autumn of 3 B.C. to the autumn of 2 B.C.

The death of King Herod, who had ordered the children of Judæa under age two to be killed, occurred shortly after the burning of

Matthias, but two months before the Passover; therefore, his death would have occurred sometime in January of 1 B.C. Obviously, the wisemen who had visited Herod because they had seen the star testifying of the birth of Jesus, would have kept their royal appointment prior to the death of Herod, and after the birth of Jesus. The eclipse of the moon which took place shortly before King Herod's death, as noted by Josephus, happened on the evening of December 29, 1 B.C. [Remember the new year began with full moon in March, and the month of Nisan extended into April.]

An ancient Jewish scroll, the Magillath Ta'anith, written during the lifetime of Jesus, gives the day and month of King Herod's death as the 1st of Shebat. The 1st of Shebat in 1 B.C., by the Julian Calendar then in use, would have been January 14th.

All of this information points to Jesus Christ being born between September and December of 2 B.C. The month, at least, can be determined from additional available historical documents. John the Baptist's birth furnishes one method of calculation. Luke 1:5 states that Zacharias was a priest of the course of Abia [Abijah]. The Levite priests were divided into twenty-four classes or courses (1 Chronicles 24:7-19) and each class officiated in the temple for one week. The courses of the priests changed duty at weekend, or in other words, from the end of the Sabbath at sundown until the next Sabbath.

Both the Talmud and the historian Josephus state that the temple was destroyed by Titus on August 5, 70 A.D. (the L.D.S. Bible Dictionary, page 645 also agrees that the siege and capture of Jerusalem occurred that year), and that the first course of priests had just taken office. The previous evening was the end of the Sabbath. The course of Abia [Abijah] was the eighth course. Thus, figuring backward we are able to determine that Zachariah ended his course on July 13, 3 B.C. John was, therefore, born around the 19th or 20th of April 2 B.C. precisely at Passover, "in the proper season" as Luke 1:20 states.

Elizabeth hid herself for five months, and at the beginning of the sixth month the angel Gabriel appeared to Mary, telling her of Elizabeth's condition. At the same time Gabriel told Mary that she, too, would conceive and bear a son who would be called Jesus. By the time she met Elizabeth, to which she had gone "with haste" (Luke 1:39) she was already with child. (Luke 1:42) Luke 3:1 clearly states that John the Baptist began his ministry in the 15th year of Tiberius Cæsar. According to the Law of Moses, a Jew was considered of age for the ministry at age thirty (Numbers 4:3). Augustus had died on August 19, 14 A.D.; thus, that year became the accession year of Tiberius, even though he had been involved in, and associated with, the Roman rulership before Augustus died. If John was born in April of 2 B.C., his thirtieth birthday would have been in April 29 A.D., or in the 15th year of Tiberius, as noted by Luke. Thus, the birth of Jesus Christ, who was five to six months younger than John the Baptist, is confirmed as being in the fall of 2 B.C., sometime between the end of September and the end of October, and is more likely closer to the end of the October, based on Mary's visit by Gabriel (See also 1 Nephi 1:42; 2 Kings 25:3).

As Jesus "began to be about thirty years of age" at the time of his baptism, which was also in the 15th year of Tiberius [as John was just beginning his ministry - Luke 3:23], then his birth is again confirmed as being in 2 B.C. As his ministry lasted through four Passovers (John 2:13; 5:1; 6:4; and 13:1), it had to have lasted for the three and one-half years prophesied in Daniel. He was crucified in April 33 A.D., during Passover, meaning he was baptized in October of 29 A.D., three and a half years earlier. If he attended the Feast of the Tabernacles on the 15th of Tishri [October 12, 29 A.D.] as required of all Jewish men [Deuteronomy 16:16], the earliest possible day he could have been baptized at the Jordan was 17th of Tishri [October 14, 29 A.D.], because immediately thereafter he went into the wilderness for forty days. Based on this scenario, it is possible that his baptism and the start of his forty days in the wilderness was October 24th (also possibly his birth date, and according to Jewish traditions, the day that Adam became mortal [4,000 years previous in 4002 B.C.].

Jesus died on April 3, 33 A.D. at 3:00 p.m. on Nisan 14 (Mark 15:34-38). The Passover lambs were always slain on the afternoon of the full moon, in other words, when the moon rose that evening it was full. New moon was always the first of the month. Full moon was always fourteen days later. Jesus was thirty-three and one-half years old when he was crucified, conforming to Daniel's prophecy and Jewish customs regarding the beginning of his ministry.

Thus we have established that Adam's fall 4,000 years earlier was in 4002 B.C., probably on October 24th as is recorded in Jewish records, and as circumstantially verified in the life of Jesus Christ. With at least a fairly substantial reason for so concluding, this will be the date from which the early chronologies will be calculated. It cannot, however, be used as the base from which to calculate all dates in *The Holy Bible* because in so doing there is a discrepancy of about 407 years. There does not appear to be a complete pedigree from Adam to David. Therefore, several other critical sign posts must be established before the full chronology can be created, or before the area of discrepancy can be isolated and calculated.

ESTABLISHING THE BIRTH YEARS

of

JOSEPH AND MOSES

and

THE CHRONOLOGY FROM DAVID TO JOSEPH

"One of the crucial problems in the history of the ancient Near East is the establishment of a cohesive and comprehensive absolute chronology for the second millennium B.C., which largely coincides with that region's Middle and Late Bronze Ages. Once securely established, such a chronological system could be extended, at least approximately, well into the third millennium. Absolute chronology means dating reigns, wars, treaties, destructions, rebuilding, and other events known from written and archaeological records, in terms of modern Western time reckoning, i.e., in years B.C. For the first millennium, this has been achieved, on the one hand, by a transmitted (and accurate) linkage between late Babylonian and Persian regnal data with Hellenistic and Roman eras, and on the other hand, by the presence of one precise astronomical datum (a sun eclipse) in the neo-Assyrian eponym list. For the second millennium, our only way of obtaining firm proceeding points for absolute datings is the utilization of preserved written references to astronomical phenomena: then the relative chronologies of ancient kingdoms, as many as are available, must be synchronized and correlated. If a system thus constructed works well, without evident contradictions and without the necessity of recurring to too many auxiliary hypotheses, this is an empirical proof of its basic soundness."[94]

Egyptian history provides some historical guides which must be taken with caution because only a few of them are exact. Cyril Aldred has provided us with a general warning as to the use of Egyptian dates. He says: "...by the time of Akhenaten, [who ascended the throne

---

[94]Michael C. Astour, *Hittite History and Absolute Chronology of the Bronze Age* (Partille, Sweden: Paul Åströms, 1989), page 1.

about 1358 B.C.], lists of such kings certainly existed among temple archives, together with the length of each reign, although the only record that now survives is a heavily damaged and incomplete papyrus in Turin, which was compiled some sixty years after the death of Akhenaten. Similar data must have been available to Manetho, the High Priest of the sun god in Heliopolis, when he was commissioned by Ptolemy I in the third century B.C. to write a history of Egypt. This work is now lost, though its king-list is preserved in copies quoted by early Christian chronographers and by the Jewish historian Josephus."[95] The real problem with using Manetho's list is that he based his chronology on consecutive dynasties. Modern research has shown some of these dynasties ruled simultaneously, however, thereby throwing Egyptian history off by hundreds of years. (See page 33 as an example of this from the 21st and 22nd dynasties). Some minor overlapping occurred in the 18th dynasty as well. Other chronologies place dates given herein up to fifty-five years earlier, but even these may be off because of the 21st-22nd dynastic discoveries just noted.

---

[95]Cyril Aldred, *Akhenaten, King of Egypt* (London, England: Thames Y. Hudson, Ltd., 1988), page 9.

Pharaohs of the New Kingdom 1540 - 1299 B.C.
The Eighteenth Dynasty (Ahmosides)

NOMEN	PRENOMEN	DATES BC	CHIEF QUEEN
Amosis	Nebpehtirē	1540-1515	Ahmose-Nefertari
Amenophis I	Djeserkarē	1515-1494	Meritamun (?)
Tuthmosis I	Aakheperkarē	1494-1482	Ahmose
Tuthmosis II	Aakherperenrē	1482-1479	Hatshepsut
Hatshepsut	Maetkarē	1479-1457	
Tuthmosis III	Menkheperrē	1479-1425	Hatshepsut
Amenophis II	Aakheperurē	1427-1393	Meritre
Tuthmosis IV	Menkheperurē	1394-1384	Tia
Amenophis III	Nebmaetrē	1384-1346	Mutemwiya
Amenophis IV			Tiye
(Akhenaten)	Neferkheperurē	1358-1340	Neferneferuaten-
Neferneferuaten/		1342-1340	Nefertiti
Smenkhkarē-			Meritaten
Djeserkheperu[96]	Ankhkheperurē		
Tutankhamun	Nebkheperurē	1340-1331	
Ay or Aye	Kheperkheperurē	1331-1326	Ankhesenamun[97]
Horemheb or	Djeserkheperurē	1326-1299	Tey, Teye or Tiy
Haremhab			Mutnodjme[98]
			or Mutnezmet

"In no case at this period does the record survive of the exact age that a pharaoh attained before he died;[99] and except in one or two cases

---

[96]Semenkhakare, brother of Akhenaten, ruled two years, and was killed by supporters of Tutankhamun, son of Akhenaten, according to some sources.

[97]Scott Woodward, "Genealogy of New Kingdom Pharaohs and Queens," *Archaeology 49 #5* (September/October 1996), page 47. Ankhensenpaaten, the wife of Tutankhamun, is given by Woodward as the daughter of Nefertiti, daughter of Aye [Ephraim], by his wife Teye.

[98]Aldred, *op. cit.*, pages 10-11.

[99]According to an article published in *Time* magazine by Michael D. Lemonick (May 29, 1995), Ramesses II took the throne at age twenty-five and ruled for sixty-seven years, from 1279 B.C. to 1212 B.C. These dates have long been in

the length of his reign is also unknown. In this predicament, Egyptologists have to depend upon medical opinion for estimates of the length of time a particular king occupied the throne. On the accuracy of such data depends the chronology not only of Egypt but also of the entire ancient Near East."[100]

"In the case of Hittite chronology and its interaction into the general chronology of Western Asia and Egypt, we are mainly dealing with what is known as the Old and Middle Hittite Kingdoms. For the New Kingdom, or Empire, both the abundant written records and the numerous synchronisms with Egypt, Assyria, and Babylonia allow a fairly accurate chronology. On the contrary, the time of the Old and Middle Kingdom is poorly documented and has few ascertainable synchronisms. Its upper time bracket is the accession of Hattushilish I, the first Hittite ruler of whom we have written records, and its lower limit is the beginning of the reign of Shuppiluliumash I. If not for Hattushilish I himself, at least for his successor Murshilish I there exists a historic and deservedly famous synchronism with Babylonia: Murshilish's sack of Babylon marked the end of the First Dynasty of that city. This event seemed to be accurately fixable in time by astronomical means, namely by the analysis and mathematical interpretation of the Neo-Assyrian copies of tablets on observations of the planet Venus in the sixth year of King Ammisaduqa. The correlation between the recorded positions of Venus and their lunar calendar dates was used for determining the year in which such coincidences could have taken place. Since the internal chronology of the First Dynasty of Babylon is perfectly known, the absolute dating of Ammisaduqa's sixth year would lead to establishing an absolute chronology for the entire dynasty. Unfortunately, the complete cycle of upper and lower conjunctions of Venus recurs every 275 years, and similar positions of the planet also repeat themselves in two shorter cycles, one of 56 years, the other of 64 years. Hence the three principal systems of Babylonian chronology, advanced and disputed since 1940 and their respective datings on the

---

dispute, but are being accepted more and more by some of the more renowned Egyptologists, among them being Dr. Kent Weeks, American University in Cairo.

[100]Aldred, *op. cit.*, page 95.

end of the First Dynasty of Babylon:

High chronology, by D. Sidersky: 1651.
Middle chronology, by J. W. S. Sewell and S. Smith: 1595.
Low chronology, by F. Cornelius and W. F. Albright: 1531....

"According to the cuneiformist-astronomer O. Neugebauer, there are too many equally possible astronomical dates from the Venus tablets (besides the ones mentioned above) to choose any of them on a purely astronomical basis; archaeology and king lists alone could provide a decision. From [the] historical point of view, high chronology, which has been recently resurrected, on the basis of complicated computer work, by P. Huber and his associates, is utterly incompatible with the Assyrian King List and even with the Babylonian King List A for the Kassite Dynasty which in itself is too long. Low chronology accommodates itself easily to the sector of the Assyrian King List between the death of Shamshi-Adad I and Year 1 of Enlil-nasir II, while middle chronology requires for it a much less probable, though not totally impossible, assumption. Taking all this into account, we must regretfully abandon the Murshilish synchronism as the pivot of Hittite absolute chronology until and unless it can be proved by independent evidence.

"There exists, however, a system of chronology which is also based on an astronomical phenomenon, but on one that is incomparably more invariable and reliable than the cycles of Venus conjunctions. We mean, of course, the Sothic calendar cycle of ancient Egypt with its discrepancy between the sacred, or true solar (Julian) year of 365½ days beginning on the heliacal rise of the Sothis star (Sirius) and the civil year of just 365 days which rotated through the seasons and whose first day coincided with the sacred New Year once in a Great Year of 1,460 Julian years. The last celebration of the Great Year is precisely dated as July 19, A.D. 139, by the testimony of the Roman scholar Censorinus. There is no need to repeat here the well-known facts about the Sothic cycle and its application to absolute chronology of Egypt, but it should be noted that:

a.   During the entire Egyptian history, from the earliest recorded Sothic dates to the end of antiquity, the sacred year started with the heliacal rise of Sirius as observed at the latitude of Memphis.

b.   The Great Year was celebrated in the first of the four consecutive years in which the heliacal rise of Sirius was visible.

c.   Egyptian priests could determine in advance at what day of the given civil year the sacred year would begin. This means that they kept the count of days, regular years, and leap years throughout the centuries, and it is inconceivable that they could change the date of the sacred New Year and reduce the number of years in the Great Year.

d.   Therefore, the assertion that during the New Kingdom, for allegedly patriotic reasons, the observation point of the heliacal rise of Sirius was transferred to Thebes, which would have changed its date and lowered the chronology by fourteen years, but was later returned to Memphis, must be declined as unwarranted and improbable.

e.   The new moon dates from the reigns of Thutmose III and Ramesses II, which were cited as supporting the years 1490 and 1290 for the accessions of, respectively, Thutmose III and Ramesses II, agree equally well, or better, with the years 1504 and 1304 (according to "Memphite" count) for those events.

f.   The fourth century A.D. Alexandrian astronomer, Theon, stated as a known fact that 1605 years had elapses from Menophres [see Ramesses I below] to the end of the era of Augustus. Theon had in mind the introduction of the era of Diocletian, which was counted in Egypt from August 29, A.D. 284. Deducting 284 from 1605, we obtain 1321 B.C., which is exactly the first year of the Sothic cycle which ended, according to Censorinus, in A.D. 139. As for Menophres, he was obviously an Egyptian king whose accession to the throne coincided with the start of a new Great Year. As considered, rejected, and finally tentatively accepted by Ed. Meyer, then convincingly presented by P. Montet, and more recently independently arrived at by J. Černý, <u>Menophrēs</u> was the Greek rendering of Men-pehti-rē^c or, even closer, Men-pehu-rē^c, the throne name of Ramesses I, the founder of the Nineteenth Dynasty, whose short reign of slightly more than one year has been dated, for independent reasons, between 1321 and 1319, following the "Memphite" reckoning.[101] [This date appears to be too high to coincide with the present study.]

M. L. Bierbrier in his excellent work says: "For the period of this study, the only universally acknowledged date is 664 B.C., which marks the accession of Psammetichis I of Dynasty XXVI and by coincidence the death of Taharqa, the penultimate ruler of Dynasty XXV. It is known from Assyrian sources that Dynasty XXV was established in Egypt by 712 B.C. and that Osorkon IV was still alive in 716 B.C. From Biblical evidence it can be estimated that the accession of Shoshenk I of Dynasty XXII took place about 945-940 B.C. with a slight possibility that it was as late as 930 B.C. Silence then prevails until the reign of Ramesses II whose accession has been dated on astronomical grounds coupled with Near Eastern synchronisms to either 1304 B.C. or 1290 B.C. The debate over the correct date has been long and inconclusive. The year 1279 B.C. is theoretically possible but has been discussed on the grounds that it conflicts with synchronisms from Assyrian, Babylonian, and Hittite sources. However, Brinkman has recently demonstrated that the Mesopotamian dates are far from as certain as some would suppose. Thus it is necessary to examine the Near Eastern evidence to see which dates should be considered before the Egyptian evidence regarding the accession of Ramesses II is investigated."

"It is accepted that 1279 B.C. cannot be used with the standard dating of Babylonian rulers, but Brinkman's new minimum dates change matters considerably. Two key pieces of evidence for dating Ramesses II through synchronisms with other Near Eastern monarchs are Hittite letter KBo I 10 and KBo I 14. The former is a letter from Hattushilish III of Hatti to Kadashman-Enlil II of Babylon. In this letter the Hittite ruler summarizes the history of Hittite-Babylonian

---

[101]Astour, *op. cit*, pages 1-3.

relations in the recent past. He declares that Kadashman-Turgu, the father of Kadashman-Enlil II, had been a loyal ally of Hattushilish III against Egypt, but on his death Itti-Marduk-balatu, the regent for the young Kadashman-Enlil II, had become hostile to the Hittite court. Now that Kadashman-Enlil II is older, the Hittite ruler hopes that he will follow the pro-Hittite policy of his father and is openly suspicious of the renewed Babylonian communications with Egypt.

"Due to the implied Hittite-Egyptian hostilities, Edel and Hornung have dated this letter prior to year 21 of Ramesses II when the well-known peace treaty between Egypt and Hatti was concluded.   In arguing for the acceptance of 1304 B.C. as the date of the accession of Ramesses II, Rowton has challenged this view on the grounds that there was not enough time between c. year 15 of Ramesses II when Hattushilish III became ruler of Hatti and year 21 for the end of the reign of Kadashman-Turgu of Babylon and the minority of his son Kadashman-Enlil II after which the letter of Hattushilish III was written. However, Rowton misses the point. It is immaterial for the chronology of this period when the letter was written since the crucial question is when Kadashman-Enlil II came to the throne, and he could easily have done so prior to year 21 of Ramesses II, perhaps c. year 19. Admittedly on this dating Hattushilish III and Kadashman-Turgu would only have been contemporaries for a short time, but Babylon's support of Hattushilish III against Egypt could have dated to just after his succession. A sudden change in Babylonian foreign policy would appear to have occurred on the death of Kadashman-Turgu, but that change might be expected if Itti-Marduk-balatu took over the regency after some trouble with pro-Hittite courtiers. The contacts between Babylon and Egypt after the peace treaty of year 21 might have proved objectionable to Hattushilish III because relations between Hatti and Egypt may still have been tense up to year 34 of Ramesses II when the Egyptian ruler married the daughter of Hattushilish III.

"It has been assumed that Kadashman-Enlil II succeeded to the throne of Babylon in year 19 of Ramesses II.   On Brinkman's minimum dating, the succession of Kadashman-Enlil II would have occurred in 1261 B.C., and if that date was year 19 of the Egyptian ruler, then Ramesses II would have succeeded to the Egyptian throne in 1279 B.C. exactly. Thus the letter of Hattushilish III cannot be used as evidence to exclude the date of 1279 B.C. as the accession date of Ramesses II. In this case, a much longer time period would elapse before the death of Kadashman-Turgu, and Kadahman-Enlil II would come to the throne some time after year 21 of Ramesses II in accordance with Rowton's arguments. The Mesopotamian maximum dates cannot be used with a 1290 B.C. accession date nor can the Babylonian minimum dates be considered with a 1304 B.C. accession date. Between the extremes of the maximum and minimum dates, certain adjustments are possible.

"The second Hittite letter KBo I 14 was written by a Hittite ruler who can only be Hattushilish III to an Assyrian monarch to complain that the Assyrian king had sent no presents to mark his accession to the throne while a previous Hittite king (Murshilish II or Muwatallish) had sent gifts to this same Assyrian king. Because there is a reference in this letter to the ruler of Hanigalbat as a vassal of Assyria, Rowton has argued that this letter must have been sent to Adad-nirari I (1307-1275 B.C.) who first subdued Mitanni and then purportedly annexed it. Hanigalbat reappears briefly late in the reign of Shalmaneser I (1274-1245 B.C.), who was Adad-nirari I's son and successor who finally eliminated it. Rowton assumes that Mitanni was then in revolt against the Assyrians and hence was never technically a vassal of Shalmaneser I. However, it is rather difficult to conceive of this state disappearing and reappearing with such persistency. Assyrian royal inscriptions should not be taken too literally, and it is not certain that Adad-nirari I definitely annexed Hanigalbat during his reign; he may merely have changed its monarch. This it is quite conceivable that Mitanni remained a vassal state of Adad-nirari I and Shalmaneser I until its final and futile revolt. In such a case, the letter of Hattushilish III could have been directed to either ruler.

"If Ramesses II ascended the Egyptian throne in 1279 B.C. and the letter was written shortly after Hattushilish III's accession c. year 15 of Ramesses II or 1265 B.C., the Assyrian ruler would have been Shalmaneser I who came to the throne on Rowton's dates in 1274 B.C. Thus Shalmaneser I would also have been briefly a contemporary of Muwatallish who died c. 1272 B.C. seven years before the accession of Hattushilish III. Indeed, the accession of

Shalmaneser I would have occurred during the reign of Muwatallish, and this fact would explain the whole point of Hattushilish III's letter. Muwatallish had sent gifts on the accession of Shalmaneser I so Shalmaneser I should send gifts on the accession of Hattushilish III. If 1290 B.C. is considered as year 1 of Ramesses II and c. 1276 B.C. as the date of the letter, it is possible that Adad-nirari I received it in his last years. In this case, the previous Hittite ruler would likely have been Murshilish II who could have been reigning in 1307 B.C. when Adad-nirari I ascended the Assyrian throne. Rowton has argued for 1304 B.C. as the accession date of Ramesses II and hence c. 1290 B.C. as that of Hattushilish III. The recipient of the letter would then have been Adad-nirari I and the previous Hittite ruler would have been Muwatallish. Unfortunately, the lengths of the reigns of the Hittite kings are not known with certainty. Rowton attempts to fix the tenth year of Murshilish II to 1335 B.C. on the grounds of a possible solar eclipse, but, even if the eclipse is genuine, later dates are possible. If the Assyrian dates should be dropped by ten years, then 1290 B.C. or 1279 B.C. would become even more feasible as the possible accession dates of Ramesses II since 1304 B.C. would be clearly impossible. Thus the evidence from other Near Eastern countries cannot be regarded as decisive in determining the accession date of Ramesses II. [However, it is obvious that 1279 B.C. weighs well in the balance.]

"The Egyptian evidence regarding this accession date consists of the minimum dating and the generation count arrived at in this study. On minimum dates 590 years elapsed between the accession of Ramesses II and the death of Taharqa in 664 B.C. (97 years for the remainder of Dynasty XIX, 114 years for Dynasty XX, 124 years for Dynasty XXI, 190 years for Dynasty XXII to the death of Shoshenk V, and 65 years for the remainder of the reign of Piankhy after the death of Shoshenk V and Dynasty XXII). When this total is added to 664 B.C., the result reached is 1254 B.C. When these figures are broken down as regards the beginning of Dynasty XXII, 664 B.C. plus 255 years yields 919 B.C. It has already been pointed out that Shoshenk I of Dynasty XXII came to the throne between 945-940 B.C. or just possibly c. 930 B.C. Thus approximately ten to twenty-five years remain to be accounted for above the minimum figures. One major adjustment might be the reign of Osorkon I to whom

Kitchen assigns an additional twenty years. However, these additional years could also be ascribed to the period between the death of Shoshenk V and the invasion of Piankhy and to the reign of Piankhy himself. Other years might be added to the reigns of Osorkon II, Takelot II, and possibly other Dynasty XXII pharaohs. The accession date of Shoshenk I is also dependent on the evidence of the dating of earlier dynasties which must now be examined.

[It should be kept in mind while reviewing this analysis that it has been proved by modern researchers that dynasties XXI and XXII had simultaneous existence, a point not considered in the present argument. See page thirty-three for proof of this dual dynastic track during this period.]

"When the minimum figures of 335 years are added to 945 B.C., this yields the date of 1280 B.C. for the accession of Ramesses II. If the accession date of Shoshenk I is lowered slightly, 1279 B.C. can be easily accommodated as an astronomically suitable date for Ramesses II. If 1290 B.C. is to be accepted as the accession date of Ramesses II, eleven years remain to be added to Dynasties XIX and XX. These years could be divided among the periods between the reigns of Merenptah and Ramesses III, Ramesses V and Ramesses IX, and Ramesses IX and Ramesses XI. It is unlikely that any years are to be added to Dynasty XXI. If 1304 B.C. is accepted as the date of the accession of Ramesses II, then another fourteen years must be fitted into Dynasties XIX and XX. The periods between the reigns of Merenptah and Ramesses III and of Ramesses V and Ramesses IX have been shown to have been of short duration, and with the distribution of the additional years between 1279 B.C. and 1290 B.C., these periods should now be complete. Another four years might perhaps be assigned to the period between Ramesses IX and Ramesses XI. However, where would the extra decade go? Unless the time span is to be stretched to the limit and several octogenarians and nonagenarians are to be created in the process, there is simply no room for these extra ten years. [It should be kept in mind that most individuals lived to about age forty during this period.] Thus on the known minimum lengths of reigns for the Ramesside period plus the calculated possible additions 1304 B.C. is very dubious as the accession date of Ramesses II. If the accession date of Shoshenk I is lowered from 945 B.C. to 930 B.C., there will be no room for these extra years in the preceding dynasties if 1304 B.C. or even 1290 B.C. is accepted as the accession date of Ramesses II. Only if 1279 B.C. is considered the accession date of Ramesses II, can that of Shoshenk I be lowered appreciably from 945 B.C.

"A second factor which may help to clarify the dating of this period is the number of generations which elapsed between the beginning of the reign of Ramesses II and the end of Dynasty XXV in 664 B.C. It has already been noted that thirteen or fourteen generations must have elapsed from Kaha i, a younger contemporary of Ramesses II who was at least half a generation older than Kaha i, to the reign of Osorkon I of Dynasty XXII. It has also been calculated that seven generations would span the period from the end of the reign of Osorkon I to the end of the reign of Shoshenk V. It has been estimated that only one generation covered the reigns of Piankhy, Osorkon IV, and Tefnakht, and that another three generations covered Dynasty XXV until 664 B.C. Thus 24 or 25 generations would have elapsed between approximately the beginning of the reign of Ramesses II and the year 664 B.C. Calculating on the minimum figure of 20 years per generation, a total of 480 or 500 years is obtained for this period. [This author opts for longer and fewer generations to arrive at basically the same point based on the simultaneous reigns during the XXI and XXII dynasties.] Obviously this total is much too low. To reach a more acceptable total of near 600 years, the number of generations would have to be raised to a minimum of 30 if the estimate of 20 years per generation is retained. On the generation analysis set forth in this study, a total of 30 generations is not possible, and thus the average number of years per generation cannot be the estimated 20 years. If each generation is estimated at 25 years, then a total of 600 or 625 years is obtained. Added to 664 B.C., the years 1264 B.C. and 1289 B.C. are obtained. Thus with some adjustments the generation analysis can accommodate either 1279 B.C. or 1290 B.C. as the accession date of Ramesses II. In order to obtain a date near 1304 B.C., it would be necessary to increase the time period of the average generation. An increase in the total number of generations by one would yield a date of 1314 B.C. which is too high for the accession of Ramesses II. In any case, the generation total of 24 or 25 is calculated from Kaha i, a presumed younger contemporary of Ramesses II, and, if both men were the same age, this generation total should date from the birth of the monarch and not his accession. Thus even the figures of 24 or 25 generation may be slightly too high. Since the number of generations should not be increased because any increase of the time span of each generation over 25 years is suspect, the generation analysis of the period from the accession of Ramesses II to 664 B.C. tends to weaken the argument in favour of 1304 B.C. as the accession date of Ramesses II."[102]

Once again, the analysis tends in favor of 1279 B.C. and once the exact generations and their ages are known, the results   will undoubtedly show fewer generations and a range around twenty-years per generation.   This calculated analysis shows that the general information regarding this time period is accurate to within a period of a generation of from 1279 to 1304 (25 years). Even getting that close to the time when the Exodus took place will place us within an acceptable margin of error over the history of the Bible and the chronology being constructed.

With this lengthy analysis to create as accurate a sign post as possible we conclude that Ramesses II acceded to the throne in 1279 B.C. This agrees, as well, with more modern thinking on this subject as noted previously. It is known that the Israelites were in Egypt at the end of the 18th Dynasty and the beginning of the 19th Dynasty; so the next step is to identify the actors in the 18th Dynasty. They have been listed above by Aldred. (page 125)

In summary then, and adding a bit of genealogy and history to the equation, Ramesses II was born in 1304 B.C., began to rule in 1279 B.C. and died in 1212 B.C., ruling for a total of 67 years. He is buried in the Valley of the Kings in Tomb 5, just across the Nile River from Luxor (Thebes).   He had eight wives and many concubines, and a total of as many as 162 children. Fifty of his sons are buried in Tomb 5 as well. His oldest son was Amen-hir-khopshef

---

[102]M. L. Bierbrier, *The Late New Kingdom in Egypt, ca. 1300 - 664 B.C.: A Genealogical and Chronological Investigation* (Warminster, England: Aris Phillips Ltd., 1975), pages 109-112.

who probably died as noted in Exodus 12:29: "at midnight the Lord smote all the firstborn in the land of Egypt, from the firstborn of Pharaoh that sat on his throne unto the firstborn of the captive that was in the dungeon."

Four years after Ramesses II succeeded his father Seti I, the Egyptians' age-old rivals the Hittites appeared on the horizon from the north. The novice pharaoh hurriedly raised an army of 20,000 soldiers, a huge number by the standards of the day, and marched up through the present-day Gaza Strip to confront a Hittite force nearly twice as big. The battle ended in a stalemate; after many more inconclusive skirmishes over the next fifteen years, Muwatallis' successor, Hattusilis (or Hattushilish) III, requested a peace treaty, and the Egyptians accepted.

The treaty lasted for the rest of Ramesses II's reign. The peace was helped along, no doubt, by his strategic marriage to Hattusilis' daughter Maat-Hor-Neferure in 1246 B.C. - a wedding that almost didn't come off when Ramesses and Hattusilis got into an argument over the dowry. The pharaoh later married another of the Hittite king's daughters, whose name is unknown.

The Hittite princesses were Ramesses' seventh and eighth wives; he had taken his first two wives, Nefertari, and Istnofret, at least a decade before he ascended the throne. By the time he took over from Seti I, Ramesses II had at least five sons and two daughters. One of Istnofret's son was Merenptah, Ramesses II's thirteenth son, who eventually succeeded him (the older ones apparently having died before their father did). Family ties were particularly close for the pharaohs: Ramesses II's remaining wives were his younger sister Henutmire and three of his daughters: Bint-Anath, Meryetamun and Nebettawy.[103]

Continuing on with the analysis of this time period in an attempt to place Moses and the Israelites in their proper place in history, we have another viewpoint, from another source. The very adept Ahmed Osman's analysis of the critical point of dating is important to this

---

[103]Dorfman, *op. cit.*

study.[104] Mr. Osman was born and raised in Egypt, with scholastic learning in the finest schools of England. His natural understanding of many things Egyptian, and the accumulation of additional knowledge through his studies, makes him one of the finest scholars quoted in this work.

"A chronology for the life of Moses clearly depends upon establishing in the first place when the Descent of the Israelites into Egypt took place and how long they remained there before the Exodus. It is generally accepted that they were in the country at the end of the Eighteenth and the start of the Nineteenth Dynasties (c. 1308 B.C.), but when they arrived and departed have both been the subject of considerable disagreement. The Old Testament is not very helpful in this matter. It does not give any dates, [n]or the names of any reigning monarch[s], referring to him [them] only as 'Pharaoh,' 'King' or 'Pharaoh, King of Egypt.' Nor does it tell us where the capital city of the [any] Pharaoh in question was situated. It also provides us with some conflicting statements about how long the Sojourn lasted [400 years, 4 generations and 430 years]:

'And he said unto Abram, Know of a surety that thy seed shall be a stranger in a land that is not theirs, and shall serve them; and they shall afflict them four hundred years.' (Genesis 15:13)'

'But in the fourth generation they shall come hither again...' (Genesis 15:16)

'Now the sojourning of the children of Israel, who dwelt in Egypt, was four hundred and thirty years.

'And it came to pass at the end of the four hundred and thirty years, even the selfsame day it came to pass, that all the hosts of the Lord went out from the land of Egypt.' (Exodus 12: 40-41)

---

[104]Ahmed Osman, *Moses: Pharaoh of Egypt: The Mystery of Akhenaten Resolved* (London, England: Grafton Books, 1990), pages 34-50; also Ahmed Osman's work on Joseph identified earlier (footnote 25).

"In addition, the Old Testament always provides us with the names of heads of tribes and the names of their descendants who are important to the story that is being related. In the case of the Sojourn we are given the names of four generations - Jacob's (Israel's) third son, Levi, and Levi's son (Kohath), grandson (Amram) and great-grandson (Moses).

"If we examine Egyptian sources we find nothing that matches precisely the broad outline of the biblical account of the Descent, Sojourn and Exodus. Yet this lack of precise evidence cannot be taken as a reason to dismiss the account as a complete fabrication or to suppose a mythological origin for these narrations. The Bible gives some inside details of the life in Egypt during the Empire (the Eighteenth and Nineteenth Dynasties) that in many cases have to be seen as originating as a result of first-hand knowledge. These details cannot be regarded as a later colouring, as some scholars maintain, for how could a Jewish priest and scribe like Ezra, returning to Jerusalem from the Exile in Babylon in the fifth century B.C., be expected to have inside details about life in Egypt during the Empire eight centuries earlier? The only logical explanation is that the biblical accounts of the Descent into Egypt and eventual Exodus have at their core real historical characters and events. It is therefore a matter of seeking clues within the Old Testament that may help us to determine to which period of Egyptian history these events belong.

"The historical period we have to examine is a long one, ranging from the seventeenth century B.C. until the thirteenth. In the seventeenth century B.C. Lower and Middle Egypt came under the control of the invading Hyksos - Asiatic shepherd rulers, with some Semitic (ethnic) elements among their followers - who set up their capital at Avaris in the Eastern Delta, where they ruled for just over a hundred years. They were eventually defeated in battle and driven from the country by Ahmosis (c. 1575 - 1550 [1540-1515 according to the previous study]), founder of the Eighteenth Dynasty, which would develop into a golden age in the history of Ancient Egypt and lasted until almost the end of the fourteenth century B.C. During this period Thebes in Upper Egypt became the capital and chief religious centre of the country, while the king's main residence was at Memphis in Lower Egypt. With the arrival of Ramses I, the first Pharaoh of the

Nineteenth Dynasty, Thebes retained its importance, but the king's main residence moved to the old city of Avaris, now rebuilt by the Israelites at Pi-Ramses and named after the Ramses kings of the dynasty. It is also from this period that the whole of the Eastern Delta area named Goshen in the Bible became known as the Land of Ramses. [This is critical to understanding that the Israelites had to have arrived during this time. There were no Ramesses pharaohs prior to this dynasty. The Israelites rebuilt Avaris and they did so at this specific point at the beginning of the nineteenth dynasty; therefore, we have them placed in time as arriving in the latter part of the eighteenth dynasty.]

"The name Ramses (spelled Rameses [and spelled Ramesses]) is also found in the Pentateuch, but not as the name of a ruling king. In Genesis 47:11, it is given as the name of the land where the Israelites were allowed to settle on their arrival in Egypt. As the Goshen area did not become known as the Land of Ramses until the Nineteenth Dynasty, and nobody disputes that the Israelites arrived in Egypt at some time before this era, it seems that the name Ramses is simply being used here as an equivalent of Goshen as it became known as 'the Land of Ramses' at the time of the Exodus. The name Rameses occurs again in Exodus 12:37, where it is described as the starting point of the Exodus. Further pointers to a northern residence at the start of the Nineteenth Dynasty are provided by the accounts of the way Moses, having returned to the Eastern Delta to rescue his people, was urged by the Lord to confront Pharaoh in the morning when he went down to the banks of the Nile (Exodus 7:15; 8:20).

"It would seem that two reasonable deductions might be made from these brief summaries of the biblical account of the Sojourn and what we know of the seat of power in ancient Egypt: firstly, that as shepherds were looked upon already as 'an abomination' when the Israelites arrived in Egypt, their appearance on the scene must have post-dated the Hyksos period, which was the root cause of the anti-shepherd hostility [an undocumented assumption]; and, secondly, the fact that they were settled in Goshen, remote from the seat of the Pharaohic power, suggests that this seat must at the time have been at Thebes, some 400 miles away in Upper Egypt, rather than Avaris, the Hyksos capital as alsothe land of Goshen in the Eastern Delta.

"However, with no archaeological evidence to help them, early Egyptologists were persuaded to believe - correctly, as it happens - that the Exodus could not be assigned to an earlier time than the Nineteenth Dynasty. It was when they attempted to decide in which reign of the Nineteenth Dynasty it took place that they went astray. Two points misled them: firstly, the figure of 430 years, given in the Old Testament as the duration of the Sojourn, which they appear to have accepted literally; and, secondly, the statement of Flavius Josephus, the Jewish historian of the first century A.D., which they also seem not to have questioned, that the Israelite arrival took place during the period of Hyksos rule. This view appeared to be justified by some elaborate mathematical guesswork, for if we add up the figures in the Bible between the start of the Sojourn and the Exodus, and compare them with the then accepted Egyptian dates, we arrive at the following totals:

Biblical Dates	Years
Joseph in prison on false charges of trying to seduce his master's wife (Genesis 41:1)	2
The good years before the famine in Egypt	7
The time when the Israelites came to Egypt after the second year of famine (Genesis 45:6)	2
The length of the Sojourn	430
Total	441

Egyptian Dates	Years
The length of the Hyksos rule	108
The length of the Eighteenth Dynasty	240
The reigns of the first four kings of the Nineteenth Dynasty:	
Ramses I	2
Seti I	14
Ramses II	67
Merenptah	10
Total	441

"The implication of these calculations is that Joseph must have arrived in Egypt as a slave, and been imprisoned in the very first year of Hyksos rule. Despite the inherent improbability of this having happened, early Egyptologists, working forward from this date, came down firmly in favour of the Exodus under Moses having taken place during the reign of Merenptah, the fourth ruler of the Nineteenth Dynasty. Furthermore, as the Bible indicates that the Pharaoh of the Oppression, during whose reign Moses fled to Sinai, died while Moses was still in exile, it followed that, if Merenptah was the ruling king at the time of the Exodus, his predecessor, Ramses II, must have been the king at the time of the Oppression.

"These assumptions were shattered in 1896 when the British Egyptologist W. M. Flinders Petrie found a great granite stela in the funerary temple of Merenptah in the west of Thebes. The stela, which had originally belonged to Amenhotep III and bore a text of his, had been later usurped by Merenptah, who recorded on the other side what some scholars believed to be two separate military campaigns - one his victory over Libyan invaders, the other an expedition into Palestine/Syria, matching the biblical account of the pursuit of the Israelites by the Egyptians. The stela, now in the Cairo Museum, has come to be known as the Israel Stela because it includes - in an epilogue to its main story - the first, and only known, mention of Israel in an Egyptian text. As this stela is dated to Year 5 of Merenptah's reign and speaks of Israel as people already resident in

Palestine, it upset completely the accepted wisdom of Egyptologists of the time. Not only had the Israelites left Egypt proper by that date, but, after spending a supposed forty years in the wilderness of Sinai, had made their way to Palestine and had been there long enough to develop into a power that posed a threat impelling the ruling Pharaoh to send troops to try to subdue them.

"This caused the scholars of the time to adjust their position. Faced with the facts, and lacking any alternative explanation, they decided that at least one of the figures in the biblical account of the Exodus, the forty years spent wandering in the wilderness, should not be taken literally. In addition they became ready to disregard the two Pharaohs of the biblical account - one for the Oppression and the other, his successor, for the time of the Exodus - and came to the conclusion that Ramses II was the Pharaoh of both events during his long reign of sixty-seven years. This belief has since become widely accepted by the majority of both biblical scholars and Egyptologists, who have come to regard it as unquestionable historical fact. However, the choice of Ramses II as the Pharaoh of the Exodus assumes that the military confrontation between the people of Israel and Egyptian forces in Palestine took place during the first five years of Merenptah, but careful examination of the Israel Stela shows that this cannot have been the case.

"In Year 5 of Merenptah's reign, Egypt was invaded by a Libyan leader named Merey, who had gathered to his banner a great army of Libyan tribes as well as five groups of 'peoples of the sea,' who are believed to have come from the Greek islands. They attacked the Western Delta. Memphis, Heliopolis and other Lower Egyptian cities were forced to shut their gates against the invaders, citizens were unable to cultivate their land in safety or move from town to town. On this occasion the invaders were not merely looking for plunder, as had been the case with previous Libyan invasions, for they brought their women, children and cattle with them, clearly intending permanent settlement. On learning of this threat, Merenptah sent an army that met the invaders in the Western Delta known as 'The Fields Of Piyer.' After six hours of fierce fighting, Merey fled, leaving his followers to their fate. The number of Libyans killed in the fighting is said to have been 6,000 with a further 9,000 taken prisoner.

"The section of the Israel Stela devoted to these events opens with the date: 'Year 5, third month of the third season (Spring), day 3.' This is followed by the tutelary and epithets of Merenptah and, after giving a general picture of Egypt after the Libyan invasion, the defeat of the enemy is described: 'Their advanced guard abandoned their rear. Their legs did not stop, except to run. Their archers abandoned their bows. The heart of their runners was weak from travelling. They untied their waterskins...their packs were loosed and cast aside. The wretched enemy prince of Rebu [Libya] was fled in the depth of the night, by himself. No feather ewas on his head' - a sign of dishonour, as Libyan warriors used to wear a feather in their head-dress - 'his feet were unshod. The loaves for his provision were seized; he had no water ... to keep him alive. The face of his brother was fierce, to slay him; among his commanders one fought his companion. Their tents were burned up, made ashes. All his goods were food for the troops.'

"Then comes some narrative sections, giving an account of the defeat of the Libyans and the saving of Memphis, which are followed by a religious composition in which the gods of Heliopolis praise Merenptah for saving Memphis and Heliopolis. The last section depicts the Egyptians joyful after their victory:

"'Jubilation has gone forth in the towns of Egypt....He [the king] was born as the one destined to [be] her protector, the King of Upper and Lower Egypt: Ba-en-Re, Meriamon; the son of Re: Merenptah Hotep-hir-Maat.'

"We have further accounts of the campaign against the Libyans in the war inscriptions of the Cairo and Heliopolis Columns, the Karnak War Inscriptions, the Athribis Stela (also called the Kom el Ahmar Stela), texts in which Merenptah has given accounts of the Libyan war in different parts of Egypt, and the Nubian Stelae, found in Nubia at Amada, Toshka, Wadi es Seboua and Amara West. With the exception of the Nubian Stelae, which describe a second war against the Nubians in Year 6 of Merenptah's reign, the only hostilities mentioned are those against the Libyans twelve months earlier.

"What distinguishes the Israel Stela is that, unlike other texts, the account of the campaign against the Libyans is followed by a separate concluding section of twelve lines (three on the original stela), naming some foreign locations and peoples:

"The princes are prostrate, saying 'Mercy!' (The word used here is the Canaanite *shalam*, meaning 'peace').
Not one raises head among the Nine Bows.
Desolation is for Tehenu; Hatti is pacified;
Plundered is Canaan with every evil;
Carried off is Ashkelon; seized upon is Gezer;
Yanoam is made as that which does not exist;
Israel is laid waste, his seed is not;
Hurru is become a widow for Egypt!
All lands together, they are pacified;
Everyone who was restless, he has been bound
By the King of Upper and Lower Egypt: Ba-en-Re
Meriamon; the son of Re: Merenptah Hotep-hir-Maat,
Given life like Re every day.

"Various interpretations have been placed upon the Israel Stela. It has been described, because of the poetic nature of its composition, as a hymn of victory. Some scholars have dismissed it as unhistorical and being rather a poetic eulogy of a universally victorious Pharaoh, while others have accepted that it provides a historical account of Merenptah's wars and victories. Although the stela is devoted almost entirely to the war against the invading Libyans, Libya (Tehenu) is also mentioned in the twelve-line epilogue. The other foreign references featured are:

■   Hatti, the land of the Hittites in Asia Minor, then extending to include northern Syria;

■   Canaan, west and south Palestine, bordering Sinai in the south, the Dead Sea to the east and the Mediterranean to the west;

■   Ashkelon, a Canaanite port on the Mediterranean north of Gaza;

■   Gezer, a Canaanite city west of Jerusalem;

■   Yanoam, an important town in northern Palestine at the southern end of the Sea of Galilee;

■   Israel: the sign used here does not indicate a land, but a people; and

■   Hurru: although this word is sometimes used to indicate the whole land of Palestine/Syria, it could also mean the land of the biblical Horites, north of Mount Seir at the foot of the Dead Sea.

"Merenptah was already an old man of about sixty when he came to the throne. [This does not coincide with information about the family. He may have been in his fifties.] At the time Egypt had enjoyed half a century of peace with Palestine/Syria since Merenptah's father, Ramses II, had concluded a treaty with the Hittites in Year 21 of his reign. No record of any major Egyptian conflict in Asia has been found during the remainder of the reign of Ramses II, and it is hardly to be believed that Merenptah, in the first five years of his reign and at his advanced age, fought these major wars against the Hittites in northern Syria and in Palestine/Syria without leaving any record of it other than the list of names in the epilogue to the Israel Stela.

"This does not mean, however, that the epilogue is without historical value. We find no claim on the part of the king that it was *he* who subdued these foreign peoples, no dates or other details of any specific confrontation are to be found, only lasting peace. Yet, as the section implies, this peace had been achieved only through the defeat of Egypt's enemies in Asia. If Merenptah was not the king who confronted and vanquished the Israelites and other peoples in Palestine/Syria, who did? To find the answer we have to go back ninety years before Merenptah's accession to the throne, back to the very beginning of the Nineteenth Dynasty.

"If, as is generally accepted, the Israelites were still in Egypt at the end of the Eighteenth and beginning of the Nineteenth Dynasties, and if Egyptian troops set out in pursuit of them after the Exodus, as the Old Testament tells us, we should expect to find some evidence of this campaign in Egyptian records.

"When Ramses I, founder of the Nineteenth Dynasty, came to the throne towards the end of the fourteenth century B.C., Egyptian influence in Asia had been weakened. The Hittite kingdom, ... which had emerged as a new power under the rule of the energetic King Suppiluliuma, had conquered first the city states of northern Syria, then Mitanni, Egypt's northern ally, thus threatening Egyptian control of central Canaan. Yet, despite this circumstance, the only stela of Ramses I, found at Wadi Halfa in Nubia, makes no mention of any campaign in the north during his short reign. A reference to 'the captivity of his majesty' is taken to imply a possible military confrontation in Nubia.

"Ramses I, already a very old man at the time of his accession, did not survive the end of his second year on the throne and was succeeded by his son, Seti I - and it is here, and in the earlier part of the reign of Seti's son and successor, Ramses II, that we find details of campaigns that match both the Exodus story and the Israel Stela.

"At some point in Seti's first regnal year, a messenger arrived with the news: 'The Shasu enemies are plotting rebellion. Their tribal leaders are gathered in one place, standing on the foothills of Khor (a general term for Palestine and Syria), and they are engaged in turmoil and uproar. Each of them is killing his fellow. They do not consider the laws of the palace.'

"There is evidence that this campaign took place immediately after the death of Rameses I, before the process of his mummification, which took seventy days, had been completed and before Seti I had been crowned as the new Pharaoh: The evidence...suggests that Seti had already returned from his first campaign (against the Shasu) when he visited Thebes in his accession year, there to attend to the burial of his predecessor and to initiate the benefactions in the Amun Temple which have been dated to his first regnal year. This reinforces the idea that Ramses I could have died while pursuing the Israelites in Sinai. The name 'Shasu' was used by the Egyptians to designate the bedouin tribes of Sinai, nomadic people who spoke a west-Semitic language, and to differentiate between them and the Palestinians, whom they called 'Aamu.' (Later on, in the early centuries A.D., the word 'Shasu' became the Coptic word *shos*, meaning shepherd). The full account of this campaign against the Shasu, here identified as a people by the determinative that can indicate either a people or a land, is found in Seti I's war reliefs which occupy the entire exterior of the northern wall of the great Hypostyle Hall in Amun's temple at Karnak. The extreme point in the king's first war, shown on the bottom row of the eastern side of the wall and dated to his first year, is the capture of the city of Pe-Kanan (Gaza).

"The second and middle row of this eastern wall shows a further war of Seti I to the north. Shortly after his coronation, Seti I set out again for western Asia. On this occasion the king marched with his army up the Mediterranean coast until he reached a point in north Palestine on the same level as the southern end of the Sea of Galilee, probably the city of Acco. He then divided his army into three divisions which moved eastward in three different branches to the cities of Yanoam in the north, Beth-Shan in the centre and Hammath in the south. The extreme end of this row shows the princes of Canaan felling the cedars in Lebanon for the sacred boat of Amun in Thebes where, in his yearly festivals, the god was carried in a celebratory procession indicating the submission of the whole of Canaan and the Phoenician coast to the Pharaoh.

"The first row of scenes at the bottom of the western wall of the Karnak temple façade depicts a war against the Hittites, who were at the time in northern Syria, where their strong centre was the city of Kadesh on the Orontes river, but the Hittite power was not broken. Although here again we have no date for the Hittite war, it is accepted that it could not have taken place in Year 1 of Seti I. The second, middle row of this western wall deals with two separate wars Seti I fought against the Libyans. No date is given, but they could have occurred any time after Year 1. The third, and top, row is again lost apart from a scene on the right extremity representing the war with the Hittites at Kadesh.

"Ramses II, who followed his father Seti I, on the throne in the early part of the thirteenth century B.C., spent the first decade fighting in Asia. His first campaign began in Year 4 when he swept through

Canaan and along the Phoenician coast, probably as far as Simyra, which had been under the control of the kingdom of Amurru, to the east in northern Syria. He then attacked Amurru itself, which had an allegiance with the Hittite king, Muwatallis.

"In the spring of the following year Ramses II returned to Syria, this time to conquer Kadesh. After fierce fighting, in which the king himself played a courageous role, he succeeded in defeating the Hittites and capturing the city. His third Asiatic campaign took place in Year 8 of his reign. On this occasion he had first to crush unrest in Galilee before embarking on other campaigns - recovery of the area of Damascus, strengthening his hold upon the Phoenician coast lands and attacking the Amurrite city of Dapur to the north of Kadesh. Two years later, in Year 10, the king engaged in a second attack upon Dapur, which had rebelled: 'Sometime in regnal Year 10, or shortly afterwards, Ramses II appears to have left Egypt; perhaps at this time he conducted the campaigns into Transjordan that are represented at the walls of Luxor since they do not fit into the accounts of his earlier campaigns.'

"Ramses II returned to Beth-Shan in Year 18, after which negotiations began between himself and Hattusili (Hattushilish) III, the new King of the Hittites, that resulted ultimately in a treaty of peace and alliance between them in Year 21. This treaty was later consolidated by a marriage between Ramses II and a Hittite princess in his Year 34 and a second princess a decade later... 'With Year 30 and the first Jubilee, a time of peace and tranquility seems to have descended upon Egypt, from that year onward, there is no reference to warfare or strife. Building activity seems to have become Ramses's primary public concern, and, as far as one can tell, the economy of this land prospered.'

"Some of the wars conducted by Ramses II were a continuation of the campaigns against the Shasu that had been initiated by his father, Seti I. There are several references to them, although no specific dates are to be found, at Tanis, one of the Ramesside cities in the northeast of the Delta, south of Lake Menzalah;...

"Where did these battles against the Shasu take place? Professor

Kenneth A. Kitchen of Liverpool University, citing various Egyptian sources, has concluded that Mount Seir formed part of the Shasu-land and is to be equated with Edom of Genesis (36:8-9)....Of a number of other names mentioned he says that Bernard Grdseloff, the Polish Egyptologist, has 'aptly conpared *Rbn* with the Laban of Deuteronomy 1:1 (and Libnah of Numbers 33:20-21) and *Sm't* with the Shimeathites of 1 Chronicles 2:55, all in the area of Seir/Edom, the Negeb, or the Araba rift valley between them,' and concludes that the evidence 'clearly suggests that Ramses or troops of his raided the Negeb, the uplands of Seir or Edom, and perhaps part of the intervening Araba rift valley.... Thus we have evidence for the activity of Ramses II (or at least of his forces) in both Edom and Moab (to the south and south-east of the Dead Sea.'

"Dr. Kitchen next proceeds to try to provide possible dates for the military confrontations between Ramses II and the Shasu: 'It is difficult to place these Transjordanian activities within the general pattern of Ramses II's Asiatic wars as at present known, and a summary must suffice. The first campaign would be that of Year 4: the middle stele at Nahr-el-Kelb, north of Beirut, gives this date clearly. The second campaign - explicitly so-called - is that of Year 5 in Syria that ended in the notorious battle of Kadesh. Then a campaign in Year 8 in Palestine, Syria and Phoenicia is commemorated on the rear face of the pylon of the Ramasseum. Then comes the south stele of Ramses II at Nahr-el-Kelb, perhaps dated Year 10, indicating further activity in Phoenicia. At some time in this general period belong the Syrian wars commemorated by the Karnak series of relief and related scenes at Luxor, besides other traces. However, the Egyptians had also to deal with matters nearer home, in Palestine. An undated scene at Karnak showing the submission of Ascalon is usually ascribed to Ramses II. And in his Year 18 is dated a stele from Beth-Shan that records virtually no concrete facts, but in itself may indicate activity in that region. This brings us to Year 21 and the Hittite Treaty, after which dated records of warfare cease.

'"The foregoing picture may suggest that for his first ten years Ramses's Asiatic activities were concentrated on Syria and the Hittite problem. Perhaps this gave way to a stalemate ending in the treaty of Year 21. In the meantime, in the Years 11-20, unrest had developed in Palestine (Ascalon relief; Beth Shan stele, Job Stone)' - inscribed stones of Ramses in Syria/Palestine - 'Perhaps one may also place the Edomite and Moabite undertakings within this period.'

"It would seem that all military confrontations in Asia came to an end for the Egyptians by Year 21 of Ramses II when the peace treaty was concluded with the Hittites. The wars with the Shasu must, consequently, all have taken place before this date.

"We therefore have the situation that, in the first year of Seti I, the Shasu were emerging from Sinai, and posing a threat to Canaan, Edom and Moab. Then, at the time of Ramses II, about two decades later, they have left Sinai and are to be found in Edom and Moab. If we compare the sudden appearance of the Shasu bedouin and their movements with the Israelite Exodus from Sinai we find that they followed the very same route. Dr. Kitchen, too, was struck by this fact: 'For Old Testament studies, the new information has some bearing on the date of the Hebrew conquest of central Transjordan and their entry into W. Palestine, not to mention the date of the Exodus.'

"And so to return to the epilogue of the Israel Stela...

"The evidence available makes it clear that Merenptah had only peace in Asia during his reign. There is no reference whatever to his having conducted any wars in Palestine/Syria. It therefore seems clear that the epilogue to the Israel Stela refers not to his own campaigns, but to the status quo he inherited, the situation created by his grandfather, Seti I, and his father, Ramses II:

■   Tehenu (Libya): Here Seti I's wars are meant, as Merenptah's own war with the invading Libyans had been described in the Israel Stela and elsewhere.

■   Hatti: The land of the Hittites. We saw how both Seti I and Ramses II fought the Hittites in northern Syria until a peace treaty was ultimately agreed. There is no account of any war after that date.

■	Canaan: The land of western Palestine, which also includes the cities of Ascalon and Gezer. It was Seti I who regained this section in the Nineteenth Dynasty and Ramses II consolidated his victory.

■	Yanoam: To the south of the Sea of Galilee in north Palestine. It was captured by Seti I in his Year 1.

■	Hurru: Whether it referred to Palestine/Syria in general or the Horite land to the south of the Dead Sea, both Seti I and Ramses II fought in these areas.

"There is one other name in the epilogue - Israel. Yet there is no mention at all of the Shasu, bedouin of Semitic origin, nomads with no fixed city or country, striking north from Sinai and threatening Canaan, Edom and Moab. On the evidence the inescapable conclusions are that Merenptah never fought Israel, but his father and grandfather did, and the terms Israelites and the Shasu are, in this particular case, one and the same people. As Moses and the tribes of Israel united in Sinai with some local Midianite elements, they were first identified as Shasu by Egyptian scribes. Later, when the Israelite identity became clear - and now that they were no longer in Sinai, but had settled in Palestine - the scribe of the Merenptah Stela was able to recognize them as such. [This certainly would tend to prove that the Israelites were not a large people as indicated in the Bible; rather, they blended into the countryside dominated by the Midianites.]

"It is the preconceptions of the majority of scholars, Dr. Kitchen among them, that have been the basic barrier to acceptance of this historical truth. They have failed to take into consideration the point made by Jean Yoyotte, one of the leading French Egyptologists of our time, that the 'biblical account of the Exodus, which was written much later by Hebrew scribes, contains literary embellishments about miraculous events of the flight.' Thus they have sought evidence of great catastrophes that befell Egypt and expected to find the names of Moses and Joshua in Egyptian texts. More misleading, through misinterpretation of the Israel Stela and their belief that the Sojourn lasted 430 years, they have sought evidence of the Exodus into Sinai in the wrong eras, the reign of Ramses II or of Merenptah.

"As long ago as the early 1900s, however, Yoyotte, who had done a great deal of work in the Delta and among the Ramesside remains, became one of the few to see through the 'embellishments' of the biblical account and identify the historical core of the story - that the Shasu wars are the only possible equivalent of the biblical story of the Exodus:

"'The persecution of the Jews was undoubtedly part of the Ramesside campaign against the Shasu (Bedouin)... The exact date of the Exodus is disputed. According to the Bible, the Jews toiled in a town called Ramses, and a stele of the time of Merenptah, a son of Ramses, speaks of the ‹annihilation› of Israel. From this evidence it has been deduced that their persecutors were Ramses II and Merenptah and that the Exodus took place under the latter in about 1200 B.C. But the ‹Israel Stele›, in fact, gives the impression that the Jews had already returned to Palestine by this time. Considering biblical chronology and the results of excavations at Jericho, it seems probable that their sufferings took place at the time of Seti I...

"'The ‹Israel Stele› is a misleading name for a document consisting of twenty-eight lines, twenty-five of which describe the triumph of the king over Libya. Mention is made of Palestine only in a three-line epilogue in which the famous name Israel appears among others. As far as the Ramesside government was concerned, the Exodus was merely a migration of Bedouin labour, the Shasu among others.' [This is further substantiated by the facts proven herein that the Sojourn lasted only between fifty and eighty years rather than 430. The numbers of 'labourers' was not significant, a few thousand at the most, certainly not the hundreds of thousands spoken of in *The Holy Bible*. Only three to four generations, with an initial pool of some seventy people are the real numbers. Given a maximum of thirty-five couples, and a total of ten children per couple {a high number} the second generation would have had potentially 175 couples, the third generation 875 couples, and the fourth generation 4,375 couples. If each of these couples had borne ten children prior to the Exodus, that is still only 43,750, plus 8,750, plus 1,750, plus 350, plus 70, or a total of 54,570 individuals belonging to the descendancy of Jacob.

That number is undoubtedly high. To it might be added a number of families from the Midianites and other Bedouins, but still the numbers would be relatively small compared to the biblical figures.]

"As we said before, there are strong indications that the Exodus did not take place before the Ramesside period of the Nineteenth Dynasty. However, as Seti I campaigned against Israel in north Sinai and south Palestine immediately on succeeding to the throne, the Israelites must have left Egypt proper during the short reign of his father, Ramses I.

"This chronology would make sense in more ways than one in the light of the Book of Exodus. As we shall see, before coming to the throne, Pa-Ramses (later Ramses I) had been appointed by Horemheb as his vizier, Commander of the Troops, Overseer of Foreign Countries, Overseer of the Fortress of Zarw, Master of the Horse. Ramses, himself said to have come from the Eastern Delta, was therefore at that time the most powerful man in Egypt after Horemheb. If the Bible, which never gives the name of the ruling Pharaoh, names the Eastern Delta city built by the harsh labour of the Israelites as Ramses, the name must derive not from Pharaoh but from vizier Ramses, who personally forced them to work. Then, while Moses was still hiding in Sinai, the Lord informed him that the King of Egypt (Horemheb) had died. In this case, the king whom Moses met after his return must have been a new king (Ramses I). Yet this new king could not have ruled for a long time as, after the difficult punishments inflicted upon him for not allowing the Israelites to depart, that by their nature take one full year as they are seasonal and follow the inundation of the Nile, they leave, he follows them and dies.

"The Bible does not state directly that the pursuing Pharaoh died in the waters although this is implied: And the waters returned, and covered the chariots, and the horsemen, and all the host of Pharaoh that came into the sea after them; there remained not so much as one of them. (Exodus 14:28)

"The Koran, however, makes it clear that the pursuing Pharaoh, too, was drowned: We took the Children of Israel across the sea: Pharaoh and his hosts followed them in insolence and spite. At length, when overwhelmed with the flood, he said: 'I believe that there is no god except him whom the Children of Israel believe in...'

"Ramses I is known to have ruled for less than two years. The biblical account of this part of the Exodus story cannot therefore agree more precisely than it does with what we know of the history of Ancient Egypt at this time. If Ramses I was the Pharaoh of the Exodus, Horemheb was the Pharaoh of the Oppression. But how long had the Israelites been in Egypt when these events took place?"

With the premise that Ramses I was the Pharaoh of the Exodus, and with his position in time placed on a firm foundation, it is now possible to approach the 18th Dynasty, that one prior to Ramesses II's 19th Dynasty. The 18th Dynasty is where Moses is found, albeit with difficulty, and where Joseph, son of Jacob is also found.

The Controversy of the 430-year Sojourn in Egypt

It is critical to the understanding of the whole premise of this work that it be understood that genealogically the information given in *The Holy Bible* is irrelevant time-wise.

This sacred record was written not as a history or as a genealogy, but as an instructive guide in spiritual matters. Great liberties have been taken in using historical events to fit into typologies, parallelisms, etc.

It is not the purpose here to criticize *The Holy Bible* in this regard, but to differentiate its purpose from that of genealogy and history as applies to the dates contained therein. If this distinction can be kept in mind it should be much easier to understand the processes that are being discussed. There have to be so many years between each generation, and gaps must be accounted for in a genealogical record for it to be relevant.

In Genesis 45:8 Joseph says "So now it was not you that sent me hither, but God: and he hath made me a *father to Pharaoh,* and lord of all his house, and a ruler throughout all the land of Egypt." (Emphasis added)

A father to Pharaoh! Who was this pharaoh to whom Joseph was father? This question is answered in detail in a book entitled *Stranger in the Valley of the Kings,* by Ahmed Osman, summarized in his subsequent book *Moses: Pharaoh of Egypt: The Mystery of Akhenaten Resolved.* But first, we must dispel the problem of the 430-year Sojourn in Egypt.

"Contradictory accounts in the Old Testament make it difficult to arrive at the precise date when the Patriarch Joseph and the Israelites arrived in Egypt. As we saw earlier, we are offered a choice of three periods for the Sojourn - 430 years, 400 years and four generations. In *Strangers in the Valley of the Kings* I argued that the figure of 430 years was wrongly arrived at by the biblical editor in the following way: firstly, he added up the four generations named in the Old Testament account of the Descent into Egypt as if each new generation were born on the very day that his father died, having lived for more than a century:

Levi	137 years
Kohath	133 years
Amram	137 years
Moses	120 years
Total:	527 years

"Then he deducted the years (fifty-seven) that Levi lived before the Descent - according to the Talmud he lived eighty years after the Descent and died at the age of 137 - plus the forty years Moses is said to have lived after the Exodus. This left him with his total of 430 years. This method of computation is obviously unsound, and I have since been pleased to find that many biblical scholars agree with my view that the figure of 430 years for the Sojourn is not to be taken literally - a variety of explanations are put forward - while it is, surprisingly, the majority of Egyptologists who appear to look upon it as a sacred figure not to be challenged.

"One eminent biblical scholar who has commented on the length of the sojourn is the late Umberto Cassuto, formerly Professor of Biblical Studies at the Hebrew University of Jerusalem, who wrote: '... the numbers given in the Torah are mostly round or symbolic figures, and their purpose is to teach us something by their harmonious character...these numbers are based on the sexagesimal system, which occupied in the ancient East a place similar to that of the decimal system in our days.

"The chronological unit in this system was a period of sixty years, which the Babylonians called a *sus*. One *sus* consisted of sixty years and two *sus* of a hundred and twenty years - a phrase that is used by Jews to this day. In order to convey that a given thing continued for a very long time, or comprised a large number of units, a round figure signifying a big amount according to the sexagesimal system was employed, for example, 600, 6000, 600,000 or 300, 3000, or 300,000 or 120, 360, 1200, 3600 and so forth. I further demonstrated there that, if it was desired to indicate a still larger amount, these figures were supplemented by seven or a multiple of seven. The number 127 [referring to the age Sarah achieved before her death], for instance (Genesis 23:1), was based on this system.' Elsewhere Professor Cassuto makes the point that the figure forty, found frequently in the Bible, is similarly used as a kind of shorthand for a period of time and is not to be taken literally.

"He then goes on to try to harmonize the two Israelite traditions - that the Sojourn lasted 430 years (six times sixty, plus seventy) and four generations. He cites as his four generations Levi, Kohath, Amram and Aaron, who is said to have been the brother of Moses, and adds together the years that they are given in the Old Testament. This approach is permissible, he argues, because: 'a) each generation endured the burden of exile throughout the times of its exile, and its distress was not diminished by the fact that it was shared by another generation during a certain portion of that period; hence in computing the total length of exile suffered, one is justified to some extent in reckoning the ordeal of each generation in its entirety, b) a similar and parallel system was used in the chronological calculations of the Mesopotamians. In the Sumerian King List, dynasties that were partly coeval, one reigning in one city and the other elsewhere, are recorded consecutively, and are reckoned as if they ruled successively. Consequently, if we add up the years that three dynasties reigned, we shall arrive at a total that is actually the sum of the periods of their kingship, although it will exceed the time that elapsed from the commencement of the first dynasty to the end of the last.' [It should be obvious to anyone looking at this approach from a genealogical point of view, that we cannot consider the numbers as they are given. From the standpoint that they are written, they serve their purpose, but from a position of identifying family numbers and sizes, it is not correct to use them: they are totally irrelevant except as rough indicator of age.]

"Professor Cassuto then proceeds to make the following calculation:

Levi	137 years
Kohath	133 years
Amram	137 years
Aaron	83 years
Total:	490 years

"Here he points out that 'upon deducting from [this total] (in order to allow for the time that Levi and Kohath dwelt in the land of Canaan before they emigrated to Egypt) one unit of time, to wit, sixty years, we obtain exactly a period of 430 years, which is the number recorded in Exodus 12:40.' The 430 years are thus the total years of the four generations and are not to be taken as representing the period of time that elapsed between the Israelites' arrival in Egypt and their departure."

Thus we arrive at another premise that will be accepted in establishing the chronology that will eventually result from this study: that the 430 years is not an actual chronological figure.

Joseph, A Father to Pharaoh

"Only two Hebrew generations of those mentioned, Amram and Moses, were actually born in Egypt - Kohath arrived with his father Levi (Genesis 46:11) - and, in working backwards from the reign of Ramses I, the Pharaoh of the Exodus, to try to establish the time of the Descent, calculation depends upon the age young Hebrew boys married at the time and had their first child. It seems reasonable to suggest that the period in which the Descent took place should be sought within the range of some fifty to eighty years earlier than the Exodus.

"It may be helpful at this point to show how this chronology accords with that arrived at, through a different approach, in *Stranger in the Valley of the Kings*, which sought to establish that Joseph the Patriarch was the same person as Yuya, vizier, Master of the Horse and Deputy of the King in the Chariotry to both Tuthmosis IV and Amenhotep III - whose mummy, despite the fact that he did not appear to be of royal blood, was found in the Valley of the Kings in 1905.[105]

"The official opening of the tomb took place on February 13, 1905.... On March 3, one hundred and twenty workmen started to carry the packing cases down to the river, where they were left overnight before

---

[105]Osman, *Stranger ... op. cit.*, pages 51-52.

being loaded onto a guarded train, bound for Cairo and Yuya's present resting place in the Egyptian capital's museum.

"Although the tomb of Yuya and Tuya was the most complete one to be found before that of Tutankhamun, nobody thought that Yuya personally was of any great importance. Davis wrote his account of the discovery, with an introduction by Maspero, in 1907: Naville published his study of Yuya's *Book of the Dead* a year later. Nothing much has been done since, other than some studies of different pieces of the funerary furniture and its texts. Yet in the case of Yuya there are enough curious facets to make it surprising that his origins were not the subject of more detailed investigation, either at the time or in the intervening eighty years.

"... he is the only person we know of from the time of the Hyksos kings onward to bear the title *it ntr n nb tawi* - the holy father of the Lord of the Two Lands (Pharaoh), the same title claimed by Joseph - and, although not apparently of Royal blood, he was buried in the Valley of the Kings rather than in the Valley of the Nobles, close to the village of Sheikh Abdel Korna. Furthermore, unlike the tombs of other nobles, Yuya's was neither decorated nor inscribed; his name, found on his sarcophagus, the three coffins and other pieces of funerary furniture, is not Egyptian and had not been discovered in Egypt before that time; unlike the ears of most Royal mummies of the New Kingdom, Yuya's were not pierced, and the position of his hands, the palms facing his neck under the chin, is different from the usual Osiris form in which the dead man's hands are crossed over his chest. Yuya, as far as is known, is the only Egyptian mummy to have been found with his hands in this position.

"Yuya bore an impressive list of titles in addition to 'the holy father of the Lord of the Two Lands':

"Father of the God, or Holy Father (This was a common priestly title which might be said to correspond to the 'Father' of the Roman Catholic Church and the High Church of England or the 'Padre' of the armed forces),
Master of the Horse,

Deputy of His Majesty in the Chariotry,
Bearer of the ring of the King of Lower Egypt,
Seal-bearer of the King of Lower Egypt,
Hereditary Noble and Count,
Overseer of the Cattle of Min, Lord of Akhmin,
Overseer of the Cattle of Amun,
Favourite of the Good God (Pharaoh),
Confidant of the King,
Confidant of the Good God,
Mouth of the King of Upper Egypt,
Ears of the King of Lower Egypt,
Prophet of the God Min,
Sole Friend (Unique Friend),
First of the Friends,
Prince,
Great Prince,
Great of Love,
Plentiful of Favours in the House of the King,
Plentiful of Favours under his Lord,
Enduring of Love under his Lord,
Beloved of the King of Upper Egypt,
Beloved of the Lord of the Two Lands,
Beloved of God,
Possessor of Favour under the Lord of the Two Lands,
Praised of the Good God,
Praised of his God,
Praised of his Lord,
Praised of his Lord Amun,
Praised of the King,
Praised of the Lord of the Two Lands
Praised One who came forth from the Body Praised,
One made rich by the King of Lower Egypt,
One made great by the King of Lower Egypt,
One made great by the Lord who does things,
First among the King's Companions,
The Wise One,
He whom the King made Great and Wise, whom the King has made
his Double.

"Unlike his wife, Tuya, who had conventional Egyptian looks, Yuya was remarkably foreign in appearance, as Arthur Weigall recorded in his book *The Life and Times of Akhnaten*, published in 1910: 'He was a person of commanding presence, whose powerful character showed itself in his face. One must picture him now as a tall man, with a fine shock of white hair; a great hooked nose like that of a Syrian; full, strong lips; and a prominent, determined jaw.'[106]

As to the name "Yuya," only four letters were used by the scribes and craftsmen who wrote Yuya's name on the objects in his tomb: *alef* (phonetic value A); *alef* or *yodh* (phonetic value A or Y); *yodh* (phonetic value Y); and *waw* (phonetic value W). There was a fifth sign, called a determinative, that has no phonetic value and was used to assist in understanding the meaning of the consonants. In the way it was used with Yuya's name it indicated that the preceding letters were to be read as a man's name. Although only four signs were used, the result in modern interpretation is dramatically varied. In all there are eleven possible spellings of his name: Ya-a, Ya, Yi-Ya, Yu-Ya, Ya-Yi, Yu, Yu-Yu, Ya-Ya, Yi-Ay, Yi-a, and Yu-y. His name is written in all but two cases as two syllables - Yu on the lid of an *ushabti* box (although inside the same syllable is repeated as *Yu-Yu*) and *Ya* on a coffin. Every syllable begins with the letter 'Y,' which in this case has to be read as a consonant because an Egyptian syllable cannot start with a vowel.

"There are two important points about the relationship between Joseph's biblical name and the name of Yuya. In the first place, Joseph's biblical name, like Yuya's, is a composite one, Yu-seph - 'Y' in Egyptian and Hebrew becomes 'J' in English, and, in both languages, 'o' and 'u' are written with the same sign - and the first syllable, which relates him to his God, *Yhwa* (Jehovah), is the same as the first syllable of Yuya's. Secondly, the variety in the spelling suggests that Yuya's name was a foreign one which the scribes found difficult to render into hieroglyphics....

"But what name were the scribes actually trying to write? Egyptian

---

[106]Osman, *Strangers, op. cit.*, pages 25-28.

names usually indicated the god under whom the person concerned was placed - Re-mos, Ptah-hotep, Tutankh-Amun and so on. The evidence suggests that, despite the years he spent in Egypt and the high office he held, Joseph remained aloof from Egyptian religious worship: most scholars believe that the sudden appearance of the name of the god Aten during the Eighteenth Dynasty is connected with Yuya although it was his grandson, Akhnaten, who later developed the worship of this god.... The first mention of Aten during the Eighteenth Dynasty occurs, in fact, on a scarab dating from the reign of Tuthmosis IV, who appointed Joseph to the post of vizier. His son, Amenhotep III, subsequently built a temple to Aten in Nubia and the barge in which he sailed on Queen Tiye's pleasure lake was named *Aten Gleams*. It seems therefore a reasonable assumption that, by the time Joseph died, Egyptians must have realised that he would not accept the protection of any Egyptian gods, only his own God, *Yhwh* (Jehovah) or *Yhwa* (the final *h* is read as an *a* in Hebrew), and what they were trying to write, following the Egyptian tradition, was the first part of the name of his God. A further cause of confusion for the scribes and craftsmen employed on Yuya's tomb may have arisen from the names of his forebears. Jacob, Joseph's father, is also said to have died in Egypt, where he was embalmed. His name must there have been known to the Egyptians, but, although again based on the divine name, it was pronounced Ya. Then in the case of Isaac it was pronounced Yi. It seems that, in the face of these differences, the Egyptian scribes used all three readings of *Yhwa*, with Yuya the most common and Yi-w the nearest to the complete form."[107]

"Although the name 'Seph' does not appear in any of the texts found in Yuya's tomb, Josephus informs us in his book *Contra Apionem* that Manetho, quoting ancient Egyptian tradition, gave the name of the leader of the Jews in Egypt during the reign of Amenophis (Amenhotep III), the eighth king in his list for the Eighteenth Dynasty, as Osarseph. Osar, the first part of this name, is a transliteration of the Egyptian *wsr* - Greek, the language used by Manetho, does not have a letter 'W' - which was the ancient Egyptian

---

[107]*Ibid.*, pages 121-123.

name for Osiris, king of the underworld, and was later used as a title, *wasir* (it is the Turkish version of this title, vizier, that has passed into English usage). We therefore have accounts of a vizier named Yu and another named Seph, both alive at the time of Amenhotep III."[108] [Manetho, whose work was based on a long oral tradition with the inevitable distortions that occur when stories are handed down by word of mouth, wrongly identified 'vizier Seph' as the leader of the Exodus, which, again wrongly, he placed in the reign of Amenhotep III. It is interesting, however, that Egyptian tradition should point to this particular point in the Eighteenth Dynasty in Egypt as one of special significance in relation to the Israelites.] So in case the point has been missed by the casual reader, **Yu-Seph** was the vizier during the time of Amenhotep III if traditions are combined. Yu-Seph can therefore be circumstantially linked to the Egyptian Yuya because of Yuya's known position as vizier to Amenhotep III.

"While we can see how Joseph could have been transcribed into Yuya, the transformation of his wife Asenath, into Tuya and his son, Ephraim, into Aye can only be a matter of conjecture. It is a fact that it was common practice at the time for the Egyptians to have several names, some of which were kept secret. Tutankhamun, for instance, had five - the one by which he is commonly known and, in addition, Ka-Nekhet Tutmes (his Horus name), Nefer-Hebo Gereh-Tawi (Nebti), Re-neb Ka-w Sehetep Neteru (Golden Horus) and Neb Kheparu-Re (Nesubet). It was also the custom to use pet names as well as abbreviated forms for longer and more complex names. Some allowances must be made, too, for the fact that many centuries passed between the events described and the time they were set down in the Bible....

"In relation to Asenath and Tuya, however, there is one striking piece of evidence. Scholars have explained that her name derives from the Egyptian *ns-nt*, which they have interpreted as meaning 'belonging to the goddess Neit.' This, as I mentioned earlier, is an arbitrary interpretation. Egyptian has no vowels: *ns-nt* could therefore be just as readily interpreted as 'belonging to the goddess Nut.' On Tuya's

---

[108]*Ibid.*, page 126.

outer coffin she is addressed as *wrt 3ht*, which appears in the texts as an epithet - as the swastika is an epithet for Nazism - of the goddess Nut."[109]

"There is an Egyptian tradition, later included in the Islamic traditions, from which it passed into Jewish literature, that the name of Potiphar's wife was Zelekha. This name is absent from both biblical and koranic narrations, but the Egyptian tradition indicates that it was she who was given to Joseph in marriage.

"One of Tuya's titles is *kheret nesw*, which, according to Alan Gardiner and T. G. H. James, means 'king's ornament.' Arthur Weigall thought that she might have been a member of the Royal family. He comments in *The Life and Times of Akhnaten:* 'She...may have been, for instance, the grand-daughter of Tuthmosis III, to whom she bears some likeness in face. Queen Tiye is often called ‹Royal Daughter› as well as ‹Royal Wife›, and it is possible that this is to be taken literally.' He goes on to remark that, after her daughter's marriage to Amenhotep III, 'Tuya...included among her titles ‹Royal Handmaid› (or lady-in-waiting), ‹the favoured one of Hathor›, ‹the favourite of the king›, a title which may indicate that she was of Royal blood.' He also thinks the fact that she and Yuya were given a fine large tomb in the Valley of the Kings makes this more likely."[110]

If the conclusion noted above is true, then Potiphar, an officer of Pharaoh, captain of the guard, an Egyptian (Genesis 39:1) and Potipherah priest of On, are one and the same person. This name has also be noted previously in The Book of Abraham 1:10, 20 as the place - Potiphar's Hill - where the priest of Pharaoh tried to sacrifice Abraham on the altar of Elkenah at the head of the plain of Olishem. So it would seem to have been an Egyptian name of some several hundred years popularity.

---

[109]*Ibid.*, pages 125-126.

[110]*Ibid.*, page 160.

A further connection between Asenath and Tuya is found in the following information. Asenath was the daughter of the priest of On. Tuya's tomb gives no indication of who her father was, but the fact that she was connected, through being Mistress of the Harem in both places, with the temples of Amun at Thebes and Min at Akhmin, indicates that she came from a priestly background.

"More significant in this respect is the priestly position held by her son Anen, whose name appears twice on her outer coffin: 'her son, the second prophet of Amun, praised of the good god, Anen.' An inscribed statue of Anen, now in Turin, identifies him also as the priest of On (Heliopolis). If this position was hereditary, as was the case with the Memphite priests, it is possible that Anen could have inherited his position as priest of On from his maternal grandfather, Tuya's father."[111] [A list of kings from the Eleventh Dynasty to the time of Shoshenk of the Twenty-second Dynasty, with the names of Memphis priests - all claiming to belong to one family - serving under every king, is described in *Egypt of the Pharaohs* by Alan Gardiner.]

"From the point of view of Egyptian history, the biblical Joseph is a misty figure. No record of the name Joseph or that of any other member of his family has been found, and there is, to date, only one recorded discovery of the name Israel. In contrast, we know a good deal, from his tomb and other sources, about Yuya - when he was alive, his family, the posts he held.

"... Tuthmosis IV (*c.* 1413-1405 B.C.) [Osman's dates] was the Pharaoh who appointed Yuya to the post of vizier.... Yuya, who had married an Egyptian woman named Tuya, possibly of Royal blood... continued to serve as vizier when Tuthmosis IV died and was succeeded by his son, Amenhotep III (*c.* 1405-1367 B.C.). Amenhotep III, who was only twelve years of age at the time, broke with Egyptian tradition by marrying first his sister Sitamun, and then Yuya's daughter, Tiye - herself thought to have been only about eight - and making her rather than Sitamun his Great Royal Wife

---

[111]*Ibid.*, page 129.

(queen)....[112]

"Yuya's name, as well as that of his wife, was first mentioned in the marriage scarab of his daughter: 'Live...King Amenhotep (III), who is given life, (and) the Great King's-Wife Tiye, who liveth. The name of her father is Yuya, the name of her mother is Tuya. She is the wife of a mighty king whose southern boundary is as far as Karoy and northern as far as Naharin.' [The mention of Karoy and Naharin basically establishes Amenhotep III's kingdom as stretching from the Nile to the Euphrates.] Although this scarab is not dated, Amenhotep III must already have been married to Tiye, whose name appears again on the wild-cattle hunt scarab, which dates from the second year of his reign and bears the inscription: 'Year 2 under the majesty of King Amenhotep (III) given life, and the Great King's-Wife Tiye, living like Re.' The name of Tiye, in fact, appears on all five scarabs and those of Yuya and Tuya on the Kirgipa marriage scarab as well as that of their daughter: '...the Son of Re, Amenhotep (III), Ruler of Thebes, who is granted life; the Great King's-Wife, Tiye, who liveth; the name of whose father was Yuya, the name of whose mother was Tuya. Marvels brought to his majesty...Kirgipa, the daughter of the chief of Naharin, Satirna; (and) the chief of her harem-ladies, (viz.) 317 persons.'

"It is interesting in the context of the scarabs to read Breasted's comments in *Ancient Records of Egypt, II:* 'The origin of the powerful Tiye is obscure; Maspero thinks her a native Egyptian, and this is the most probable conclusion, but the persistent publication of the names of her untitled parents on these and other scarabs is in that case remarkable, although paralleled by scarabs of the Thirteenth Dynasty. This difficulty is, however, not relieved by supposing her of foreign birth. It is incredible that anyone could identify her with Kirgipa, on

---

[112]Woodward, *op. cit.*, page 47. Based on DNA studies, it is possible that Sitamun was Amenhotep III and Tiye's daughter; that he married his own daughter. Analysis of tissue from the two mummies of Tutankhamun and Sitamun show a very close similarity, and that both had a relatively rare blood type for ancient Egypt. It is speculated that Tutankhamun was either the son or brother of Akhenaten. If a son, it was possibly from a secondary wife Kiya. If he was a son of Amenhotep III, then his mother was likely his sister Sitamun.

whose marriage scarab she already appears in the titulary as queen. She is the first queen who is thus recognised by the regular insertion of her name in the titulary. The innovation was continued by Amenhotep IV, who inserted his queen's name in the same way. His ephemeral successors show the same inclination, and the whole period from the time of Amenhotep III to the close of the Eighteenth Dynasty is characterised by the mention and prominent representation of the queens on all state occasions, in such a manner as is never found later.'

"Further evidence that Yuya lived during this period, and died during his son-in-law's reign, is provided by the objects found in his tomb with Amenhotep III's name on them - the jewel-box, the chest and the alabaster vase - and the absence of any gifts from the ruler who succeeded him, Akhenaten. When it comes to trying to establish the precise year of his death, however, we encounter a major difficulty. There is no date of any kind to be found among the inscriptions on Yuya's funerary furniture; nor is there any record of a name or an event that can help us to establish the year. In fact, the latest precise date we have for Yuya being alive is the scarab recording the construction of the pleasure lake in the eleventh year of Amenhotep III's reign. [The copy of this scarab in the Vatican is described by Rosellini, *Monumenti Storici.*]

"One of the most significant pieces of evidence is the three chairs, found in his tomb, that belonged to Princess Sitamun. The variations in the height, width and depth of the chairs suggest that they were made for the princess at three different stages of her growing up:

	Height	*Width*	*Depth*
First chair	595mm	400mm	370mm
Second chair	615mm	380mm	410mm
Third chair	770mm	520mm	540mm

"The first chair has no inscription, but has scenes representing the cat goddess Bes, dancing with her tambourine between two lion-headed figures of Tueris, the hippopotamus goddess, on the back. The second chair has Bes and Tueris on the sides, plus a boat containing Sitamun, offering a bouquet of lotus flowers to the seated Queen

Tiye, with a cat under the queen's chair and another princess standing behind.   Above the queen is her name inscribed inside a Royal cartouche (an oval ring containing hieroglyphic names and titles) - 'The Great Royal Wife, Tiye' - while, behind Sitamun, is her name, also written in a cartouche: 'Praised of the Lord of the Two Lands, Sitamun.' Only part of the inscription relating to the other princess in the scene can be read: 'The daughter of the king...' According to Theodore M. Davis, the dimensions of this second chair prove that it must have been made for a child, and, as the gold has been rubbed off and patched again in places, it is probable that the princess used it in her younger years.   The third and largest of the chairs, is sufficiently large to have been used by a grown person - has, on the inside of the back, a double scene of Sitamun, seated and receiving a necklace of gold from a maiden.   Her name, this time without a cartouche, is written above her.

"Scholars have identified Sitamun as the daughter of Amenhotep III and Tiye, and claim that the king married her. I believe, as I said earlier, that she was the infant sister, perhaps about three at the time, whom Amenhotep III married in order to inherit the throne. Tuthmosis IV is known to have had at least two sons, Amenemhet and Amenhotep, and four daughters, Tentamun, Amenipet, Tia, and Sitamun.   Amenemhet and Tentamun both died early and were buried with their father in his tomb. Sitamun was therefore still alive at the time of her father's death.

"Her name appears along with that of Amenhotep III inside a cartouche on a kohl-tube that is in the Metropolitan Museum in New York as well as inside the cartouche on one of the three chairs. The inscription on the bright blue, glazed faience tube, which probably came from Sitamun's palace at the King's Malkata complex at Thebes, is one of the main reasons that have led scholars to take the view - mistaken in my opinion - that Sitamun was Amenhotep's daughter as well his wife. It reads: *ntr nfr (nb m'at Re) s3t-nsw-hmt-nsw wrt (St Amn),* which is translated as 'the good god (*Neb-maat-Re*), king's daughter, king's great wife (Sit-Amun).' It is the reference to 'king's daughter' which has persuaded scholars that she was the daughter of Amenhotep III.   However, as in many other cases when a princess or a queen is described as being the daughter of a king, the name of the king is not given. Why then the assumption that it was Amenhotep III rather than his father Tuthmosis IV? Moreover, by claiming to be the 'king's great wife,' which was Tiye's title, Sitamun is challenging Tiye's position, reinforcing the idea that she was the heiress her brother married in order to inherit the throne.

"The presence of the chairs also indicates that, after her father's early death, Sitamun was reared by Tuya and must have been *at least* about fifteen years of age - and the possessor of yet a fourth chair - when she gave these three chairs to be included in the funerary furniture. This, and the evidence of the scarabs, suggest that Yuya's death could not have occurred earlier than Year 12 or 13 ... of Amenhotep's reign. This, of course, is not to say that it did not take place later in his son-in-law's reign, which lasted according to the conjectural dates (1405-1367 B.C.) for thirty-eight or thirty-nine years. Opinions differ in the matter. Arthur Weigall asserts - without giving any reason - in his book *The Life and Times of Akhnaten* that 'it must have been somewhere about the year 1390 B.C. that Tiye's father, Yuya, died; and Tuya soon followed him to the grave.' In contrast, Christiane Desroches-Noblecourt, the former curator of the Egyptian section of the Louvre Museum, makes the statement - again without giving any reason - in her book *Tutankhamen* that Yuya died in Year 31...of Amenhotep's reign.

"The situation is not made any clearer by the fact that we do not know how old Yuya was when he died. Until modern techniques are used to examine his mummy and some of the contents of his tomb, we have nothing to go on except the opinions of Sir Grafton Elliot Smith, the anatomist who conducted the initial examination, and Gaston Maspero, the Director-General of Cairo Museum at the time. Elliot Smith said, in a report published in James Quibell's book, *Catalogue général des antiquités du Musée du Caire*, in 1908, three years after the discovery of Yuya's tomb: 'The mummy of Yuaa is that of an old, white-haired man... His hair, now stained yellow by embalming materials, was perfectly white at the time of his death... The skin of the forehead, as well as that of the cheeks, is wrinkled. In attempting to determine the age that Yuaa had attained at the time of his death there is little to rely on beyond his general appearance, his white hair and wrinkled skin. If, on these slight grounds, we estimate his age as about sixty years, it must be understood that the mention of such a figure is little more than guesswork.' Gaston Maspero had been less cautious in the foreward he wrote to Theodore M. Davis's book, *The Tomb of Iouiya and Touiyou*, published a year earlier: 'Iouiya and Touyiyou died at a fairly advanced age: their hairs are white, and the examination of their bodies does not contradict the verdict of their hair. It will not be a mistake to state that they had reached an age over sixty. From the relative position of the two sarcophagi in the tomb, it seems that the husband was the first to die; but the material is lacking to decide this question.'

"Although Amenhotep III's name is the only king's name to be found in Yuya's tomb, this should not be taken as signifying automatically that it was Amenhotep III who first appointed Yuya as vizier and gave him his many titles. The fact that the new king, just after acceding to the throne, made Yuya's daughter his queen indicates that they must have known each other well as children. This would have been possible only if it was Tuthmosis IV who appointed Yuya to his post. Yuya's titles included Master of the Horse and Deputy of His Majesty in the Chariotry, while Tuya was the king's 'ornament' (*khrt nsw*), a post which might be said to combine the duties of a modern butler and lady-in-waiting. Yuya's titles and the position of his wife would have required them to live in the Royal residence. In those circumstances we can understand how the young prince grew up with Tiye, became enchanted with her and made her his queen when he came to the throne."[113]

"The Bible states that Joseph's Egyptian wife bore him two sons, Manasseh and Ephraim. No mention is made of a daughter. This is not unusual, however. The Bible does not usually refer to female descendants unless it is relevant to the story being told. Therefore the absence of any mention of a daughter cannot be taken as proof that Joseph did not have one: otherwise we should be forced to the conclusion that, apart from the few women who are mentioned, the Hebrews fathered only male descendants....

---

[113]*Ibid.*, pages 62-68.

"As for the two sons, we know from an inscription on Tuya's sarcophagus that she had a son named Anen, who was the second prophet of Amun [noted above]. There is no mention of another son, but the argument has been strong in favour of there having been one, Aye. Scott Woodward adds a piece to the puzzle when he states, based on his DNA studies, that Yuya and Thuya "were the parents of Tiye, who was the wife of Amenhotep III, and Ay, who succeeded Tutankhamun."[114]   Alan Gardiner commented in *Egypt of the Pharaohs*: 'Yuya in his tomb at Thebes bore the title of Overseer of Horses, while Aye at el-Amarna is Overseer of all the Horses of His Majesty. Even more remarkable is the connection of both with the town of Akhmin, where Yuya was a prophet of Min as well as superintendent of that god's cattle, and where King Aye erected a shrine and left a long inscription. Just as Yuya's wife Tuya was the mother of Queen Tiye, the spouse of King Aye had previously been the nurse of Queen Nefertiti. Little wonder if, in view of these facts, Percy E. Newberry proposed that Yuya and Aye, as well as their wives Tuya and Tey, were actually one and the same. It must be understood that the names which, in a purely conventional manner, we render in different ways, offer no real obstacle to this theory: such is the nature of hieroglyphic writing at this period that we cannot be sure that what appears to be written as Yuya may not have been pronounced Aye, and similarly with the names of the wives. Chronologically, however, Newberry's view, which he himself never published, is absolutely impossible: since, moreover, the mummies of both Yuya and Tuya, evidently very aged people, were discovered in their Theban tomb, it would be necessary to assume that Yuya and Aye, whichever pronunciation we might prefer for him, had before his death been forced to renounce his kingly title and to revert to the position of a commoner. Cyril Aldred has made the plausible suggestion that the future monarch Aye was the son of Yuya: this certainly would explain the similarity of their titles and their close connection with Akhmin. The author also noted a striking resemblance between Yuya's mummy and a portrait of Aye as king, depicted as the Nile God, at the base of a statue now in the Museum of Fine Arts in Boston.'

---

[114]Woodward, *op. cit.*, page 45.

"If, as is now generally thought, Yuya, like Joseph, had two sons, and it was the younger one who reached the higher position when he became king of Egypt after Tutankhamun's death, this would explain - which the Bible itself does not do - the biblical story of Jacob's blessing for Joseph's younger son."[115]

Now as to the age and burial of Joseph as they are described in the Bible. The conflict between his mummy (in the form of Tuya) being found in Egypt and his being carried out of Egypt by Moses at the Exodus must be reconciled in order for all of this to fit.

"Genesis tells us that Joseph died 'being an hundred and ten years old' (Genesis 50:26). Ancient Egyptians considered old age to be a sign of wisdom and those who attained long life were looked upon as being holy figures. In our case, both Joseph and Yuya were considered wise by Pharaoh. Of Joseph, he said: '...there is none so discreet and wise as thou art' (Genesis 41:39). Yuya is also described on his funerary papyrus as 'the only wise, who loves his god.' The age the Egyptians gave to those who lived to be wise was one hundred and ten years, irrespective of their real age when they died. Amenhotep son of Habu, an Egyptian magician in Yuya's time, was said to have lived one hundred and ten years although the last information we have of him puts his age at eighty. Since 1865, when Charles W. Goodwin suggested that the age the biblical narrator assigned to Joseph at the time of his death was a reflection of the Egyptian tradition, this idea has become more and more accepted by Egyptologists and was further reinforced when Gustave Lefebvre and Josef M. Janssen were able to show from Egyptian texts that at least twenty-seven characters were said to have reached the age of one hundred and ten years.

"From the medical report made by Grafton Elliot Smith, we know that Yuya probably was not less than sixty at his death. Smith was unable, judging by facial appearance alone, to decide the exact age, ...

---

[115]*Ibid.*, pages 130-132.

"The last verse of the Book of Genesis describes the final rites of Joseph: So Joseph died, being an hundred and ten years old: and they embalmed him, and he was put in a coffin in Egypt. (Genesis 50:26) But, because of the two preceding verses, the story of Joseph does not end there: And Joseph said unto his brethren, I die: and God will surely visit you, and bring you out of this land unto the land which he sware to Abraham, to Isaac, and to Jacob. And Joseph took an oath of the children of Israel, saying, God will surely visit you, and ye shall carry up my bones from hence. (Genesis 50:24-25)

"This is a complete change in Joseph's attitude to settling in Egypt. He arrived in the country, according to the Bible, at the age of seventeen and was appointed vizier, the most powerful post in the country after that of Pharaoh, when he was thirty. He made no attempt to contact his family and it was only when his brothers came to Egypt to buy corn that he was eventually reunited with them. In addition, by accepting an Egyptian woman as his wife he knew that his children would be brought up as Egyptians, for it was the Israelite custom that the children followed their mother, not their father. Even when his father, Jacob, died and Joseph went up to Canaan with all his brothers to bury him, he still came back, as did all the Israelites, to live in Egypt, their new home. Why, then should he change his mind suddenly at the time of his death? Or did he? When Jacob felt that his end was near, he asked Joseph to 'bury me with my fathers' and his wish was carried out. Why did not Joseph do the same if he wished to be buried in Canaan? Furthermore, if he foresaw trouble for the Israelites in the future should they continue to live in Egypt, why did he not advise them not only to take his body back to his homeland but themselves leave forthwith? Otherwise, of what value was his prophecy? He took practical steps to deal with the famine he foretold from Pharaoh's dreams: why did he not do the same here? [A contradictory chronology for these events comes from rabbinical sources to the effect that it was the second generation of the Israelites who, after Joseph's death, went up to Canaan to bury Jacob's other sons, leaving Joseph still buried in Egypt.]

"Then again, as Egyptians used to place some valuable objects in their tombs, they took the precaution of keeping the whereabouts of the tomb a secret. We are even told that in some cases kings buried the architect who had planned their tomb inside it so as to keep the entrances completely unknown. In the face of such customs, how would the fourth generation of Israelites have known where to find the tomb of Joseph?

"Donald B. Redford believes that the verses reporting Joseph's death were not included in the original story, but are the work of a later editor. How did this come about? Redford explains in *A Study of the Biblical Story of Joseph*: 'With the pattern of Jacob's death and burial before him, the Genesis editor could have made the family trek a second time to Palestine to bury Joseph. This would have been the most reasonable procedure. But he did not choose such an expedient. Instead, he adopted the most unlikely course of having Joseph's body kept in a coffin in Egypt for five hundred-odd years until, after the Israelite Exodus and Conquest, it was finally buried at Shechem. Why? Because the Genesis editor had no authorisation in his sources to do otherwise...the Joseph story told of only one trip to Palestine with the purpose of burying Jacob: another source, the Exodus tradition, told of a second trip, viz. the Exodus. Between these two egressions from Egypt, the Genesis editor had no evidence for another, and could not invent one.

"'In order to reinforce the implications of the two verses mentioned above, the biblical editor introduced two later verses, one in the Book of Exodus, the second in Joshua:

And Moses took the bones of Joseph with him: for he had straightly sworn the children of Israel, saying, God will surely visit you; and ye shall carry up my bones away hence with you. (Exodus 13:19)

And the bones of Joseph, which the children of Israel brought up out of Egypt, buried they in Shechem, in a parcel of ground which Jacob bought of the sons of Hamor, the father of Shechem... (Joshua 24:32)

"'Two points need to be made before examining the original Hebrew texts relating to the removal of Joseph's bones. The first is the use of the word ‹bones› for Joseph's mummy. It is obvious that the scribe who edited the story had no idea of how an embalmed body would look: Yuya, after thirty-three centuries, looked as if he had just died a few days ago. The second point concerns the position of the intruding verse in the Book of Joshua. It comes not as soon as the Israelites arrive in Canaan, but at the very end (Joshua 24:32), three verses after Joshua has been reported dead (Joshua 24:29). This suggests that it was not part of the original story, and such a view is reinforced by the original Hebrew text. The divine name is not mentioned in the Joshua reference to the bones of Joseph, but it occurs nineteen times in Chapter 13 of Exodus. In fifteen cases it is given as Jehovah and in four - all relating to the Exodus and the removal of Joseph's bones - as Elohim. This again indicates a later insertion.

"'It would seem that the later editors did not like the idea that the Patriarch was still buried in the land of the oppressors when the Exodus had become the cornerstone in the new religion of the Jews. How else would it be possible to understand how Moses, the greatest Israelite leader, who supposedly carried Joseph's bones with him to Sinai, was himself left buried in an unmarked grave when he died? ‹So Moses the servant of the Lord died in the land of Moab, according to the word of the Lord. And he (Joshua) buried him in a valley in the land of Moab, over against Beth-pe-or: but no man knoweth of his sepulchre unto this day›. (Deuteronomy 34: 5-6)'"[116]

What Mr. Osman does not realize in his analysis, is that even the addition of the verse regarding the burial of Moses is a false statement made for similar reasons by later scribes. Modern revelation of an original copy of the Old Testament record provides dynamic proof that this whole scenario just discussed was contrived by later authors.

"The Old Testament account that Moses died and was buried by the hand of the Lord in an unknown grave is an error (Deuteronomy 34:5-7.) It is true that he may have been 'buried by the hand of the Lord,' if that expression is a figure of speech which means that he was translated. But the Book of Mormon account, in recording that Alma 'was taken up by the Spirit,' says, 'the scriptures saith the Lord took

---

[116]*Ibid.*, pages 133-136.

Moses unto himself; and we suppose that he has also received Alma in the spirit, unto himself.' (Alma 45:18-19.)   It should be remembered that the Nephites had the Brass Plates and that they were the 'scriptures' which gave the account of Moses being taken by way of translation."[117] Thus we can say with certainty that the changes made in the original record were made after 598 B.C., the year in which the family of Lehi left Jerusalem for the New World. As the verses regarding Joseph are not quoted in *The Book of Mormon*, we can't say at this point which ones were inserted, but the inferences have already been made as to which these were.

"According to the Book of Genesis, the total number of Israelites who settled in Egypt was seventy. Yet we are provided with only sixty-nine names - sixty-six of whom made the Descent, plus Joseph and his two sons, Manasseh (Egyptian, Anen) and Ephraim (Egyptian, Aye). It is a reasonable deduction that the seventieth member of the tribe of Israel was also already in Egypt. I believe that she was a daughter of Joseph, Tiye. Why would her name be omitted? It may be because it is common in the Bible not to mention the names of women unless they are particularly important to the story that is being told. Alternatively, in the lingering bitterness surrounding the Exodus, her name may have been suppressed centuries later by the biblical editor in order to conceal this historical link between the royal house of Egypt and the tribe of Israel which would show that Moses, their greatest leader, was of mixed Egyptian-Israelite origins....

Moses was the Pharaoh Akhenaten

"While the second chapter of the Book of Exodus describes the daughter of Pharaoh as being the royal mother of Moses, the Koran claims that the mother was the queen, Pharaoh's wife. It is strange that, as both holy books must have had the same origin, whether God's inspiration or a literary source, they should not agree in this important matter, particularly when Egyptian custom would not have allowed an unmarried princess to adopt a child. How then has the variation arisen?

---

[117]Bruce R. McConkie, *Mormon Doctrine,* 2nd edition (Salt Lake City, Utah: Bookcraft, 1966), page 805.

"There are two sources for the misunderstanding. In the first place, the scribe who wrote down the Book of Exodus was faced with two traditions - that the mother of Moses was an Israelite and that she was *b-t Phar'a*, literally 'the house of Pharaoh.' Unaware, as she had already been omitted from the Joseph story in the Book of Genesis, that Joseph had a daughter named Tiye, who became Pharaoh's wife, he resolved this initial difficulty by creating two mothers, one Hebrew, who gave birth to Moses, and one royal, who adopted him and brought him up as her son. That he chose to identify this adoptive mother as a princess rather than a queen has a philological explanation.

"The word for 'daughter' and the word for 'house' were written identically *b-t* in early Hebrew and open to misconstruction by anyone not familiar with Egyptian usage. To an Egyptian the word 'house' was also used - and indeed, still is - to signify a wife: to a Hebrew it meant either 'house' in the sense of a building or 'household.' Later, both Hebrew and the language of Ancient Egypt, which had no written vowels, began to use some consonants like *y* to indicate long vowels. Thus, for example, we find a slightly different spelling of *b-t Phar'a* in the Book of Genesis account of events when Jacob, the father of Joseph, died. Joseph, who wanted permission to take him back to Canaan for burial, did not speak to the king directly but to *b-y-t Phar'a*, the Hebrew word signifying 'the house of Pharaoh': 'And when the days of his mourning were past, Joseph spake unto the house of Pharaoh, saying, If now I have found grace in your eyes, speak, I pray you, in the ears of Pharaoh...' (Genesis 50:4). 'Pharaoh' itself means literally 'the great house.' Thus *b-y-t Phar'a* signifies the 'house of the great house,' which in the Egyptian sense would mean the queen, whom in this case I regard as Joseph's own daughter, Tiye, whose intercession he sought in the matter of his father's burial....

"The royal mother of Moses was therefore the Queen of Egypt. But which queen? As we saw earlier,... Manetho, the third century B.C. historian, identified the reign of Amenhotep III and Queen Tiye - while son of Habu was still alive, some time before the king's Year 34 - as the right time for the religious rebellion that led to the persecution of Akhenaten's followers, and Redford has made the point that it is not built simply on popular tales and traditions of

Manetho's time, but on old traditions, passed on orally at first, then set down in writing, that he found in his temple library...."

In comparing the Book of Exodus and the Koran, the significant differences in these accounts are:

■   The Koran story does not give us the names of Moses' parents;

■   While the biblical story tells us that the rush basket was left by the river, the Koran refers to 'the water,' which could be a lake joined to the river;

■   While Pharaoh's daughter (or wife, as we saw before) is said by the Bible to have been the child's rescuer, it was the 'Pharaoh's people' according to the Koran;

■   The biblical version says that Moses' sister watches events while the child is in its basket, hidden in the reeds outside Pharaoh's palace, but this is not the case in the Koran; there it is only after the child was in the possession of 'Pharaoh's people' that his sister is asked by the mother, who must have been in the vicinity at the time, to follow after him, which she does secretly, indicating that this incident must have taken place in the palace itself;

■   Pharaoh's wife, who, according to the Koran, had nothing to do with the child until he had fallen into the hands of 'Pharaoh's people,' then intervened to prevent them - probably the guards - from killing him;

■   Once the child was in the custody of 'Pharaoh's people,' we are told in the Koran that the child's mother became worried about what might happen to him. Why would she be worried unless she was in a position to know what was going on inside the palace?

■   The mother, according to the Koran, was about to reveal her hidden fears for the safety of the child. This is the strongest indication so far that the child's mother and Pharaoh's wife were one and the same person. After her intervention to prevent him from being killed, he was taken away from her. She then became so worried that she was about to reveal that she was the mother of the baby, but instead she sent the sister to find out what was happening inside the palace;

■　　Rather than killing the child, Moses' sister, according to the Koran, succeeded in persuading 'Pharaoh's people' to place him in the care of a family that would look after him. Here there is another crucial point. Where the Bible indicates that the child was later returned to Pharaoh's daughter to be brought up by her, the Koran, makes it clear that this event was the actual return of Moses to his real mother;

■　　The Koran story states that Moses went out of the palace and 'entered the city,' thus implying that the palace was not far from the city, and use of the word 'unnoticed' here can only mean that he was neither dressed in princely attire at the time, nor was he attended by guards.

■　　While the biblical account of the slaying incident describes the two men who were fighting as an Egyptian and a Hebrew, the Koran version of the story makes them a follower of Moses' religion and an enemy, implying that at this stage, even before his flight to Sinai, Moses had a different religion that had followers as well as enemies.

"If we assume for the moment what is as yet far from proved - that Moses and Akhenaten were the same person - it is possible to assemble a brief outline of the historical facts behind the varied, and at times extravagant, accounts of the life of the greatest Jewish hero that we find in the Old Testament and other holy books, and to offer an explanation of why the world should have remembered him by the name of Moses.

"Moses, the second son of Amenhotep III and Queen Tiye, was born, I believe, at the frontier fortified city of Zarw, probably in 1394 B.C.... His eldest brother, Tuthmosis, had already disappeared mysteriously, and, in view of the threats that were about to be made to the life of Moses, it seems more than likely that the disappearance of Tuthmosis was not the result of natural causes. The reason for the king's hostility to the young princes was the fact that Tiye, their mother, was not the legitimate heiress. She could therefore not be accepted as the consort of the State god Amun. (See page 185 for further attempts on the life of other royal offspring - Sinuhe.)

"Furthermore, as she herself was of mixed Egyptian-Israelite blood, her children would not, by Egyptian custom, be regarded as heirs to the throne. If her son acceded to the throne, this would be regarded as forming a new dynasty of non-Egyptian, non-Amunite, part-Israelite kings over Egypt. This is exactly the light in which the Amunite priests and nobles of Egypt, the watchdogs of old traditions, regarded Akhenaten. It was not he who first rejected the position of son of Amun; it was they, the Amunists, who refused to accept him as the legitimate heir to the throne.

"Consequently, the king, motivated by the possible threat to the dynasty and confrontation with the priesthood, instructed the midwives to kill Tiye's child in secrecy if it proved to be a boy. The Talmud story confirms that it was the survival of Moses that Pharaoh wanted to prevent, because, once he knew that Moses had been born and survived, his attempt to kill all the male Israelite children at birth was abandoned: 'After Moses was placed in the Nile, they [Pharaoh's astrologers] told Pharaoh that the redeemer had already been cast into the water, whereupon Pharaoh rescinded his decree that the male children should be put to death. Not only were all the future children saved, but even the ... children [who had already been] cast into the Nile with Moses.'

"Zarw was largely surrounded by lakes and a branch of the Nile. On learning - perhaps from the midwives - that her son's life was in danger, Tiye sent Moses by water to the safe-keeping of her Israelite relations at nearby Goshen. Yet the biblical story makes it clear that the king was still afraid of Moses. Why should the mighty Pharaoh fear Moses if he was simply a child of the despised Asiatic shepherds? In those circumstances, how could he have posed a threat to the Dynasty?

"Moses spent most of his youth in the Eastern Delta where he absorbed the traditional Israelite beliefs in a God without an image [This is a misconception of the doctrine that was believed at that time. The Israelites worshipped a corporeal God]. It was not until he was a grown boy that he was finally allowed to take up residence at Thebes, the capital city in Upper Egypt and the principal centre of worship of the State god, Amun. By this time the health of his father had begun to deteriorate and Tiye's power had increased correspondingly. In order to ensure her son's ultimate inheritance of the throne, she therefore arranged for him to marry his half-sister Nefertiti - the daughter of Amenhotep III by his sister, Sitamun, the legitimate heiress - and to be appointed his father's coregent, with special emphasis on Nefertiti's role in order to placate the priests and nobles.

"Moses, whose religious ideas were already well developed offended the Amunite priesthood from the start of the coregency by building temples to his monotheistic God, the Aten, at Karnak and Luxor. In a climate becoming increasingly hostile, Tiye eventually persuaded him to leave Thebes and found a new capital for himself at Tell el-Amarna, some 200 miles to the north, roughly halfway between Thebes and the Eastern Delta. Moses named his new city Akhenaten - the city of the horizon of the Aten - in honour of his new God.

"It was during this period that the old king became concerned about the growing power of the Israelites and sought advice about how to deal with them. But this cannot be simply because they had grown in number and might side with his enemies. The growth in their numbers would simply have provided him with more slaves to work for him and made him stronger in the face of foreign aggressors. What we are dealing with is a religious revolution. The vast [not so vast] increase in the numbers of the Israelites by this time was not simply a matter of their birth rate: the declaration by Moses that the Aten, his God, was the only true God, had attracted many Egyptian adherents who, as a result of their conversion to the new religion, became regarded as Israelites. [Herein may lie part of the number of "Israelites" that were involved in the Exodus.] Other evidence suggests that the Israelites had also achieved political importance and high position in the land, with, according to Manetho, priests, and learned people in their ranks. At the same time, those of Moses' followers who did not follow him to Amarna were, according to Manetho, set to harsh work in the stone quarries.

"At Amarna the monotheistic ideas of Moses underwent further development and, when he became sole ruler on the death of his father, Amenhotep III, after the end of his Year 38 - Year 12 of Moses - he shut down the temples of the ancient gods of Egypt, cut off all financial support for them and sent the priests home. These actions caused so much bitter resentment that, in his Year 15, Moses was forced to install his brother, Semenkhkare, as his coregent at Thebes. This action served only to delay the eventual showdown. In his Year 17 Moses was warned by his uncle, Aye (Ephraim), the second son of the Patriarch Joseph (Yuya), of a plot against his life, and he abdicated and fled to Sinai, taking with him his pharaonic symbol of authority, the staff topped by a bronze serpent. Semenkhkare did not long survive the departure of Moses - perhaps only a few days [more likely up to two years] - and was replaced on the throne by Moses' son, the boy king Tutankhamun, who restored the old gods, but attempted a compromise by allowing the Aten to be worshipped alongside them. Tutankhamun ruled for at least nine, and perhaps ten, years and was succeeded by Aye, his great-uncle [granduncle is the proper term], who ruled for four years before the army leader, Horemheb, brought the era of Amarna rule to an end.

"The bitterness which divided the country at the time is indicated by the actions of Horemheb and the Ramesside kings who followed him. The names of the Amarna kings were excised from king lists and monuments in a studied campaign to try to remove all trace of them from Egypt's memory, and it was forbidden even to mention in conversation the name of Akhenaten. In addition, the Israelites were put to the harsh work of building the treasure cities of Pithom and Ramses.

"On the death of Horemheb, there was no legitimate Eighteenth Dynasty heir. Ramses, Horemheb's elderly vizier, took power as Ramses I, the first ruler of the Nineteenth Dynasty. On hearing of Horemheb's death, Moses returned from Sinai to challenge Ramses' right to the throne. With him he brought his sceptre of authority, the bronze serpent. The wise men of Egypt were assembled to decide between the rival claimants to the throne, but, while they chose Moses as the rightful heir, Ramses controlled the army, which was to prove the decisive factor in the power struggle. For a short time, however, Moses did succeed in establishing his followers as a community in Zarw, which for the Israelites may be likened to the Paris Commune briefly established in the French capital in 1871. Then, having failed in his attempt to restore his former position as ruler, Moses eventually persuaded Ramses I to allow him and the Israelites to leave the country.

"How long was the Oppression? If the chronology in the Book of Exodus was correct, it would have begun before Moses was born, lasted during the eighteen or twenty years he was growing up, and continued during the years of his exile before his eventual return to lead the Exodus - a period of several decades, which seems an unduly long time to build the two store cities. The Oppression story in the Book of Exodus, in fact, links three separate events that happened at different periods - the first the plan to murder the Israelite male children; the second related to the religious upheaval caused by Akhenaten that was already in full flow at the time he was forced to build his new capital at Amarna to avoid further confrontation with the Theban priests; the third the rigorous Oppression of the Israelites by Horemheb after the final overthrow of Amarna rule.

"It seems therefore that it was the scribes, working from what Cassuto has called 'an epic poem describing the enslavement of the Israelites in Egypt and their liberation' - whether it was oral or written, or partly oral and partly written, in Egyptian - who rearranged the chronology, especially in the opening chapter of the Book of Exodus, which was regarded as an introduction to that book as well as a link with the preceding Book of Genesis.[118]

We have now established the setting for Moses and his relationship (a grandson) to Joseph the Patriarch. To recap this analysis, a summary is contained in Osman's work on Moses,[119] quoted in part

---

[118]Osman, *op. cit.*, pages 52-64.

[119]Osman, *op. cit.*, pages 180-185.

as follows:

"If Moses and Akhenaten were the same person, it must be possible to match some biblical characters with characters we know of in Egyptian history. We can best begin with Jochebed, the daughter of Levi, who is described in the Book of Exodus as Moses' nurse. She is, I think, to be identified as Tiy, the wife of Aye (identified earlier as Ephraim, son of Joseph), last of the Amarna kings.

The American scholar Keith C. Seele has noted the special importance attached to Aye's wife at his Amarna tomb: 'The tomb of Aye and Tiy at Amarna is the only one in which both husband and wife are depicted with so nearly equal prominence. This exceptional treatment of the wife suggests the possibility that Aye owned his favour at court to her, or even that she was his superior in rank and family.'

"What strikes us first is that Tiy seems to have been named after Queen Tiye. We know from the Amarna tomb that she was 'nurse and tutress of the queen,' Nefertiti. She was also, as Baikie noted: 'The great nurse, nourisher of the god (king), adorner of the king (Akhenaten).'

"Scholars have long debated the identity of Queen Nefertiti's parents. As we saw earlier, some have suggested that she was Tadukhipa, the daughter of the Mitannian king Tushratta sent to Amenhotep III as a bride towards the end of his days, and that she could then have married his son, Akhenaten, instead; others that she was, in fact, Aye's daughter by an earlier wife who had died. Neither of these hypotheses has any grounds for support. Akhenaten, himself rejected on account of the non-royal origins of his mother, would not have married someone other than the heiress, the eldest daughter of Amenhotep III, and he had, in any case, married Nefertiti in his Year 28, eight years before the arrival of Tadukhipa in Egypt. Nor can Nefertiti have been Queen Tiye's daughter, otherwise she would not have been the heiress.

"Seele has argued that, as Nefertiti became 'Great Royal Wife of the King,' it is probable that she was a princess of royal blood. In addition, Ray Winfield Smith, reporting on the reconstruction work of the temple project of Akhenaten at Karnak, makes the point: 'An astonishing emphasis on Nefertiti is demonstrated by the frequency of her name in the cartouches on offering tables, as contrasted with the relatively few cartouches of Amenhotep IV. The queen's name alone occurs sixty-seven times, whereas only thirteen tables carry both names, and a mere three show only the king's name.' He goes on to discuss the appearance of statues of the king and queen on offering tables that appear on the *talalat*, the small stones used in building Akhenaten's Karnak temple and later re-used by Horemheb after the temple's destruction. 'There are sixty-three Nefertiti statues and thirty-eight Amenhotep IV statues, with eleven unidentified. Significant is not only the preponderance of Nefertiti, but even more important the extraordinary domination of the larger offering tables by Nefertiti statues....

"The greater importance attached to Nefertiti than even the king himself agree with Seele's theory that she must have been a daughter of Amenhotep III, not by Tiye but by one of his other wives. As Horemheb later married Nefertiti's sister Mutnezmet, to strengthen his claim to the throne, this reinforces the view that Nefertiti's mother was Sitamun, Amenhotep's III's sister and wife, who, from the traditional point of view, would have been regarded as the real Queen of Egypt, being the heiress daughter of Tuthmosis IV.

"Tiy, then, was Nefertiti's nurse and also nursed her [Nefertiti's] half-brother, Akhenaten, and Seele goes on to explain: 'It would be especially understandable if, as I have indicated, Nefertiti was the daughter of Amenhotep III. In that case, Nefertiti and her half-brother, Akhenaten, perhaps from childhood destined to be her husband, would have grown from infancy to maturity in close association with both Tiy and Aye. Egyptian history presents repeated precedents for the reward of royal nurses and their families at the hands of Pharaoh.'"

As a side note there is a tradition that Sinuhe's father was the father of the half-sister of Akhenaten. This may be Nefertiti whose mother was probably Sitamun and whose father was Amenhotep III. Thus Sinuhe may have been the full brother of Nefertiti. Tradition has it that Caphtor secreted the royal blood away to protect it from destruction.   Thus the story of Sinuhe takes on possible royal significance, close to the whole story we are treating here.   But back to the main story.

Seele also indicates that the nurse of Nefertiti and Akhenaten must have had another child of her own: 'The Egyptian word for nurse employed in her title almost certainly means that Tiy was the actual nurse - wet-nurse - of Nefertiti during her babyhood.   If this interpretation be correct, it is evident that Tiy had been the mother of a child - presumably the child also of Aye [but not necessarily; it may have been the case that Jochebed was the wife of Amram as it states in the Bible, and later of Aye or Ephraim] - and thus became available as the nurse of the princess, Nefertiti.'   Because Jochebed and Amram were the same age (see page 191) and Amram lived for 137 years (Exodus 6:20), Jochebed would have to have left her marriage to him if she became the wife of Ephraim.   This is possible but cannot be speculated or proved.

"Even today, Bedouin children thus nursed by a woman call her 'mother,' the same name that they use for their real mother.   The naming of Akhenaten's nurse after his real mother, Tiye, confirms [circumstantially] the relationship, and at the Amarna tomb of Aye and Tiy the king is seen bestowing honour on his nurse as well as on her husband.

"If Nefertiti were the eldest daughter, she could have been a few years older than Akhenaten, which would explain why she is more prominent in the scenes of the king's Karnak temple.   Although we do not know for certain whether the child Tiy nursed at the same time as Nefertiti was a boy or a girl, if the other elements of the biblical story can be identified from Egyptian evidence, then it must have been Aaron, about three years before the birth of Akhenaten.   Thus Nefertiti would stand for the biblical character of Miriam, while the nurse's real son, Aaron, was simply what the Bedouin call 'a feeding brother' to Moses.

"Such a relationship would explain the strange way he is introduced in the Book of Exodus, for, after the birth of Moses is reported in the second chapter, a long time elapses before we hear of Aaron. He makes his appearance in the story only after Moses had grown to manhood, fled to Sinai and is resisting the Lord's orders to return to Egypt to rescue the Israelites, pleading that he is 'slow of speech, and of a slow tongue.' It is only then that we learn of Aaron, and in a very strange way, when the Lord asks: 'Is not Aaron the Levite thy brother? I know that he can speak well.' (Exodus 4:10, 14)

"The Koran also confirms that Moses and Aaron were related only through the feeding-mother relationship. When Moses comes back from the Mount to find the Israelites worshipping a golden calf, he becomes very angry, so he: seized his brother by (the hair of) his head and dragged him to him: Aaron said "Son of my mother!" (Sura VII:150)

"In Manetho's account it was Amenhotep III who fled to Ethiopia (Nubia): in the Talmud it was Moses. The strange name given to Moses' queen, Aten-it, relates her to Akhenaten's God. No doubt what is meant by the Talmud reference to Ethiopia, which is described as being a city, is the Amarna location, and the queen's desire to place her son on the throne instead of Moses could represent Tutankhamun replacing his father, Akhenaten, whose policies had placed the whole dynasty in the possible danger of being overthrown....

"Analysis of the origins of the tribe of Israel and of the Levites would need a book in itself. Here it is worth making a few points briefly.

"Contrary to the general view, the name Amarna does not derive from a Muslim Arab tribe which settled in the area later. No evidence of such an event exists. The name derives from the name in the second cartouche of Akhenaten's god - *Im-r-n*. Amram, or Imran, was the name given in the Bible to Moses' father and it is the name Akhenaten gave to his 'father,' the Aten.

"Across the river from Amarna there is the modern city of Mal-lawi (Mallevi), which means literally 'The City of the Levites.' This could be explained by the fact that the Levites, who held priestly positions with Moses, held the same positions with Akhenaten at Amarna. For example, Meryre II was the High Priest of the Aten at his Amarna temple: the Hebrew equivalent of this name is Merari, who is described (Genesis 46:11) as one of the sons of Levi. Similarly, Panehesy was the Chief Servitor of the Aten at Akhenaten's temple: the Hebrew equivalent of this name is Phinehas, the son of Eleazar and grandson of Aaron (Exodus 6:25) in whose family the priesthood was to remain: Wherefore say, Behold, I give unto him (Phinehas) my covenant of peace. And he shall have it, and his seed after him, even the covenant of an everlasting priesthood; because he was zealous for his God, and made an atonement for the children of Israel. (Numbers 25:12-13)

"It is therefore a possibility that we are dealing here with the same people who served Akhenaten at Amarna and then followed him to Sinai after his fall from power.

"Discovery late in 1989 of the tomb, almost intact, of Aper-el, the hitherto unknown vizier to Akhenaten, also provides a semantic link between the Israelites and the Amarna regime.

"Similar names are known to have existed in Egypt at this time, but never in the case of high officials. The name 'Aper' corresponds to the Egyptian word for 'Hebrew' [which meant to ancient Egyptians a nomad], and the final 'el' is the short form of 'Elohim,' one of the words used in the Bible as the name of 'the Lord.'

"The fact that Akhenaten's vizier was a Hebrew worshipper of El confirms the link between the king and the Israelites living in Egypt at the time. Furthermore, the fact that Queen Tiye was associated with her husband, Amenhotep III, in donating a box to the funerary furniture of Aper-el indicates the possibility that the vizier was a relation of the queen's, most probably through her Israelite father, Yuya (Joseph)."

There is additional information to consider here as it pertains to the names being used by the Jews and Egyptians of the period, or more to the point, by Ezra as he wrote the history of this era. Albright points out that in the House of Aaron, Egyptian personal names were in use for at least 200 years after the Exile. The names of Eli's two sons were Hophni and Pinehas. Pinehas mean Pi-nehase: or "the Nubian."[120]

The name of Moses is also obviously Egyptian. It appears as the second half of Egyptian compound theophoric names such as Ahmose (also Amosis), Tutmose (also Tuthmosis), Ramose (Graecised as Ramesses or Rameses), and Amenophis the first part representing the state god Amun (of whom Amenophis IV was Akhenaten). In Toynbee's words: "The Israelites would hardly have given an Egyptian name to their national hero if he was not an authentic figure by whom this name had actually been borne. On the other hand, if their historical figure leader did bear an Egyptian compound theophoric name, they might well have docked the name, retrospectively, of its first element, since this would have been the name of some Egyptian god," in this case Amun.[121] Thus Amenophis could have become Mophis or Mosis or Moses. Of course this seems to more easily apply to an earlier pharaoh Ahmose or Ahmosis. But whatever the reality, there is definite circumstantial evidence of Moses being Egyptian because of his name, and of the connection of his name to pharaoh Akenaten.

Finally, from Albright's writings the Egyptian name *sbâyet* was that name applied to Akenaten's monotheistic doctrine. It has the same meaning, i.e. "teaching" as does the Hebrew word *torah*.[122] He then summarizes: "It is also credible that a new religion which in Egypt, had been invented and imposed by a sovereign, and which did not there outlast its author's lifetime, should have survived, outside Egypt, among non-Egyptian voluntary converts,... and if Moses himself was born and brought up in Egypt, he might have been predisposed in this originally Egyptian religion's favour by some echo of it that might have come to his ears in Egypt when he was a child." Indeed! He could just as easily have been the author, or recipient, as noted in *The*

---

[120]Arnold J. Toynbee, *A Study of History* (London: Oxford University Press, 1961), volume 12, page 416, footnote 3).

[121]Ibid.

[122]Ibid., page 415, footnote 2.

Holy Bible. However, even with the supposition by Albright, all the facts he noted circumstantially support our premise that Moses was Akenaten. When combined with the other material included herein, they form a solid case.

As a final straw on the camel's back, the prophecy of Joseph in Egypt as interpreted by modern revelation gives us a dramatic new piece of primary evidence. Upon his death bed, Joseph told his brethren of a revelation the Lord had given him. The original revelation has been taken out of the current Genesis texts. Joseph Smith in his revision of the Old Testament made it Genesis 40:24-34. The verses quoted below are 24, 28 and 29.

"And Joseph said unto his brethren, I die, and go unto my father; and I go down to my grave with joy. The God of my father Jacob be with you to deliver you out of affliction in the days of your bondage; for the Lord hath visited me, and I have obtained a promise of the Lord, that out of the fruit of my loins, the Lord God will raise up a righteous branch out of my loins; and unto thee, whom my father Jacob hath named Israel, a prophet; (not the Messiah who is called Shilo;) and this prophet shall deliver my people out of Egypt in the days of thy bondage.

"And he shall bring them to the knowledge of the covenants which I have made with thy fathers; and he shall do whatsoever work I shall command him.

"And I will make him great in mine eyes, for he shall do my work; and he shall be great like unto him whom I have said I would raise up unto you, to deliver my people, O house of Israel, out of the land of Egypt; for a seer will I raise up to deliver my people out of the land of Egypt; and he shall be called Moses. And by this name he shall know that he is of thy house; for he shall be nursed by the king's daughter, and shall be called her son."[123]

---

[123]This quotation is taken from the "Joseph Smith Translation: Excerpts too Lengthy for Inclusion in Footnotes," under Genesis 50:24-38 (page 799) of *The Holy Bible*, King James Version (Salt Lake City, Utah: The Church of Jesus Christ of Latter-day Saints, 1979).

The latter part of this quotation has apparently been left vague on purpose. How can Moses be of the house of Joseph by being nursed by the king's daughter, and being called her son? This has been answered on pages 178-180.

In summary, then, for purposes principally of chronological verification at this time, we have shown through modern revelation that Moses was a descendant of Joseph, not of Levi; we have shown circumstantially that Moses was born as the second son of Amenhotep (also Amenophis) III and Queen Tiye (daughter of Tuya and Yuya), probably at the frontier fortified city of Zarw, probably in 1394 B.C. As Moses was raised during his youth among the Hebrews, he may have been confused as to his true parentage until later. We have shown that Aaron was his "feeding brother" not his literal blood brother, but that *Im-r-n,* Amram, or Imran, was the name given in the Bible to Moses' father and it is the name Akhenaten gave to his 'father,' the Aten. Amram was probably the literal father of Aaron. He would had to have been in order for the Aaronic Priesthood to continue in his lineage. Amram probably lived 137 years (Exodus 6:20), was the son of Kohath who lived 133 years (Exodus 6:18), who was the son of Levi who lived 137 years (Exodus 6:16), who was the son of Jacob.

In *The Testament of the Twelve Patriarchs, the Sons of Jacob,* Levi states: "At eight and twenty years I took a wife, and at forty years old I entered into Egypt." It also states that he died at age 137. The Torah says that he was 57 at the time of the Descent into Egypt. The discrepancy is 17 years, but gives us a general time frame within which to work. However, it is important to try to resolve the discrepancy at some point because it matters a great deal as to the age difference between Jochebed, Aye (Ephraim) and Amram. Jochebed was born in Egypt, as noted below, either when Levi was sixty-four, or when he was eighty-one.

Kohath was the second son of Levi, unmarried at the Descent, because no wife is listed among those who entered Egypt. Levi states in his testament that "[his] second [son] was Kohath, who was born in my five and thirtieth year," making Kohath either 5 or 22 at the time of the Descent, and making Levi about thirty when he married.

Levi goes on to say "And in the sixty-fourth year of my life was my daughter Jochebed born in Egypt." He then says "The sons of Kohath were Amram, Yshvat, Hebron, and Uziel....In the ninety-fourth year of my life Amram took unto wife my daughter Jochebed, because that they were born both on a day."

Amram, the eldest son of Kohath (Numbers 3:19) would have been born also in the ninety-fourth year of Levi's age, on the same day as Jochebed. They were both thirty when they married. If we take literally the statement that Amram and Jochebed were both born on the same day (and the same year), then the statements of age as recorded in *The Testament of the Twelve Patriarchs, the Sons of Jacob* would be more likely correct, and the Koran faulty. If Levi was thirty-five when Kohath was born, and Kohath was fifty-nine when Amram was married (Levi being ninety-four: 94-35=59), Kohath was twenty-nine or thirty when he married. This would show a fairly constant tradition of marriage at about the age of thirty for three generations.

Assuming that Aaron was born several years later, and that he was approximately the same age as Moses [we saw above that he could have been three years older], Aaron would have been born about the year 1397 B.C., given the birth year of Moses at 1394 B.C. as noted above. With these premises in place, it is possible to make the following chronology.

Aaron,   born 1397 B.C.
Amram,   born 1431 B.C.
Kohath,   born 1461 B.C.
Levi,   born 1506 B.C.

It should be noted that the difference in age between Amram and Aaron is about thirty-four years, showing that Amram and Jochebed had been married about four years when Aaron was born. If this chronology is turned around and traced from Judah, brother of Levi, to David it appears approximately as follows:

Levi,	b. 1506 B.C.	←brothers→	Judah	b. abt. 1503 B.C.
Kohath,	b. 1461 B.C.		Pharaz	b. abt. 1448 B.C.
Amram,	b. 1431 B.C.		Esrom	b. abt. 1415 B.C.
Aaron,	b. 1397 B.C.		Arom	b. abt. 1380 B.C.
			Aminadab	b. abt. 1350 B.C.
			Nasbon	b. abt. 1320 B.C.
			Salmon	b. abt. 1280 B.C.
			Boaz	b. ab.t 1240 B.C.
			Obed	b. abt. 1200 B.C.
			Jesse	b. abt. 1160 B.C.
			David	b. abt. 1085 B.C.

This shows a very likely sequence of generations from David to Judah, taking into consideration in several instances where the sons fit into lists of children as stated in *The Holy Bible*. The years between the generations are not excessive; in fact, they are based on a normal standard. We can now show a more correct genealogy and time frame back to Abraham and Noah, hopefully identifying where the problem exists in the chronologies of *The Holy Bible*.

One of the first dramatic, apparent clues in pointing to the discrepancy is the number of generations cited in *The Holy Bible* between David and Abraham, the number being fourteen, a holy number, a number which usually does not literally mean fourteen, but is of religious significance only. St. Matthew 1:17 says: "So all the generations from Abraham to David are fourteen generations; and from David until the carrying away into Babylon are fourteen generations; and from the carrying away into Babylon unto Christ are fourteen generations." Let us quote again the late Umberto Cassuto, formerly Professor of Biblical Studies at the Hebrew University of Jerusalem:

"... the numbers given in the Torah are mostly round or symbolic figures, and their purpose is to teach us something by their harmonious character...these numbers are based on the sexagesimal system, which occupied in the ancient East a place similar to that of the decimal system in our days.

"The chronological unit in this system was a period of sixty years, which the Babylonians called a *sus*. One *sus* consisted of sixty years and two *sus* of a hundred and twenty years - a phrase that is used by

Jews to this day. In order to convey that a given thing continued for a very long time, or comprised a large number of units, a round figure signifying a big amount according to the sexagesimal system was employed, for example, 600; 6000; 600,000 or 300; 3000; or 300,000 or 120; 360; 1200; 3600 and so forth. I further demonstrated there that, if it was desired to indicate a still larger amount, these figures were supplemented by seven or a multiple of seven. The number 127 [Sarah's age at death], for instance (Genesis 23:1), was based on this system." Elsewhere Professor Cassuto makes the point that the figure forty, found frequently in the Bible, is similarly used as a kind of shorthand for a period of time and is not to be taken literally.

Based on the harmonious character of St. Matthew 1:17, of three periods of fourteen generations, or a long time at indicated by Professor Cassuto, it stands to reason that somewhere within at least one of the three fourteen-generations periods given in St. Matthew, there are real, missing generations. Just a perusal and calculation of the generations from Jesus Christ to David shows obvious missing generations. These will not be discussed in this volume.

We have shown a reasonable pedigree from Jacob to David, with historical verification that David fits within the time frame stated. Thus the next step is to examine the generations from Judah to Abraham where missing generations are also identified.

ESTABLISHING THE YEARS OF BIRTH

OF

ABRAHAM, ISAAC, AND JACOB

Jacob, father of Judah and Levi was born, according to *The Testament of the Twelve Patriarchs, the Sons of Jacob,* in the year of the world 2108, or approximately 1894 B.C. Using the Bible chronology from Adam, his birth is placed at about 1922 B.C., showing a discrepancy of twenty-eight years, between these two sources. However, when compared with the years noted on page 192, his sons being born about 1500 B.C., there is a serious discrepancy. With the facts established through secular history as to David's and Moses' birth dates, it must necessarily be that Jacob was born in the period of the 1500's rather than in the 1800's or 1900s B.C. Jacob was 147 years old when he died. According to his testament he lived seventeen years in Egypt (arriving there at age 130), had lived thirty-three years in Canaan (arriving there at age 97), seventeen years in the house of Laban in Mesopotamia, which by deduction, shows that he arrived in Mesopotamia from Beersheba, the home of his father, at the age of eighty. Looking at it another way, if he left his father's home at the age of eighty, he having been born when his father was 60, Isaac was age 140 at the time of his departure, living until after he returned from Mesopotamia.

We must point out the 60 years - one *sus* - noted as Isaac's age; 140, being two 70's, and his death at 180 (three *sus*) as being suspect of being real dates. This may point to the fact that Jacob was not a son of Isaac, and that the missing generations are between them.

Jacob's testament states that he was born in the sixtieth year of his father's age. Isaac, father of Jacob and Esau, was forty years old when he took Rebekah to wife (Genesis 25:20) He was 180 years old when he died (Genesis 35:28). He and Rebekah were unable to have children for some time, "because she was barren" (Genesis 25:21). How long this was is unknown. If Jacob's testament is correct, it had been twenty years.

In Genesis 26:34, it shows that Esau was forty years old when he married Judith the daughter of Beeri the Hittite and Bashemath the daughter of Elon the Hittite. Chronologically this event takes place prior to Isaac's blessing of his twin sons. At the time Isaac "was old" (Genesis 27:1) "And he said, Behold now, I am old, I know not the day of my death." (Genesis 27:2) It is obvious that some time passed after the blessing before Isaac died, if we follow the biblical story.

If Jacob was eighty years of age when he arrived in Mesopotamia, and served seventeen in the house of Laban, then we have the following chronology.

Jacob was ninety when Leah was given to him as a wife. Shortly thereafter he was also given Rachel, although he then had to serve another seven years for her [remembering that he arrived back in Canaan when he was ninety-seven]. Initially the Lord made Rachel barren because Jacob hated Leah. Leah's womb was opened and she conceived Reuben, probably in about the ninety-third year of Jacob's life. She then conceived again and bare Simeon, probably in the ninety-fifth year of his life. Then she bare Levi, and then Judah, likely in the ninety-eighth and one hundred and fourth years of Jacob's life. With Judah having been identified above as being born in approximately the year 1490 B.C., we can now determine that Jacob was born about the year 1594 B.C. and Isaac in the year 1654 B.C., if he was the father of Jacob.

Thus we come to Abraham, who was 100 years old when Isaac was born (Genesis 21:4), making his birth year in about 1754 B.C, according to the chronological sequence from David to Abraham as we have established so far. However, we are forced by the evidence to make a departure from the Bible at this point, and take a position that must stand on its own merits. The position or premise is that the stories of Abraham and Isaac as contained in the Bible are basically allegorical, and that either Abraham was not the father of Isaac, or that Isaac was not the father of Jacob. We will take the position that the gap is between Abraham and Isaac, but it could just as easily be between Isaac and Jacob.

The reason for taking this position is that there are about 307 years separating Abraham from his descendant Isaac's birth date if Abraham was 100 when Isaac was born, or 407 years from Isaac's birth in 1654 and Abraham's birth in 2061 (to be shown later); and there is more evidence for Abraham being associated with Noah and Shem, than with Isaac and Jacob. This will be explored further in the following analysis. This premise is critical to the development of the chronology contained herein and is not made lightly. Other sources will be quoted to show that experts have long suspected missing generations in the Bible. Why they are missing will be explained. Where they are missing is a calculated guess based on the reasoning presented below.

Standard biblical chronologies place the birth of Moses in 1571, the Exodus in 1491, the birth of Joseph in 1745, the birth of Jacob in 1836, the birth of Isaac in 1896, and the birth of Abraham in 1996, over a 200-year variant from the chronology developed herein. All premises in the revised chronology are based on historical records, on circumstantial evidence, and on detailed analysis of the events of the times in question. Even if this revised chronology is wrong it isn't likely that it is off by more than a generation. Therefore, the revised chronology will be used in this study, rather than the biblical chronology, which can now be safely said to be erroneous. In the revised chronology, after Abraham, there can be little certainty as to the time periods, although an attempt will be made to show where the biblical chronology is errant. We will assume that the chronology from Adam to Noah is correct because of the sources and reasons state previously.

CHRONOLOGICAL INFORMATION
REGARDING ABRAHAM'S ERA

Another premise, then, is that Israel was not in Egypt for 430 years, but rather for a much reduced period. Based on the information regarding the birth dates of Jacob and Levi, the Descent should have been in the year 1464 or 1466, or 1449 if the Torah's date for Levi's birth is used. We will use the date 1464 B.C. as the year of the Descent. Amram and Jochebed were both born in Egypt in 1431 B.C. Moses and Aaron were born in Egypt in 1397 and 1394 B.C. respectively. Some of the third generation, the children of the generation of Moses were also born in Egypt and it is possible that part of the fourth generation was born there as well. The estimated totals were given above.

The information just given raises a serious question concerning the total number of Israelites that left Egypt. The numbers, once again, must be highly inflated in *The Holy Bible*, because seventy-one souls do not grow to hundreds of thousands in three to four generations. There is circumstantial evidence creating a serious doubt, because of this time revision as it applies to the Sojourn, regarding the place in history of those patriarchs who lived just prior to the Descent, raising the possibility that the discrepancy in the chronology of *The Holy Bible* is centered around Abraham. Based on the above references to Salim in the Ebla tablets, and the fact the Melchizedek was the King of Salem and one to whom Abraham paid tithing, it is more likely that Abraham was a contemporary of Noah and Shem than that he was a contemporary of his stated grandson Jacob. This will be outlined in more detail. Thus, the fourteen generations from David to Abraham, which are likely instructional or of religious significance rather than chronological, combined with other facts, point to the time discrepancy being centered around Abraham. Let's repeat this so that it is not misunderstood: **the fact that this 14-generation cycle ends with Abraham, points to Abraham as to where the generations are missing.** We previously determined some other facts about Abraham (pages 82-88) and now continue with his key role in the revised chronology. A detailed analysis of all the evidence placing him in his true historical setting is given on pages 209-211.

One of the early centers of the post-Flood civilization as it pertained to the righteous, patriarchal lineage, was Ur of the Chaldees. There is some discrepancy as to where this was. The following is important in establishing the location, as it may have been the home of Noah and Shem during the lifetime of Noah. Another possibility is that they lived in Ebla. Some accounts also have Noah going to China, and Shem to Egypt.

According to The Book of Abraham (1:1), Abraham lived in the land of the Chaldeans, at the residence of his fathers (plural). He was apparently born in Ur, of Chaldea. After some great wickedness in the land, a curse of famine was sent upon the land by God. Given the time period in question, it was most likely the famine sent prior to the confusion of tongues at the Tower of Babel in 1996, that caused Abraham, along with other righteous men, to be inspired as to the locations to which they were to travel. His grandfather Nahor died in the year 2005, and his brother Nahor, as well as the patriarch Peleg and Father Noah also died in this same general period as has been noted. It would appear that Abraham's group, and the Jaredites, and the Chinese, and very likely others, were all commissioned by Jehovah in the same way. Probably because they left before the confusion of tongues, and also because they were under the watchful care of the Lord these groups were blessed with an ability to continue to understand one another.

"Now the Lord God caused the famine to wax sore in the land of Ur, insomuch that Haran, my brother, died; but Terah, my father, yet lived in the land of Ur, of the Chaldees. And it came to pass that I, Abraham, took Sarai to wife, and Nahor, my brother, took Milcah to wife, who was the daughter of Haran. Now the Lord had said unto me: Abraham, get thee out of thy country, and from thy kindred, and from thy father's house, unto a land that I will show thee. Therefore I left the land of Ur, of the Chaldees, to go into the land of Canaan; and I took Lot, my brother's son, and his wife, and Sarai my wife; and also my father followed after me, unto the land which we denominated Haran. And the famine abated; and my father tarried in Haran and dwelt there, as there were many flocks in Haran; and my father turned again unto his idolatry, therefore he continued in Haran....So I, Abraham, departed as the Lord had said unto me, and Lot with me; and I, Abraham, was sixty and two years old when I departed out of Haran. And I took Sarai, whom I took to wife when I was in Ur, in Chaldea, and Lot, my brother's son, and all our substance that we had gathered, and the souls that we had won in Haran, and came forth in the way to the land of Canaan, and dwelt in tents as we came on our way; therefore, eternity was our covering and our rock and our salvation, as we journeyed from Haran by the way of Jershon, to come to the land of Canaan....And...we passed from Jershon through the land unto the place of Shechem; it was situated in the plains of Moreh, and we had already come into the borders of the land of the Canaanites, and I offered sacrifice there in the plains of Moreh...." (The Book of Abraham 2:1-5; 14-16; 18)

Haran is located in Turkey, approximately to the northeast of Aleppo, Syria, just north of the modern-day border between Syria and Turkey. We do not know where the Ur is in which Abraham was born, but more and more scholars today assume that it was in Turkey, near the site of Haran, the location of which we know with certainty. Others maintain that the Ur of the Chaldeas is the southern Ur. The two positions will be discussed below. Given the fact that Haran is mentioned in the tablets of Ebla, according to Pettinato referenced in the second paragraph below, this requires that we place Abraham in this early period contemporary to the city of Ebla and the written tablets discovered in its archives; original records containing primary evidence of important facts pertinent to the discussion at hand. Thus we have not circumstantial evidence but primary evidence pointing to a discrepancy in the Biblical chronology and in favor of the revised chronology contained herein. Abraham's statement is also primary evidence as it refers to Haran, because Abraham himself testifies to naming Haran, and we know that The Book of Abraham is an inspired translation based on spiritual empirical data as noted in the Introduction. Abraham stated in his narrative that it was his company that named the land of Haran initially, in honor of their deceased brother, or in other words, before his travels to Haran, the name did not exist.

"The biblical narrative itself (e.g. Genesis 12:1, 5; 24:4, 7; Joshua 24:2-3) clearly denotes Haran and the area of northern Mesopotamia in general as the land of Abraham's and of his ancestors' births. The narrative describing his journey to Canaan, from Ur of the Chaldees via Haran, surely does not imply a long journey up the Euphrates from Sumerian Ur to Haran, and from there southwest to Canaan. The narrative implies that "Ur of the Chaldees" and Haran are in the same geographical region. This was the view held for many years by scholars until Sir Leonard Woolley popularized the notion that Sumerian Ur was Abraham's birthplace, based on Woolley's excavations at Ur (Tell el Mukayyar) during the 1920's and 1930's.

"More recently, Cyrus Gordon has called our attention to a Hittite city of "Ura," in Anatolia, along with the northern Armenian referent of 'Chaldean.' Indeed, Giovanni Pettinato, the former epigrapher of the excavations at Ebla, reported the appearance in the third millennium-B.C. Ebla texts of the city 'Haran in the territory of Ur.' Although Pettinato's identification of this text is contested, the fact remains that much evidence exists for the placement of 'Ur of the Chaldees' in Anatolia (Turkey) near Haran.

"The Book of Abraham itself is clear on this point, placing Potiphar's Hill 'in the land of Ur, of Chaldea' (Abraham 1:20). Potiphar's Hill was 'at the head of the plain of Olishem' (Abraham 1:10), which Olishem has been identified in texts of the Akkadian King Naram Sin as being located in northern Syria, in the region of ancient Ebla."[124] The text of Naram Sin itself reads as follows: "Never, since the time of the creation of mankind, did any king, whatever, set Arman and Ebla to sword and flame. Now did Nergal [which is a deity] open up the path of Naram Sin the strong and he gave him Arman and Ebla. He also presented him with the Amanus, the Mountain of Cedars and the upper sea. And with the weapon of Dagon, who aggrandizes his kingdom, Naram Sin the strong, defeated Arman and Ebla and from the banks of the Euphrates **as far as Ulisum** [emphasis added], he subdued the peoples whom Dagon had given him, so that they carried the corvee basket for his god, Aba, and he could control the Amanus, the Mountain of Cedars.

"Now this is the famous text which Professor Matthiae uses to associate the destruction level of the palace at Ebla, which he dates about 2250 B.C., with Naram Sin as the conqueror. The thing that interests me in this text is the word Ulisum. The Akkadian text makes it clear that Ulisum, in this instance, is the name of a place, and furthermore that it is the name of a place near Ebla in northern Syria. In Abr[aham] 1:10 we read: 'Even the thank-offering of a child did the priest of Pharaoh offer upon the altar which stood by the hill called Potiphar's Hill, at the head of the plain of Olishem.' It is very possible that Ulisum of the Akkadian text of Naram Sin, and Olishem of the Book of Abraham are linguistically the same form. Both the "u" of the Naram Sin name, and the "o" of the Book of Abraham

---

[124]Lundquist, *op. cit.,* pages 226-227.

term, as well as the "s" of the Naram Sin word, and the "sh" of the Book of Abraham word can be explained as equivalent on linguistic grounds. It's very possible that the "s," in fact, can be explained on the basis that in the time of Naram Sin, texts which used the letter "s" were, in fact, pronounced "sh" and probably in later times were written with an "sh" instead of an "s."

"It should be noted that the Book of Abraham speaks of the *plain* of Olishem and not the *city* of Olishem. A Sumerian text of Gudea, king of Lagash, a southern Sumerian city, states, "from the city of Ursu situated on the Plateau of Ebla, he imported pine logs, large fir trees, trunks of plain trees and mountain trees." That means that a city can also give its name to the surrounding plain. Olishem, then, would be a city, and the plain that it controls or dominates would be given the same name, Olishem. I think that this has most significant possibilities."[125]

One thing Lundquist has not mentioned, that is interesting in its genealogical potential is the derivation of the name Olishem. We know that Shem lived in the immediate vicinity, possibly even founding the town of Olishem, because this was the land of first discovery after the Flood.

It would appear from the evidence that the preponderance rests with the northern Ur being the birthplace of Abraham. We can assume from this evidence, which could be backed with a great deal more, that Noah and his wife and the more righteous part of his family continued to reside in this region of Turkey which they called Ur of Chaldea and Ur of the Chaldees.

According to Abraham's own writings, he was sixty-two years old when he left Haran for Canaan. This must be considered primary evidence. According to Genesis 11:26, Terah lived seventy years, and begat Abram, Nahor, and Haran. Given the chronology noted above, with Abraham's birth in the year 1754 B.C., Terah would have been born about 1816 B.C. However, we will depart from this chronology and separate Abraham from his descendants, showing a discrepancy

---

[125]Lundquist, *op. cit.,* page 234.

of about 407 years in the chronology of *The Holy Bible*. His wife Sarah's age is also questionable as a genealogical fact. In Genesis 17:17 Sarah is given as being age ninety years old, yet in chapter twenty she is the target of King Abimelech's advances. Tradition says she was beautiful, but she was past the normal bearing years of even her generation, and we must raise the possibility that some of what is given in the story of Abraham in allegorical only.

Chaim Bermant and Michael Weitzman have written[126] regarding the early history of the Bible, and discuss in their writings that the composition of the Bible is from a number of sources, by obviously divergent writers, in different styles, and then say:

"Analysis, then, moved on from the documents of the various units - such as poems, codes of law, narrative - embedded in each. Thus much of the Pentateuch came to be considered far more ancient than earlier critics would have conceded, *but not necessarily more trustworthy as history*. [emphasis added] Two examples from the work of Gunkel, the pioneer in this area, will be instructive. The story of Jacob and Esau in Genesis chapters 25-28 originated as a popular tale which contrasts two different occupations, represented by two brothers - shepherd and hunter. The tale commends the shepherd: he always had food to eat, and thus he has the advantage over the hunter, who has to find his living day by day. Only later was this tale recast and referred to Jacob and Esau, in the light of very different competition between Israel and Esau's supposed descendants, the Edomites. Again the historical meaning of Genesis 38 is that the tribe of Judah once had three clans, Er, Onan and Shela. The first two died out, but two new clans (Perez and Zerah) emerged. Hence a tale which represented each clan or tribe as an individual, and which is held together by the purely fictional motif - familiar also from the book of Ruth - of the widow (Tamar) who requires issue from her late husband's kin.

"Many conservative scholars have stressed that, for all the discrepancies, the overall correspondence in content (regarding the

---

[126]Chaim Bermant and Michael Weitzman, *op. cit.,* pages 54-55.

narrative passages at least) between the different 'documents' is impressively close. They have inferred that the channels of oral prehistory that lead back from each 'document' meet ultimately in a single main stream of living tradition which continued unbroken from the days of Moses or even of Abraham. On that basis, one may resort to any part of the Pentateuch for an historical reconstruction, because all spring from the same source. Through such treatment of biblical passages, in combination with archaeological evidence, scholars such as W. F. Albright have maintained, for example, the historicity of the three Patriarchs.

"Yet two of the most recent studies, by T. L. Thompson and J. van Seters, though concerned primarily with the accounts of the Patriarchs, have pleaded for a return to something like Wellhausen's view of the character of the documents and argue that the only sort of oral traditions on which the documents need to be supposed to have drawn are the folklore motifs of the first millennium Canaanite/Israelite world - motifs which had not originally had anything to do with the Patriarchs. This judgment on the literary background, together with their own reassessment of the archaeological evidence, has led them to doubt whether the Patriarchs ever lived at all."

Although we are not willing to accept that Abraham, Isaac and Jacob did not exist, for we have modern revelation to show that they did *The Pearl of Great Price* and *The Doctrine and Covenants* of The Church of Jesus Christ of Latter-day Saints), given the approximately 407 year discrepancy in the biblical record, the archaeologists have some claim on the truth as to the stories and traditions as they are currently found. They cannot all be true. It is factually impossible.

In *The Book of Jasher* 13:9, it says: "At that time, at the end of three years of Abram's dwelling in the land of Canaan, in that year Noah died, which was the fifty-eighth year of the life of Abram; and all the days that Noah lived were nine hundred and fifty years and he died." Noah died in the year 1996 B.C. according to the chronology calculated from the dates given in the Book of Genesis (Genesis 9:29), or in 1998 according to the Bible Dictionary found in the L.D.S. version of the King James edition, page 636. If Abraham was fifty-eight when Noah died, then Abraham was born in 2054 B.C. If Abraham was sixty-five (he says he was sixty-two when he left Haran), three years after residing in Canaan when Noah died, then Abraham was born in 2061.

The stated fact in *The Book of Jasher* that Abraham had lived three years in Canaan when Noah died is consistent with the facts, but the age is not. If Abraham was fifty-eight and born in 2054, his father would have been seventy-one, which goes against the statement that he was seventy and had by then had his three sons. However, Abraham's statement is more likely correct, that he left Haran at age sixty-two. If, then, after three years in Canaan, Noah died in 1996, and Abraham was sixty-five in that year, then Abraham was born when his father was sixty-four, in the year 2061, not in 1754 according to the figures that must be assumed if he is the father of Isaac. The discrepancy as to the time error in *The Holy Bible* must necessarily be during the time of Abraham if we can prove he was contemporary with Noah and Shem (or Melchizedek). We have already linked him with Ebla, and Haran which in his own words he named.

The Mormon philosophy that Shem, son of Noah, and Melchizedek, King of Salem were the same person, and that, therefore, Shem lived to see the life of Abraham, as Abraham paid tithes to Melchizedek, King of Salem, appears to be based on Jewish tradition, and *The Book of Jasher* rather than on modern revelation. There appears to be nothing in the literature pointing to modern revelation on this subject.

The following summarizes Mormon thought.[127] "In the 600th year of Noah's life the flood came and swallowed up the wicked, including all of Noah's posterity except his three sons and their wives. Through them 'from Noah came all the families of the earth.' The foremost in blessings was Shem. It is clear that Noah pronounced upon Shem the blessings of the chosen seed. 'Blessed be the God of Shem; and Canaan shall be his servant. God shall enlarge Japheth, and he shall dwell in the tents of Shem.' (Genesis 9:26-27)

---

[127]The Church of Jesus Christ of Latter-day Saints, *Birthright Blessings* (Salt Lake City, Utah: Deseret Sunday School Union Board, 1942), pages 112-113.

"Noah and Shem both lived until the time of Abraham, and Shem actually outlived Abraham. Noah died 1996 years after creation; Abraham 2123; and Shem 2158. 'Jewish tradition pronounces Melchizedek to be a survivor of the Deluge, the patriarch Shem.' (Smith, *Bible Dictionary*, page 630) This same view was held by Luther, Melancthon, Bishop Lightfoot, and other scriptorians and commentators. A quotation from *The Book of Jasher*, which the Prophet [Joseph Smith] said was profitable for study, and had not been disproved as a good authority, and may be safely classed as Jewish tradition, is interesting in this connection:

"'And Adonizedek, king of Jerusalem, the same was Shem, went out to meet Abram and his people, with bread and wine, and they remained together in the valley of Melech. And Adonizedek blessed Abram and Abram gave him a tenth from all that he had brought from the spoil of his enemies, for Adonizedek was a priest before God.' (*The Book of Jasher* 16:11-12) Compare this account with Genesis 14:18-19, where the same character is called Melchizedek, King of Salem. [Compare, also, in Joshua 10:1 where Adonizedek, king of Jerusalem, is a contemporary of Joshua.]

"The following is an excerpt from an editorial by President John Taylor published in the *Times and Seasons*, December 15, 1844:

"'Therefore is the name of it called Babel; because the Lord did there confound the language of all the earth; and from thence did the Lord scatter them abroad upon the face of all the earth.

"'From this definite account of driving the ‹nations apart, when the ancient hills did bow› all reflecting minds may judge that *man was scattered over the whole face of the earth*: And with the superior knowledge of men like Noah, Shem, (who was Melchisedec) and Abram, the father of the faithful, three contemporaries, holding the keys of the highest order of the Priesthood: connecting the creation, and fall.'"[128]   Elsewhere, the argument is fairly conclusive that

---

[128]John Taylor, "Ancient Ruins," *Times & Seasons,* Volume 5, Number 23, page 746, under date of December 15, 1844 at Nauvoo, Illinois.

Abraham's statement that he was a "follower of righteousness" can be linked scripturally through parallelisms to Melchizedek. Malki and Sedeq combine to mean "Righteousness is my King."[129]

"If this identification is correct, then *The Book of Mormon* gives further interesting data on Shem [and certainly on Melchizedek, regardless]. Salem is now known as Jerusalem. [Jerusalem means "the city of Salem."] 'Now this Melchizedek was a king over the land of Salem; and his people had waxed strong in iniquity and abomination; yea, they had all gone astray; they were full of all manner of wickedness. But Melchizedek having exercised mighty faith, and received the office of the high priesthood according to the holy order of God, did preach repentance unto his people. And behold, they did repent; and Melchizedek did establish peace in the land in his days; therefore he was called the prince of peace, for he was king of Salem; and he did reign under his father. Now, there were many before him, and also there were many afterwards, but none were greater." (Alma 13:17-19)

It should be noted here, in light of the Ebla tablets' distinctions of Salim and Urusalima as two separate cities, that it does not say in Alma that Melchizedek was king of the city of Salem, but of the land of Salem, which apparently included the cities of Salim and Urusalima of the Ebla tablets.

Finally, as a possible proof of the time period in which Abraham lived, there is the very old tradition, that Nimrod coveted the priesthood of Abraham. Nimrod, born about 2319 B.C., a son of Cush, the son of Ham and Egyptus. Nimrod was initially born in Africa, and associated with the court of the pharaohs. In his wandering he finally settled in the lower Mesopotamian valley and began to build the mighty cities mentioned previously and ruled with great unrighteousness. He would have been 258 at the time of Abraham's birth. He may have been the one who tried to have Abraham killed, recognizing in him a spiritual giant, one who would

---

[129]Stephen D. Ricks, "The Early Ministry of Abraham," *Studies in Scripture*, pages 217-219. This volume is edited by Robert L. Millet and Kent P. Jackson. It is Volume 2 of *Studies in Scriptures: The Pearl of Great Price*.

destroy his wicked powers, and one who, like Moses, and Christ, would hold great priesthood powers.[130]

In conclusion to this presentation on the chronology of *The Holy Bible*, the renowned Hugh Nibley, has left us with this summation: "The first chapter of our Ether text gives us warning not to be dogmatic about chronology. In the genealogical list of thirty names running back to 'the great tower' the word 'descendant' occurs, once where several generations may be spanned (Ether 1:23; 10:9), and twice interchangeably with the word 'son' (Ether 1:6, 16; cf. 10:31; 11:23). As you know, in Hebrew and other languages 'son' and 'descendant' are both rendered by one very common word. One and the same word describes a modern Jew and Father Isaac as 'sons' of Abraham - the word is understood differently in each case, but is not written differently. A person confined to a written text would have no means of knowing when *ben* should be taken to mean 'son' in a literal sense and when it means merely 'descendant.' The ancient Hebrews knew perfectly well when to make the distinction: like the Arabs and Maoris they kept their records in their heads, and in mentioning a particular patriarch, it was assumed that the hearer was familiar with his line down to his next important descendant, the written lists being a mere outline to establish connections between particular lines - the name of a patriarch was enough to indicate his line, which did not have to be written out in full. Sir Leonard Woolley has some interesting things to say on this subject in his book *Abraham*. Now Ether proves, at least to Latter-day Saints, that 'son' and 'descendant' were both used in the ancient genealogies, which thus do not present an unbroken father-to-son relationship. We are told that the genealogy in Ether belongs to the second part of a record and that 'the first part of this record...is had among the Jews' (Ether 1:3). So we may regard the Old Testament genealogies as the earlier part of this same list and are thus faced with the possibility, long suspected by many, that in Biblical genealogies *ben* must sometimes be read 'son' and sometimes 'descendant,' though men have long since lost the knowledge that enabled the ancient ruler to

---

[130]Hugh Nibley, "The World of the Jaredites," *The Collected Works of Hugh Nibley*, Volume 5 (Salt Lake City, Utah: Deseret Book Company, 1988, page 170.

make the necessary distinction. The result is, of course, that our Biblical genealogies as we read them today may be much too short."[131]

Thus, until other evidence surfaces to prove false the premise contained herein, we have shown to a certain degree of probability, using both primary and circumstantial evidence, that between Abraham's birth in 2061 and Isaac's birth in 1654 there are 407 missing years genealogically. This could mean anywhere from six to thirteen generations are missing from the biblical pedigrees.

As one looks at Ishmael's genealogy, he being the son of Abraham and Hagar, there is a possibility for interpreting therein a clue to the number of generations that were missing. Given Dr. Nibley's discussion, just noted, how should the following be understood?

"Now these are the generations of Ishmael, Abraham's son, whom Hagar the Egyptian, Sarah's handmaid, bare unto Abraham: And these are the names of the sons of Ishmael, by their names, according to their generations: the firstborn of Ishmael, Nebajoth; and Kedar, and Adbeel, and Mibsam, and Mishma, and Dumah, and Massa, Hadar, and Tema, Jetur, Naphish, and Kedemah: these are the sons of Ishmael, and these are their names, by their towns, and by their castles; twelve princes according to their nations." (Genesis 25:12-16) Is it possible the biblical composers gave here, by association, the number of missing generations in the covenant line? Notice the use of "sons" and "generations." Generations are not given, only one generation is given based on the normal interpretation. Should "sons" be interpreted as "descendants" here? There is no way of knowing, but the point is raised as a consideration. It cannot be used even as circumstantial evidence.

We have shown evidence linking Abraham to the earlier period with Noah and Shem rather than the later period with Isaac and Jacob as follows:

---

[131]Nibley, "The World of the Jaredites," *op. cit.,* pages 158-158.

Primary Evidence

1)   Haran is identified in the Ebla tablets which have been shown to be from a period around 2000 B.C. Abraham states that his family named Haran.

2)   The cities of the plains are identified in the Ebla tablets and in the writings of Abraham, both pointing to the early period. Sodom and Gomorrah had been destroyed (1961 B.C.) before the days of Isaac and Jacob if they fit into the later period, but clearly the cities existed in the days of Ebla and in the days of Abraham, which by inference are the same days.

Circumstantial Evidence

1)   Amraphel and Hammurabi have been determined to be the same person. Amraphel was a contemporary of Abraham. The time period in question is the early period.

2)   Melchizedek and Shem are given as the same person.

3)   Abraham paid tithes to Melchizedek, King of Salem. Salim and Urusalima are identified in the Ebla tablets. Abraham was a follower of Righteousness which title refers to Melchizedek.

4)   Olishem and Ulisum, possibly the same name, were both in the vicinity of Ebla. Olishem in the writings of Abraham connects him to Ebla and the early period. Potiphar's Hill, at the head of the plain of Olishem, was in the land of Ur of Chaldea. (Abraham 1:10, 20)

5)   The Book of Jasher says that Abraham lived with Noah after his father tried to sacrifice him. This circumstantial evidence has not been presented previously and is the least valid of the information proposed.

6)   Hugh Nibley shows that the word *ben* is used to denote both *son* and *descendant*; thereby creating potentially missing generations in the biblical genealogies.

7)   Nimrod coveted the priesthood of Abraham according to tradition. Nimrod was a grandson of Ham.

8)   The time revision of the Sojourn (page 198) points to the possibility of the patriarchs prior to that time being misplaced in time as well. Abraham is one of those patriarchs.

9)   The 3 14-generation pedigrees, ending with Abraham, point to Abraham being the one to look to for missing generations.

KNOWN DEATHS

BETWEEN THE BEGINNING OF CIVILIZATION

AFTER THE FLOOD

AND THE DISPERSION AT THE TOWER OF BABEL

2345 B.C. TO 1996 B.C.

2017 B.C.	Approximate death year of the three virgin daughters of Onitah, descendants in the royal line of Ham. They were sacrificed at Potiphar's Hill, in Ur of the Chaldees. (Abraham 1:10-11)
2017 B.C.	Approximate death year of the priest of Elkenah and Pharaoh at Potiphar's Hill, at the head of the plain of Olishem in the land of Ur of Chaldea (Abraham 1:20)
2015 B.C.	Approximate death year of Haran, brother of Abraham at Ur of Chaldea (Abraham 2:1)
2206 B.C.	Death of Peleg, son of Eber (Genesis 11:19)
2205 B.C.	Death of Nahor, grandfather of Abraham (Genesis 11:24)
2205 B.C.	Probable year of death of Nahor, brother of Abraham
1996 B.C.	Death of Noah

"The weather of Asia is the great central driving mechanism of world history. It is only in recent years that men have begun to correlate the great migrations of history, with their attendant wars and revolutions [and death], with those major weather crises such as the great wind and drought of 2300-2200 B.C. and the world floods of 1300 B.C., which we now know to have taken place in the course or recorded history."[132]

This statement by Dr. Nibley shows the mechanism by which the dispersion at the Tower of Babel likely was instituted. It also shows that there would have been a large number of deaths at this time, in this one hundred year disaster, between 2300 and 2200 B.C. It was

---

[132]Nibley, "The World of the Jaredites," *op. cit.*, page 175.

undoubtedly the single largest deterrent to normal reproduction patterns for this period, and is one of the reasons why lower birth numbers have been used in calculating the development of the human race after the Flood, as given in the statistics below.

LINGUISTIC HISTORY

FROM THE FLOOD TO THE BIRTH OF JESUS CHRIST

2345 B.C. TO 2 B.C.

The 349-year period immediately after the Flood was a period of mutual understanding and of a common spoken language. All the people of the earth as they expanded had full use of the technologies and knowledge of Noah, Japheth, Shem, Ham and their wives. The language spoken was the Adamic language. As nearly as can be determined, this language has been identified by modern philologists as the Keltemin language. This was the language of the patriarchs. "For death hath come upon our fathers; nevertheless we know them, and cannot deny, and even the first of all we know, even Adam. For a book of remembrance we have written among us, according to the pattern given by the finger of God; and it is given in our own language." (*The Pearl of Great Price,* The Book of Moses 6: 45-46.) In another place it states: " And a book of remembrance was kept, in the which was recorded, in the language of Adam, for it was given unto as many as called upon God to write by the spirit of inspiration; and by them their children were taught to read and write, having a language which was pure and undefiled." (The Book of Moses 6:5-6)

It is accepted as a possibility that a diversity of languages developed in the 1657 years prior to the Flood among those nations who lost contact with Adam and his righteous posterity. In the writings of Enoch (The Book of Moses 6:40-41) Enoch says he came upon a people who had lost all knowledge of Adam, and this during the lifetime of Adam. Nevertheless, this diversity in spoken languages was wiped out in the Flood. It is a premise within this work, therefore, that there was no diversity of spoken languages immediately after the Flood, but that diversity began to develop in the 349 years between then and 1996, as the grandchildren and later generations began to distance themselves from the ways of Noah and his children.

However, as pertains to the written records being found in the archeological digs of our era that show that a great diversity of languages existed on the earth during a period prior to the Tower of Babel, it is possible Noah brought more than one writing system with him, and that these diversified early after the Flood. Some of these discoveries may also be pre-Flood.

We have seen above, that Adam was given writing by the finger of God. At Uruk, presumably a post-Flood discovery has been made where "the parent forms" of writing appear, not by any gradual process of evolution, but "suddenly and without warning there appear fifteen hundred signs and pictographs scratched on clay. They seem to have been written and used without any signs of hesitancy," showing that writing was already well-established *somewhere* in the world, and that somewhere would seem to be in the region to the north of Mesopotamia.[133]

There are a number of secular and scriptural scholars who maintain a position of a common language. Hutton Webster says, for example: "More than a century ago Occidental philologists discovered that Sanskrit, the ancient speech of the Aryans in India, was distantly connected with the classic Greek and Latin. All the Indo-European languages, both living and 'dead,' have now been shown to be related. They must have sprung from some parent language no longer adequately represented by any one of them. Their likeness is illustrated in the case of such terms as 'father,' 'mother,' 'brother,' and 'sister.' Thus 'father' in Sanskrit is *pitar*, in ancient Persian, *pidar*, in Greek, *pater*, in Latin, *pater*, and in German, *vater*."[134]

Because of the intermixing of the Nordic or Aryan tribes (see below) with the peoples of Greece and Italy, it stands to reason that the Sanskrit language of the Nordic or Aryans would have influenced and helped shape the Greek and Latin alphabets and language. Most historians and anthropologists claim that these northern tribes were uncivilized, but this fact of language shows a strong influence that proclaims other factors usually claimed as originating with the

---

[133]Nibley, "The World of the Jaredites," *op. cit.*, page 257.

[134]Webster, *op. cit.*, page 29.

Mediterraneans, short, dark, long-headed peoples who these professionals call collectively, the Mediter-ranean race, or more specifically, the Egyptians, Sumerians, and Minoans.

Hugh Nibley discusses this very subject in some lengthy insights. Paraphrasing his words: The Book of Ether [in *The Book of Mormon*], depicting the uprooting and scattering from the tower of a numerous population, shows them going forth not individually but in groups, and not merely family groups but groups of friends and associates: "thy friends and their families, and the friends of Jared and their families" (Ether 1:41). There was no point in having Jared's language unconfounded if there was to be no one he could talk to, and his brother cried to the Lord that his friends might also retain the language. The same, however, would apply to any other language: If every individual were to speak a tongue all of his own and so go off entirely by himself, the races would have been not merely scattered but quite annihilated. We must not fall into the old vice of reading into the scripture things that are not there. There is nothing said in our text about every man suddenly speaking a new language. We are told in The Book of Ether that languages were confounded with and *by* the "confounding" of the people: "Cry unto the Lord," says Jared (Ether 1:34), "that he will not confound us that we may not understand our *words*" (italics added). The statement is significant for more than one thing. How can it possibly be said that "*we* may not understand *our* words"? Words we cannot understand may be nonsense syllables or may be in some foreign language, but in either case they are not *our* words. The only way we can fail to understand our own words is to have words that are actually ours change their meaning among us. That is exactly what happens when people, and hence languages, are either "confounded," that is, mixed up, or scattered. In Ether's account, the confounding of *people* is not to be separated from the confounding of the languages; they are, and have always been, one and the same process: the Lord, we are told (Ether 1:35-37), "did not confound the language of Jared; and Jared and his brother were not confounded...and the Lord had compassion upon their friends and their families also, that they were not confounded."

Yet another important biblical expression receives welcome elucidation from our text: though Ether says nothing about "the whole earth" being "of one language and one speech" (Genesis 11:1), he does give us an interesting hint as to how those words may be taken. Just as "son" and "descendant" are the same word in Hebrew and so may easily be confused by translators, so "earth" and "land" are the same word, the well-known *eretz*. In view of the fact that The Book of Ether, speaking only of the Jaredites, notes that "there were none of the fair sons and daughters upon the face of the whole earth who repented of their sins" (Ether 13:17), it would seem that the common "whole earth" (*kil ha-aretz*) of the Old Testament need not always be taken to mean the entire globe.

One of the most surprising discoveries of recent years has been the revelation that wherever the experts search, in Babylon, Thebes, Ras Shamra, Central Asia, or the Far East, they are met at *every period* of history by an almost unbelievable mix-up of physical and linguistic types. And as the biological picture becomes more complex, the cultural one seems to become more simple, the whole civilized world at any moment of its history seeming to share in a general sort of way in a single common world civilization. This is also the picture we get in Ether, where the nations and tribes are already thoroughly "confounded" in Jared's day, while certain institutions and practices are described as being common to "the ancients" as a whole and as flourishing among all nations.[135]

Another example of the commonality of cultures and therefore of languages can be seen in modern language systems. In the 2,000 years that have elapsed since the Roman conquest of Western Europe, Latin has evolved into an entire family of languages of which French, Italian, Portuguese, Romanian, and Spanish are the principal representatives. If we did not know of the existence of Latin through historical records we would be obliged to postulate its existence of the basis of the sound correspondences within the Romance family. It is obvious that every contemporary spoken language is nothing but a transformed version of an earlier language and even in the absence of written records, languages can be grouped together on the basis of their "descent" from a common ancestor. In like manner, those speaking these languages can be classified as to their ancestral origins

---

[135]Nibley, "The World of the Jaredites," *op. cit.*, pages 172-173, 286-287.

in part. Thus, in a more remote period, Proto-West Germanic was undifferentiated from Latin and a large number of additional languages including the ancestral forms of Hindi, Persian, Greek, Russian, and Gaelic also show a common origin. This group of languages constitutes the Indo-European family of languages. Inferences based upon the sound correspondence among the Indo-European languages have led linguists to reconstruct the sound system of the protolanguage from which they all ultimately derive. This language is called Proto-Indo-European,[136] or Keltemin on other fronts. Hugh Nibley has stated: "The newly discovered Kelteminarian culture, for example, would seem to bind together all the major languages of Europe and central Asia in a single, vast, prehistoric continuum that embraces not only the Indo-European family but the Turanian as well and even the ancient non-Aryan languages of India."[137]

Many languages exist and existed only in spoken form and leave and have left no material for historians or genealogists. Some of these languages are much older than their known history. Some are preserved in written records but extinct in their spoken form. Extinction, in practice, means that for one reason or another a language is overshadowed and gradually and imperceptibly superseded by another. Characteristically, what has been preserved is contained in religious and dynastic histories.

Ten different peoples in various parts of the world developed a system of writing that has been preserved. These people were the Tokhari, the Sumerians, the Babylonians, the Eblaites, the Egyptians, the Hittites, the Chinese, the Jaredites, the Incas, the Mayas and the Aztecs. These will each be discussed in more detail in their proper places in volume two of this work. At this point only summarial information is being given.

Quoting from Calvin Kephart's work we find the following: "After

---

[136]Harris, *op. cit.,* page 132.

[137]Nibley, "The World of the Jaredites," *op. cit.,* pages 182-183.

about 1000 B.C., because of pressure from Turks on the north, the Massagetae (later called the Tokhari, at least in part) moved southward and eastward and finally settled in Bactriana, as far as the Pamirs and southeast of the Hissar Mountains, and the Sakae settled in Sogdiana (Bukhara and Ferghana). Apparently, it was the Tokhari who originally introduced the Sanskrit language into western India, and the two nations later jointly established the great Scytho-Indian Empire, when the Sanskrit dialect was reintroduced into India. This nation long endured." This shows that the origins of Sanskrit comes from the Nordic tribes (Suebian, Kimmerians, Getae, Massagetae and Sakae) who were descendants of Gomer, son of Japheth, son of Noah.[138] However, it does not show anything in contradiction to our major premise. All of this exchange could have taken place after 1996 B.C. and originated north of Mesopotamia, or in northern Mesopotamia.

For the cradle of civilization, a chart of some of the principal language grouping shows that the Semitic languages include Western and Eastern (Akkadian). From this latter derived the Assyrian, Chaldean and Babylonian. The original Egyptians, also descended from the Chaldeans, were Semitic in speech or writing but Hamitic ethnically, as will be seen later, and spoke the Chaldean, now called Akkadian, language. Akkad was a chief city of the first Semitic speaking empire in Mesopotamia. (Genesis 10:10) The Babylonians, the Chaldeans and the Assyrians adopted the cuneiform writings of the Sumerians for their own Semitic writing. The Sumerians were associated politically from time to time with Akkad, but were a non-Semitic people who had lived previously in Mesopotamia.

The people which have spoken or speak one of the Semitic languages as their main language are known as Semitic peoples. Divisions between the branches of these people have been subject to much controversy. The following, therefore, is a general outline that is not always as straightforward as it appears.

The Semitic languages are generally divided into three main

---

[138]Kephart, *op. cit.,* pages 250-251, 263.

groupings: 1) Eastern Semitic, 2) Western or Northwestern Semitic, and 3) Southern or Southwestern Semitic. For purposes of geography here, east is Mesopotamia, west or northwest is the Middle East proper, or Syro-Palestine, and south or southwest is the Arabian peninsula and Ethiopia.

The eastern Semitic consists of only Akkadian. Akkadian was spoken in parts of what is today Iraq. From about 2000 B.C., two dialects of Akkadian are known: 1) Babylonian, which was spoken in southern Mesopotamia and 2) Assyrian, which was spoken in the north. As spoken languages, these were replaced with Aramaic in the 6th century B.C., but as a written language Akkadian survived until the end of this study, the beginning of the Christian era.

In the 1970's a previously unknown language was discovered south of Aleppo in Syria and has been named Eblaite after the site of its discovery. Passages in this language are interspersed with Sumerian texts. Research is not at all complete on deciphering this language. It resembles Akkadian in many ways but has a number of similarities to the languages of the western Semitic.

Western Semitic has four main groupings: 1) Amorite and Ugaritic, 2) Canaanite, 3) Aramaic, and 4) Phoenician.

Amorite is a general term for a language known from the first half of the 2nd millennium B.C. Many of its proper nouns and found in extant Akkadian and Egyptian texts. The first speakers of Amorite were probably nomadic shepherds.

Ugaritic appears to be an early form of Canaanite. It was spoken and written in and to an unknown extent near the ancient city of Ugarit on the coast of Syria in the 14th and 13th centuries B.C., before that city was sacked. The first Ugaritic texts were discovered in the excavation of Ras Shamra in the late 1920's. Most of the texts were written with alphabetic characters resembling cuneiform script.

The Canaanite language constitutes a group of closely-related languages and dialects spoken in Palestine. Written records go back to about 1500 B.C. Current research indicates that alphabetic script was invented by one of the Canaanite peoples in Palestine during the 17th century B.C.

A branch of the Canaanite language where the Semitic was mixed with modified Egyptian hieroglyphic characters is the Byblos Syllabic language of the eighteenth century B.C. from the city of Byblos on the Phoenician coast. This is an important link between the hieroglyphs and the Canaanite alphabet.

Classical, or Biblical, Hebrew was spoken virtually throughout the area of modern Israel. The language is known mainly from the Old Testament, which contains texts in Hebrew from over a period of almost 1,000 years. The earliest known inscription, the Gezer calendar, has been dated to around 925 B.C. Hebrew was originally written in the Canaanite-Phoenician alphabet, but in the 4th century B.C. the Jews adopted from Aramaic the square alphabet still in use. By the 3rd century B.C., Hebrew was spoken only in Judaea, and even there in a modified form known as Mishnaic. This language also died out around 200 A.D., giving way to Aramaic.

Phoenician records extend from inscriptions dating from around 1000 B.C. and found in Lebanon to the last pre-Christian centuries. Almost all known texts are short tombstone inscriptions; no literature proper has survived. Much the same applies to Punic, a language that developed from Phoenician in Carthage (in present-day Tunisia), settled by Phoenicians in the 9th century B.C. Punic was still spoken in the 5th century A.D.

Semitic speakers of early second millennium B.C. Syria and Palestine seem to have adopted reformed or modified versions of both Egyptian hieroglyphs and Mesopotamian cuneiform into syllabic and alphabetic systems of writing. Ultimately, this reformed Egyptian script became the basis for the Phoenician alphabet, from which nearly all subsequent alphabets derive. These Proto-Sinitic inscriptions were written in a Semitic language, and their letters were the prototypes for the Phoenician alphabet. This Canaanite/Phoenician syllabary formed the basis of the Greek alphabet, which in turn gave Latin its basis.

Moabite, Edomite, and Ammonite were spoken in the area of present-day Jordan. Only a handful of short inscriptions and seals from the 9th to the 5th centuries B.C. survive in these language, which were probably supplanted by Aramaic. The best-known text, in Moabite, is inscribed on the Mesha Stone from about 840 B.C. On this stone, Mesha, King of Moab, recounts his battles against King Omri of Israel.

Aramaic appears among the ranks of known languages around 850 B.C. in Syria and is found at that time on the Tell Fekheriye stela. Aramaic spread with tremendous speed, and by the 6th century B.C. was being used as the administrative language and principal spoken language of the Middle East, from Afghanistan to Egypt. Many ancient Semitic languages, including Akkadian and Hebrew, died out and were supplanted by Aramaic. Only Greek rivalled Aramaic for dominance in the Middle East until the Arab conquest of the 7th century A.D.

Aramaic of the pre-Christian era, known as ancient Aramaic or imperial Aramaic is known from inscriptions, papyrus letters and documents, and from the Old Testament books of Ezra and Daniel. A small number of literary texts are also known. The Aramaic alphabet was derived from Canaanite script. By the time of Christ's birth, written Aramaic had divided into several different forms based on the various types of script adopted by different religions. All the languages come under the general headings of West Aramaic and East Aramaic, west referring to the Middle East (Syro-Palestine) and east to Mesopotamia (Iraq).

The West Aramaic languages include Nabataean, Palmyrene, Aramaic of Hatra, Jewish Palestine Aramaic, also called Galilean Aramaic, Samaritan Aramaic, and Christian Palestine Aramaic, also called Palestinian Syriac. The inhabitants of the Nabataean kingdom of Petra and surrounding area in southern Jordan, Palmyra (Tadmor in northeastern Syria) and Hatra (el-Hadr in northern Iraq, were mainly Arabs, but between 100 B.C. and 350 A.D. they wrote epitaphs and other short texts in Aramaic, using their own variant scripts.

East Aramaic is divided into three distinct languages. These are the

Syriac language of the Christians, Jewish Babylonian Aramaic and Mandaean, the language of the Mandaean Gnostic sect.

The center of the Syriac language was the city of Edessa, modern Urfa, in present-day Turkey, but the language was also spoken in Mesopotamia proper. There is a wealth of literature in Syriac, which is still the liturgical language of the Syriac churches. Syriac script is cursive and looks rather like Arabic.

Hebrew script was used to write Jewish Babylonian Aramaic, the main cultural centers of which were in the central part of modern-day Iraq. The most important literary work in this language is the Babylonian Talmud, still of great importance in Judaism, consisting of the Mishnah, which is in Hebrew, and the extensive Gemara, in Aramaic. Syriac and Babylonian Aramaic died out as spoken languages around the year 1000 A.D. and were replaced by Arabic.

The Mandaeans lived in southern Iraq and parts of Iran. Their literature flourished from the 3rd to the 8th centuries A.D. and do not form part of our present study.

The southern or southwestern Semitic languages include: 1) the South Arabian languages, 2) Arabic, and 3) the Ethiopian languages.

The South Arabian languages consist of the languages of ancient inscriptions, on the one hand, and of living vernacular languages in present-day Yeman and Oman, on the other. The monumental forms of the South Arabian alphabet were probably derived from Canaanite consonant script, brought into the area around 1300 B.C. by the peoples of the northern Arabian peninsula. South Arabian inscriptions consist of short epitaphs, promises and deeds, dating from between 700 B.C. to 500 A.D. The language comprised several dialects, the most important of which were Sabaean, Minaean, Qatabanian and Hadramauth.

The precursors of Arabic proper were the languages or dialects spoken by the tribes of Dedan, Liyn, Thamd and Saf, thousands of short petroglyphs and graffiti of whom have survived from the period 700 B.C. to 400 A.D. The other early forms of Arabic were discussed above in conjunction with West Aramaic (the Nabataeans, etc.). The oldest texts in Arabic proper, which use a script derived from the Nabataean alphabet, date from the 4th century A.D.

The Ethiopian languages bear a closer resemblance to the South Arabian languages than to Arabic proper. At least some of the Semitic peoples of Ethiopia originally moved there from the Arabian peninsula, and the writing system still used by all of the Ethiopian languages is based on the South Arabian script of the immigrants.

The earliest known Ethiopian language is Ge'ez, commonly called Ethiopian. It diverged from the South Arabian languages around the beginning of the Christian era, reaching its greatest extension in the 4th century A.D.

The language of ancient Egypt stood geographically between the Semitic languages of the Middle East and the Hamatic languages of northern and eastern Africa. Traditionally, Egyptian has been termed an hamito-semitic language, since it contained significant characteristics of Semitic languages, as well as elements of Berber and Chad, which are hamatic.

Initially, some Egyptologists suggested that the Egyptian language represented a stage or linguistic development which predated the division of the languages of the Near East and Africa into Semitic and Hamitic branches. In this way, Egyptian was some great parent language of these two great language groups, in order words a mother tongue from which they all descended. This theory has been disproved because Egyptian per se was contemporary with its so-called daughter languages and at the same time contained grammatical formations at variance with those of its daughter languages.

This theory has been replaced with a comprehensive reassessment of all the languages of western Asia and Africa which showed similarities. Linguists now agree in the identification of a super family called Afro-Asiatic or Hamito-Semitic. It encompasses nearly all the languages of the Near East and northern Africa. The Afro-Asiatic family consists of six coordinate branches, each branch with its own set languages:

Egyptian (ancient Egypt): Old Egyptian, Middle Egyptian, Late Egyptian, Demotic, and Coptic;

Over the course of its 4,000 year history, the written language of ancient Egypt went through five successive stages. In the texts, each stage or phase is identified by peculiarities of grammar, vocabulary and spelling, and in later times by the script. At different periods of Egyptian history, different phases of the language were employed in the inscriptions. These phases are:

Old Egyptian (about 2686-2160 B.C.), being hieroglyphic (monument script) and hieratic (modified form of hieroglyphics used to write formal documents on papyrus with brush and ink).

Middle Egyptian (about 2060 - 1293 B.C.), being hieroglyphic and hieratic.

Late Egyptian (about 1293-715 B.C.), being hieroglyphic and hieratic.

Demotic (about 715 B.C. - 470 A.D.), this written language being used from the 25th dynasty through the Roman Period, the script being Demotic (a cursive script).

Within this time period a reformed Egyptian was taken by the people of Lehi (*The Book of Mormon*), the Egyptian being altered by them and handed down from generation to generation and "none other people knoweth our language." (Mormon 9: 32, 34)

Coptic (about 470 - 640 A.D.), being used until the Arab conquest, after which Arabic was imposed upon Egypt. Scripts were Coptic and Demotic.

Berber (North Africa west of Egypt): Numidian, Tureg, and Riff;

Cushitic (East Africa south of the Sahara): Galla, Somali, Oromo, Bedawiye, and Hadya;

Chadic (West Africa south of the Sahara): Hausa, and others.

Omotic (southern Ethiopia): Omotic.

Semitic (Western Asia): Akkadian, Aramaic, South Arabic, Arabic, Hebrew, Eblaite, Amorite, Maltese, Ugaritic, Amharic, Canaanite, and Phoenician;

The Chinese were a religiously-oriented group with a belief in a God as the Supreme Ruler of Heaven. Their leaving Mesopotamia appears to have been in a religious group. Very early in their history as a separate people, they found a need to communicate with a written language, probably as early as 2250 B.C. If their own time table is correct, they would have arrived in China with the language of Adam as their mother tongue. This language was clearly a written language as shown from two modern scriptures. "For a book of remembrance we have written among us, according to the pattern given by the finger of God; and it is given in our own language." *(The Pearl of Great Price,* Moses 6:46) Further it says: "And God revealed himself unto Seth, and he rebelled not, but offered an acceptable sacrifice, like unto his brother Abel. And to him also was born a son, and he called his name Enos. And then began these men to call upon the name of the Lord, and the Lord blessed them; and a book of remembrance was kept, in the which was recorded, in the language of Adam, for it was given as many as called upon God to write by the spirit of inspiration; and by them their children were taught to read and write, having a language that was pure and undefiled." (Moses 6:3-6) Given this introduction, however, Chinese writing descends in part from the Sumerian culture.

They developed a system of word pictures in keeping with the characteristic calligraphy of the ancient world. True to all these early languages, these so-called pictographs were satisfactory for representing objects but carried limitations in expressing abstract concepts. The early graphic symbols, therefore, were combined in meaningful ways to convey ideas, called ideograms, and these "picture stories" of necessity had to contain common knowledge in order to be understood. These ancient picture writings of the Chinese language embodied memories of man's earliest beginnings.

The Chinese ideographic system exhibits peculiarities which depend upon the language that it was formed to represent. At the point where the symbols attained a phonetic value, serious difficulty arose from the fact that a single monosyllabic word might have many distinct meanings, distinguished in speech only by intonation, which for a time, was impossible to represent in writing. The difficulty was felt in the spoken language as well, and one homonym was distinguished from another by the addition of a second word which made the meaning clear, a kind of compound being thus formed. In the course of time the original pictographs have deteriorated, but they are capable of analysis into their original constituent parts without undue difficulty.

All ancient scripts such as the Chinese, and the Jaredite undoubtedly, begin with simple line drawings of familiar objects. Word picture systems were developed by many pre-Tower civilizations including the Sumerian people in the Mesopotamian Valley and the Egyptians. In the evolution of most scripts, ideograms emerged at the demand for more abstract ideas of size, movement, thought, and feeling.

Since the pictographs and ideographs had corresponding sounds of the spoken language, they were also phonetic. The most cumbersome drawings of most early languages were abbreviated into shortened forms for the sake of rapid writing until letters evolved and phonetic alphabets were born.

Whereas most written languages construct words from the letters of an alphabet, the Chinese written language uses radicals, also called keys, roots or primitives, as the basic units and buildings blocks for the word characters. Each character contains one or more root symbols.[139]

As recent as 1993 historians, writing for university students about the civilizations of the Americas, continue to make statements such as: "No surviving writing systems ever *developed* (emphasis added) in North and South America. Mesoamerica, on the other hand, did

---

[139]C. H. Kang and Ethel R. Nelson, *The Discovery of Genesis* (St. Louis, Missouri: Concordia Publishing House, 1979), pages ix, xiii, 3, 22-23.

have a hieroglyphic writing system."[140] This type of statement in a world where a mountain of evidence to the contrary continues to grow, is misleading. The author has in his possession, and several great eastern and western universities have had in their possession proof of writing systems that *developed* in both North and South America, as well as in Mesoamerica. Characters, which will be shown under the Jaredite, Inca, and Nephite sections of the subsequent volume, prove that not only the Nephites but also the Jaredites came to the Americas with writing systems fully intact. There are individuals, such as the gentlemen noted above, who disclaim the mention of writings having been preserved on gold plates or any other plates, such as silver, copper or bronze. Briefly, as an introduction to this kind of evidence found among many cultures worldwide, a few examples will suffice to show that both the Jaredite, and the Nephite cultures came from that region of the world where writing on metal plates was a common practice.

1.   The gold wafer called the Tablet of Shalmaneser III (842 B.C. from Kalat Shergat in modern Iraq, now housed at the Oriental Institute, University of Chicago Museum.

2.   The Plates of Darius I (Persian ruler from 518-515 B.C.) found at Persopolis, consisting of two gold plates and two silver plates, now housed at the National Archaeological Museum, Tehran, Iran.

3.   The gold plate from Lambayeque, Peru housed in the Hugo Cohen collection in Lima, Peru.

4.   Gold plates found at Pyrgi, Italy (500 B.C.) housed at the National Museum of Villa Guilia, Rome.

5.   Rolled copper scrolls, Qumran, Dead Sea (2nd century B.C.) now in the National Museum, Amman, Jordan.

---

[140]Jay Pascal Angelin and William J. Hamblin, *HarperCollins College Outline World History to 1648* (New York City: HarperCollins Publishers, Inc., 1993), page 346.

6.   Small gold plate from Djokha Umma (2450 B.C.) housed at the Louvre, Paris, France.

7.   The Korean Plates, a book of nineteen gold metal sheets, hinged and folded on top of each other and inscribed with Buddhist scriptures and engraved with Chinese characters, currently housed in the National Museum in Seoul, Korea.

8.   A bronze plaque found at Styria, Greece, containing laws for the distribution of land, now housed at the National Archaeological Museum in Athens, Greece.

9.   A gold disc taken from the sacred well at Chichen Itzá on the Yucatán peninsula, with Mayan writing around the edge, housed at the Peabody Museum at Harvard University.

10.   Brass and copper plates containing prophetic writings of the Ispogogee Indians at Tuckabatchee, Alabama.[141]

11.   A Maya book containing the complete history of their ancestors, inscribed on gold plates.[142]

12.   An ancestral record of the Indians of Chiapas, Mexico, engraved on gold leaves, supposedly concealed in the vault of some ancient city at the time of the Conquest.[143]

---

[141]Edward King, viscount Kingsborough, *Antiquities of Mexico* (London: James Moyes, 1831-1848), Volume 8, pages 357-358.

[142]Alpeus Hyatt Verrill and Ruth Verrill, *America's Ancient Civilizations* (New York: G. P. Putnam's Son, 1953), page 23: According to traditions a complete history of Maya was recorded in the Golden Book of the Mayas which, if it actually existed, as it probably did, was so carefully hidden to prevent it from falling into the hands of the Spaniards that it never has been found. [The author has been told of similar records had even today among the Indians of Guatemala and Oaxaca, Mexico.]

[143]Harold T. Wilkins, *Mysteries of Ancient South America* (New York City: Citadel Press, 1956), page 180.

13.   Isaiah was commanded to engrave his prophecies on brass (Isaiah 8:1) called "a great roll" in the King James Bible, "a great Gillayon" in other bibles, which Dr. Adam Clarke, a celebrated Biblical scholar has noted means a polished tablet of metal.

14.   According to Flavius Josephus in his *Antiquities* XI, Chapter 5, verse 2, during the time of Moses the ancient Israelites used a kind of brass which was an alloy of copper and gold, upon which they wrote.

Many books with confusing and alternate conclusions have been written about the native civilizations of Latin America. It is quite possible to read about an individual who is claimed to have lived in any one of three or four centuries. Traditions, folklore, archeological interpretations, and speculation have caused this plethora of positions. Most professionals admit they do not know where the people originated or how or when they arrived at their various points in history. Some generally agreed-upon information, however, is helpful to place the following studies into a somewhat understandable structure. Most archeologists and historians accept the following time scale for purposes of coordinating their studies: 1) Archaic Period - pre-3000 B.C.; 2) Pre-Classic Period - 2999 B.C. to 300 A.D.; 3) Early Classic Period - 299 - 500 A.D.; 4) Late Classic Period - 501 - 900 A.D.; 5) Early Post-Classic Period 901 - 1200 A.D.; 6) Late Post-Classic Period - 1201 - 1520 A.D. For purposes of our study, the known migrations to the Americas are the Jaredite in about 1985 B.C., the Nephite in 600 B.C. and the Mulekite in 587 B.C. It is also obvious from archeological finds that migrations of groups have taken place in periods later than our current study, over the Bering Strait, that the Phoenicians made colonies in both North and South America, that the Scandinavians and Welsh made inroads and intermixed with the native populations of North America, and possibly others.

Muriel Porter Weaver[144] says: "An excellent summary of languages and their history is found in the volume by Wolf (1959), which is

---

[144]Muriel Porter Weaver, *The Aztecs, Maya, and their Predecessors: Archaeology of Mesoamerica* (New York: Seminar Press, 1972), page 7.

briefly summarized here. Prior to 4000 B.C. all languages in Mesoamerica may have been related, but soon after that, the great Uto-Aztecan strain can be distinguished....This group in turn split into many subdivisions. Nahua being the most important, and its close relative, Náhuatl, became the language of the Aztecs and is still spoken today....Another large group was made up of Macro-Mayan speakers who spread through the southern lowlands of the Gulf Coast and the eastern highlands. Huastec and Mayan languages are closely related."

Joel C. Janetski, professor of anthropology at Brigham Young University in Provo, Utah[145] states: "The Ute, along with the Southern Paiute, speak Numic (Miller, 1986), a branch of the Uto-Aztecan language spoken by all Great Basin Native Americans except the Hokan, who speak Washo (Lamb, 1958)."

Lewis Spense adds: "The area covered by the ancient Nahuan or Mexican race, both in its fluctuant and settled conditions, extended in its utmost limits from British Columbia in the north to Costa Rica in the south,..."[146]

Norman A. McQuown states his belief that the very first Maya were a small Indian tribe of North American origin, distantly affiliated with some peoples of southern Oregon and northern California, and more closely to the Totonacan and Zoquean speakers of Mexico.[147]

Father Alonzo de Posada, a Franciscan missionary in New Mexico from 1650 to 1660, spent much of his ministry "in the most remote parts of the province." During those years he had the additional duty as *custodia* or administrator of the Franciscan Order. This position

---

[145]Joel C. Janetski, *The Ute of Utah Lake* (Salt Lake City: The University of Utah Press, 1991), page 18.

[146]Lewis Spence, *The Civilization of Ancient Mexico* (Cambridge: Cambridge University Press. 1912), page 2.

[147]Norman A. McQuown, "The classification of the Maya languages," *International Journal of American Linguistics* 22 (1956); pages 191-195.

gave him access to many official records. In the year 1686, as part of his official report to the Council of the Indies, he indicated that "according to their [Indian] traditions it [the Valley of Teguayo] is the place where all Indians originated, even the Aztecs and Incas."[148]

"Aztec legend holds that their forefathers migrated to Mexico City from a land to the north - a land of red rocks and four rivers." Cecilio Orosco of Cal State Fresno and Alfonso Rivas-Salmon, a respected Mexican anthropologist at the Universidad Autónoma de Guadalajara, contend that the land of red rocks spoken of are [is] Utah's maze of canyonlands. "Futhermore, they claim ancient paintings on Utah's canyon walls reflect many of the same symbols and figures found in the Aztec calendar. [These] experts say the Barrier Canyon-style rock art in Utah is believed to date to a time well before the time of Christ. According to Orosco, the Mexica migrated from their northern homeland about 502 B.C. 'Utah is sitting on a treasure, a missing link in the prehistory of man in this hemisphere,' said Orosco.... 'It's right there on the canyon walls. Utah is the home of Quetzal-coatl.'...Orosco and Rivas recently returned from an expedition down the Green River to examine Barrier Canyon-style rock art. They say common symbols to both the Aztec calendar and Utah rock art include snakes with four rattles, knotted rope symbols and other figures dividing time according to the four-year and eight-year cycles of Venus. Bug-eyed figures common to Utah pictographs have been interpreted by Orosco and Rivas as representing the duality of Venus as the morning and evening star. The use of knots of strings to represent numbers has been attributed exclusively to the Incas of South America, but 'I found this numerical representation in many of the pictographs' in Utah. Orosco and Rivas have identified the calendrical formula symbols on pictographs at Head of Sinbad, Black Dragon Canyon, Barrier Creek and Horseshoe Canyon, all in the canyonlands area of southern Utah. They believe these sites represent celestial observatories. Legend holds the Mexica were forced from their northern homelands by a prolonged drought, called the *Rain of Fire*. A series of migrations took the ancient ones south, eventually to build Tenochtitlán more

---

[148]George A. Thompson, *Faded Footprints* (Salt Lake City: Roaming the West Publications, Inc., 1969), page 3.

than 1000 years later on the site of modern-day Mexico City....The Mexica spoke Náhuatl, a language rooted in an Uto-Aztecan family of languages. Uto Aztecan is a common language shared by many different Mexican and South-western cultures, including all Great Basin tribes. The Mexica migration out of Utah would have occurred before the emergence of the more advanced Anasazi and Fremont cultures in Utah. Orosco and Rivas believe the Mexica possessed a detailed knowledge of a calendar centuries before these cultures. "We must re-evaluate much of our thinking about the greatness and antiquity of Native American civilization,' Orosco said."[149]

Finally, as a summary note to this section, the languages of the modern Europe descended from Latin, which developed from Etruscan, which developed from Greek, which developed from a combination of Aramaic, Sanskrit, and Phoenician. On another front they developed from the incursions from Asia into German, France, and Scandinavia. This history will be more fully developed in volume two, as will the variants of these languages for the period and countries pertinent to this part of our study. For our purposes at this time, what has been written is sufficient to show the general development of world languages prior to the Christian era.

---

[149]Jerry Spangler, "Researchers say Aztec Homeland was in Utah," *The Deseret News*, March 24, 1990, B1, B6.

THE DISPERSION
FROM THE TOWER OF BABEL IN 1996 B.C.

From the time of the Flood in 2345 B.C. to the building of the Tower of Babel, estimated at 1996 B.C. there was a gradual dispersion of the family of Noah. Based on the physical evidence, the following scenario is likely prior to the general dispersion.

The time period in question, 2345 B.C. to 1996 B.C. was a period of 349 years. Given the advanced nature of mankind in 2345 (Noah and his sons undoubtedly brought a great deal of knowledge with them through the Flood, which would have allowed for maximum development technologically), and given the more normal lifespans after the Flood, it is possible that the following numbers existed during this period of ten generations (an actual count from Shem to Abraham, and an estimated account using thirty-year generations. Pre-flood estimates noted above were based on eighteen children per mother. Post-flood estimates, given the polygamous nature of many of the couples, is calculated at eight living children per mother, or four female children per mother, the percentage of male/female being given as equal. Shem, Ham, and Japheth had sixteen boys between them; therefore, they likely had sixteen girls. This number will be used instead of twelve in the first generation, which would have been the number of three wives times four daughters. Also as a reference during this period, there are two known families from the latter part of this era that have left a record of the number of their children. These were Mahonri with twenty-two children, and his brother Jared with four sons and eight daughters. (*The Book of Mormon*, The Book of Ether 6:20)

First generation	6
Second generation	32
Third generation	128
Fourth generation	512
Fifth generation	2048
Sixth generation	8196
Seventh generation	32,768
Eighth generation	131,072

Ninth generation	8,388,608
Tenth generation	33,554,432

The first, obvious position that can be taken from an analysis of these population statistics, is that given the fact that Noah and some of the antediluvians were still alive at the time of the Tower of Babel because of their longer lifespan capability, it is obvious that many of those who were born after the Flood were still alive also. The next obvious position is that it is highly likely that there had been a worldwide dispersion, or at least a hemisphere-wide dispersion of this huge population by the time of the Tower of Babel. It cannot be assumed that the dispersion of the tongues at the Tower of Babel had to do with the entire population of the earth. That there was a confusion of tongues is granted, but it is also obvious that there are many linguistic similarities in a number of the cultures, which would indicate prior diffusion. These linguistic similarities have been discussed previously. It is more likely that Jehovah confused the tongues of the wicked who were trying to build the Tower of Babel. Finally, it must be assumed that there were a great number of this population who died as a result of the serious drought which, according to the sources quoted previously, began about 2300 B.C., causing loss of life not only from want of sustenance and disease, but from wars and wanderings. In Abraham's family alone, we know of the death of his grandfather and brother. And, if our data is correct, Noah and Peleg may have both died as a result of the drought and famine associated with the dispersion.

SAMPLE DISPERSION TECHNIQUE EMPLOYED BY GOD: THE JAREDITES

Jared, and Mahonri Moriancumer were brothers who lived at the time of the Tower of Babel. They were born about 2056 B.C., being therefore, of the tenth generation. As Noah and Shem were still alive, it is very likely that they knew them as well, and that they were blessed by them with the blessing of the priesthood, and given great knowledge concerning the things of the former generations. We now have two migrations identified in the same generation: were there others? Is there a general dispersal of the righteous at this period just prior to The Tower of Babel? We have suggested that the Chinese might have been part of this dispersion, but it is also likely, even probable, that they were already gone by 1996. But then so was Abraham.

In about 485 B.C. on this American continent there was a prophet named Ether who compiled a record written on twenty-four gold plates. That record was part of the repository maintained by the Nephites at the end of their civilization in 421 A.D. Moroni, the prophet at that time states the following, beginning in The Book of Ether 1:1. Where the word "descendant" is used in this list, it is sometimes shown elsewhere in Ether to mean "son."

"And now I, Moroni, proceed to give an account of those ancient inhabitants who were destroyed by the hand of the Lord upon the face of this north country [north country here has been interpreted to mean north of Central America by some, and by others the area of the modern United States]. And I take mine account from the twenty and four plates which were found by the people of Limhi, which is called The Book of Ether." (Ether 1:1-2)

"And on this wise do I give the account. He that wrote this record was Ether, and he was a descendant Coriantor. Coriantor was a son of Moron. And Moron was the son of Ethem. And Ethem was the son of Ahah. And Ahah was the son of Seth. And Seth was the son of Shiblon. And Shiblon was the son of Com. And Com was the son of Coriantum. And Coriantum was the son of Amnigaddah. And Amnigaddah was the son of Aaron. And Aaron was a descendant Heth, who was the son of Hearthom. And Hearthom was the son of Lib. And Lib was the son of Kish. And Kish was the son of Corom. And Corom was the son of Levi. And Levi was the son of Kim. And Kim was the son of Morianton. And Morianton was a descendant Riplakish. And Riplakish was the son of Shez. And Shez was the son of Heth." (Ether 1:6-25)

Now this Heth "...had perished by the famine and all his household save it were Shez - wherefore, Shez began to build up again a broken people. And it came to pass that Shez did remember the destruction of his fathers, and he did build up a righteous kingdom; for he remembered what the Lord had done in bringing Jared and his brother across the deep; and he did walk in the ways of the Lord; and he begat sons and daughters." (Ether 10:1-2)

"And Heth was the son of Com. And Com was the son of Coriantum. And Coriantum was the son of Emer. And Emer was the son of Omer. And Omer was the son of Shule. And Shule was the son of Kib. And Kib was the son or Orihah, who was the son of Jared; which Jared came forth with his brother and their families, with some others and their families, from the great tower, at the time the Lord confounded the language of the people, and swore in his wrath that they should be scattered upon all the face of the earth; and according to the word of the Lord the people were scattered." (Ether 1:26-33)

"And Jared had four sons; and they were called Jacom, and Gilgah, and Mahah, and Orihad. And the brother of Jared also begat sons and daughters. And the friends of Jared and his brother were in number about twenty and two souls; and they also begat sons and daughters before they came to the promised land; and therefore they began to be many." (Ether 6:14-16)

"And it came to pass that the brother of Jared did cry unto the Lord, and the Lord had compassion upon Jared; therefore he did not confound the language of Jared; and Jared and his brother were not confounded.

"Then Jared said unto his brother: Cry again unto the Lord, and it may be that he will turn away his anger from them who are our friends, that he confound not their language.

"And it came to pass that the brother of Jared did cry unto the Lord, and the Lord had compassion upon their friends and their families also, that they were not confounded.

"And it came to pass that Jared spake again unto his brother, saying: Go and inquire of the Lord whether he will drive us out of the land, and if he will drive us out of the land, cry unto him whither we shall go." (Ether 1:35-38)

And they were driven out of the Mesopotamian Valley into the land northward where the waters had not yet receded from the earth, into that quarter of the land where there never had man been [since the Flood]. Their journey was one of crossing not only the ocean, but many waters. "And it came to pass that they did travel in the wilderness, and did build barges, in which they did cross many waters, being directed continually by the hand of the Lord. And the Lord would not suffer that they should stop beyond *the sea* in the wilderness, but he would that they should come forth even unto the land of promise." (Ether 2:6-8; italics added). It is a fact that in ancient times the plains of Asia were covered with "many waters," which have now disappeared but are recorded as existing well down into historic times; they were of course far more abundant in Jared's time. Even as late as Herodotus, the land of the Scythians (the region into which Jared's people first advanced) presented formidable water barriers to migration.[150]

And after crossing the vast steppes of central Asia they arrived at the great ocean and prepared for four years to cross the waters to North America. This Jaredite crossing took place sometime around the year 1985 B.C. Most Mormon archeologists and anthropologists have guessed that the landing was anywhere from Ecuador to Central Mexico. The claims theorized by this author point to a North American landing. There were several places in modern California where access was possible to the great inland sea later called Lake Lahontan and Lake Bonneville. Entry near either Los Angeles or San Francisco would undoubtedly have been possible at that time, with less than ninety miles of present land mass needed to cross to its known shores. With California's many upthrusts known to have taken place along its hundreds of fault lines, it is very plausible that there was direct access at that time. As noted in *The Book of Mormon,* Third Nephi 8:11-18 regarding the changes in the land masses of the Americas at the death of Jesus Christ: "And there was a great destruction in the land southward. But, behold there was a more great and terrible destruction in the land northward; for behold, the whole face of the land was changed, because of the tempest and the whirlwinds, and the thunderings and the lightnings, and the

---

[150]Nibley, "The World of the Jaredites," *op. cit.,* page 183.

exceedingly great quaking of the whole earth; and the highways were broken up, and the level roads were spoiled, and many smooth places became rough.... And thus the face of the whole earth became deformed.... And behold, the rocks were rent in twain; they were broken up upon the face of the whole earth, insomuch that they were found in broken fragments, and in seams and in cracks, upon all the face of the land."

This vast inland waterway stretched from central Oregon to near Los Angeles and from Southeastern Idaho and Southwestern Wyoming through Utah and Nevada to near San Francisco.[151] Their initial landing, therefore, after having traversed what is now desert but was then ocean, was in north-central Utah, and they settled in the Sanpete Valley or as it was called at the time by them, the land of Moron.

"Now the land of Moron, where the king dwelt, was near the land which is called Desolation by the Nephites." (Ether 7:6) The "land of their first inheritance" is linked through descriptions of warfare to the land of Moron. (Ether 7:16-17) Discoveries of ancient artifacts, photographs of over 100 of which are in the hands of the author, show this people to have had a written language, using a mixture of pictographs, and a simple alphabet. Drawings of two of the mummies found with the records show them to have been a large people, of a royal caste, with armor and crowns showing definite Asiatic influences. The sword of the male mummy is over seven feet in length. Additional information will be given about these people in the appropriate place in volume two. Suffice it to say that this people had knowledge of the mummification process of the Egyptians, of the working in fine metals, of record keeping, and had definite connections to Asia.

The chronology of the Jaredite nation is critical to an understanding of the development of the Olmecs, the Toltecs, the Mayas, the Aztecs, the Cherokees, and other nations of North America. This chronology will also be more fully developed in Volume 2. At this point only a summary of their genealogy will be given. The following genealogy is from father to son, for the most part, although the word

---

[151]Janetski, *op. cit.,* pages 6-10.

"descendant" is used in several incidents. The text of The Book of Ether, however, clarifies these relationships on at least one occasion where both terms have the same meaning. We have already discussed Nibley's analysis of this.

Jared, tenth generation from Noah through the lineage of Seth born about 2056 B.C.

Orihah, son of Jared
Kib, son of Orihah
Shule, son of Kib
Omer, son of Shule
Emer, son of Omer
Coriantum, son of Emer
Com, son of Coriantum
Heth, son of Com
Shez, son of Heth
Riplakish, son of Shez
Morianton, descendant of Riplakish
Kim, son of Morianton
Levi, son of Kim
Corom, son of Levi
Kish, son of Corom
Lib, son of Kish
Hearthom, son of Lib
Heth, son of Hearthom
Aaron, descendant of Heth
Amnigaddah, son of Aaron
Coriantum, son of Amnigaddah
Com, son of Coriantum
Shiblon, son of Com
Seth, son of Shiblon
Ahah, son of Seth
Ethem, son of Ahah
Moron, son of Ethem
Coriantor, "descendant" of Moron, born about
Ether, son of Coriantor, born about 485 B.C.

In closing this first volume of *The World Book of Generations* it should be obvious from the reading of this material that much remains unknown and probably always will concerning what has happened in the world both prior to and after the Flood. However, it should also be apparent that much more is known than might have been supposed. As Volume 2 of this series unfolds, the actual development of each nation will be revealed in as much pertinent detail as possible, in preparation for placing individuals in their time and circumstances. Subsequent volumes will then deal with the individuals themselves, and every effort will be made to document each person's connections to their parents and to their children. But if we only have an obscure reference to an individual in Sumer or Ebla, that person will be given equal weight and recorded in their proper place and time, with the hope that someday further information will be found concerning their place in the genealogy of man.

SUMMARY

In summary then, we have shown in Volume 1 critical pieces of information that will serve as foundation blocks upon which to build a genealogical history of the world. A number of positions and premises have been established:

1)   The universal methodology using spiritually empirical data is necessary to unravel much of the uncertainty that exists in ancient records and histories, some of which have been purposefully changed or distorted to hide what really happened.

2)   This world since the Fall of Adam in 4002 B.C., has passed through nearly 6,000 years or the full period of its temporal existence. One more 1,000 year period is need to complete the divine plan.[152]

---

[152]Time and the concept of time is extremely relevant to understanding the past. The reader should consider the possibility that there may be two time frames with which we are dealing as we look at the genealogical past and those historical events that affected it: *prophetic time* and *earth time*. The latter diverged from the former at a specific point in ancient history. If the creator considers the 360-day year as a perfect and original cycle for earth time, and the 365.2564-day year as a distortion of that time, he would continue to use the system he set up, when he gives revelations, as his main reference when speaking to his prophets: *prophetic time*. Our discussion of the birth date of Jesus Christ using the 360-day *prophetic time* proves this position quite dramatically. The catastrophic time, that time created when a planetary encounter or other pole-shifting event of the past caused the earth's orbit around the sun to change, would be the present *earth time*. This present time is distinct from *prophetic time*.

For purposes then of clarification, 1998 is not the end of the 6,000 years of this earth's temporal existence. This book is not claiming that the Millennium begins in 1998. When it begins is not pertinent to this study. No one has identified the exact time when the earth changed its orbit. It is unlikely that they ever will as it was undoubtedly a transitional period lasting for a period of months or even years. At whatever point it happened in the remote past the total number of years between then and when the calculation is made are multiplied by 5.2564, which is the difference in total number of days between the old earth rotation time around the sun and the new yearly rotation. The resultant figure is the additional days that must be added to the present calendar. The figure thus arrived at must be divided by 365.2564 to determine the years that the present Gregorian Calendar is ahead of the prophetic calendar.

3)   Even though all land life was destroyed by the Flood, and the face of the world was dramatically changed in many places, in others there was little cataclysmic activity by comparison.

4)   It is a premise within this work that there was no diversity of spoken languages immediately after the Flood, but that diversity began to develop in the 349 years between then and 1996, as the grandchildren and later generations began to distance themselves from the ways of Noah and his children.

5)   The genealogy of the patriarchs from Adam to Abraham is complete, being a record from father to son for twenty generations.

6)   The story of Abraham as contained in the Bible as it pertains to his son Isaac is allegorical. He was probably not Isaac's father. The reason for taking this position is that there are about 307 years separating Abraham from his descendant Isaac's birth date if Abraham was 100 when Isaac was born, or 407 years from Isaac's birth in 1654 and Abraham's birth in 2061. There is more evidence for Abraham being associated with Noah and Shem, than with Isaac and Jacob. It may be that the missing generations are between Isaac and Jacob, but the premise herein is that they are between Abraham and Isaac for the purposes stated.

7)   All premises in the revised chronology are based on historical records, on circumstantial evidence, and on detailed analysis of the events of the times in question. Even if this revised chronology is wrong it isn't likely that it is off by more than a generation. Therefore, the revised chronology is given more weight that the biblical chronology, which can now be safely said to be erroneous.

8)   Thus, until other evidence surfaces to prove false the premises contained herein, we have shown to a certain degree of probability, using both primary and circumstantial evidence, that between Abraham's birth in 2061 and Isaac's birth in 1654 there are 407 missing years genealogically. This could mean anywhere from six to thirteen generations are missing from the biblical pedigrees.

9)   The Patriarch Joseph was the vizier Yuya who served under Tuthmosis IV, and Amenophis III, who was his son-in-law, husband of his daughter Tiye, mother of Moses who was also Akhenaten.

10)   The 430 years stated in the Bible was not a chronological figure, but an instructive figure only. Genealogically speaking it is irrelevant.

11)   Seti I was the Pharaoh of the Oppression; Ramses II was the Pharaoh of the Exodus.

12)   Israel was not in Egypt for 430 years, but for a shorter period. Based on the information regarding the birth dates established for Jacob and Levi, the Descent should have been in the year 1464 or 1466, or 1449 if the Torah's date for Levi's birth is used. We have used the date 1464 B.C. as the year of the Descent.

13)   The genealogy from Judah to David, as given in the Bible, is correct.

14)   The birth year of Jesus Christ was 2 B.C.

With these premises in place, we have established posts along the path of history from which we can measure any event, and identify any individual associated with the events of that period. This will allow us, within a reasonable degree of error, to begin to compile the history of nations and people - individuals - into a realistic framework, with as much documentation as may be available. When discoveries of ancient archives, artifacts, or other important evidence are made, these will necessarily, and gladly, be added to the puzzle. Where errors have been made in the analysis noted herein, when any of the premises are shown to be wrong, they will be changed and revisions will be made respectively to all areas affected by the new data.

BIBLIOGRAPHY

Books

Ager, Derek V. *The New Catastrophism: The Importance of the Rare Event in Geological History.* New York City, New York and Cambridge, England: Cambridge University Press, 1993. 231 pages.

Aldred, Cyril. *Akhenaten: King of Egypt.* London, England: Thames and Hudson, Ltd., 1988. 320 pages.

Andrus, Hyrum L. *Doctrinal Commentary on the Pearl of Great Price.* Salt Lake City, Utah: Deseret Book Company, 1973. 522 pages.

Angelin, Jay Pascal, and Hamblin, William J. *HarperCollins College Outline World History to 1648.* New York City, New York: HarperCollins Publishers, Inc., 1993. 472 pages.

Astour, Michael C. *Hittite History and Absolute Chronology of the Bronze Age.* Partille, Sweden: Paul Åstöms, 1989. 152 pages.

Baines, John and Málek, Jaromir. *Atlas of Ancient Egypt.* New York City, New York: Facts on File Publications, 1983. No page numbers.

Bermant, Chaim and Weitzman, Michael. *Ebla: A Revelation in Archaeology.* New York City, New York: Times Books, 1979. 249 pages.

Bierbrier, M. L. *The Late New Kingdom in Egypt, ca. 1300 - 664 B.C.: A Genealogical and Chronological Investigation.* Warminster, England: Aris & Phillips Ltd., 1975. 160 pages.

Bone, Robert G. *Ancient History.* Ames, Iowa: Littlefield, Adams & Co., 1957. 289 pages.

Brownrigg, Ronald, and Comay, Joan. *Who's Who in the Bible: Two Volume in One (Who's Who in the Old Testament with the Apocrypha; Who's Who in the New Testament).* New York City, New York;

Avenel, New Jersey: Wings Books, 1980. 432 pages each.

Charlesworth, James H., editor. *The Old Testament Pseudepigrapha*. Volume 1. New York City, New York: Doubleday, 1983. 995 pages.

Childress, David H. *Lost Cities and Ancient Mysteries of Africa and Arabia*. Stelle, Illinois: Adventures Unlimited Press, 1989. 414 pages.

Clay, Albert T. *The Empire of the Amorites*. New Haven, Connecticut: Yale University Press, 1919. 192 pages. Reprinted New York City, New York: AMS Press, 1980.

Clayton, Peter A. *Chronicle of the Pharaohs: The Reign-by-Reign Record of the Rulers and Dynasties of Ancient Egypt*. London: Thames and Hudson Ltd., 1994. 224 pages.

Comay, Joan. *Who's Who in the Bible: Who in the Old Testament together with the Apocrypha*. New York City, New York and Avenel, New Jersey: Wings Books, 1980. 432 pages.

Daly, Reginald A. "Rise and Fall of Floodwaters - Historical Record," *Earth's Most Challenging Mysteries*. Nutley, New Jersey, 1975. 200 pages.

Davidovits, Joseph and Morris, Margie. *The Pyramids: An Enigma Solved*. New York City, New York: Hippocrene Books, 1988. 263 pages.

Dyer, Alvin R. *The Refiner's Fire*. Salt Lake City, Utah: Deseret Book Co., 1976. 141 pages.

Eban, Abba. *Heritage: Civilization and the Jews*. New York City, New York: Summit Books, 1984. 354 pages.

Garber, Janet Serlin, editor. *The Concise Encyclopedia of Ancient Civilizations*. New York City, New York and London, England: Franklin Watts, 1978. 850 pages.

Gates, Susa Young. *Surname Book and Racial History*. Salt Lake

City, Utah: General Board of the Relief Society, 1918. 572 pages.

Harris, James R. *Studies in Scriptures: The Pearl of Great Price.* Salt Lake City, Utah: Randall Book Co., 1985. 446 pages.

Harris, Marvin. *Culture, Man, and Nature: An Introduction to General Anthropology.* New York City, New York: Thomas & Crowell Company, 1971. 660 pages.

Hoagland, Richard C. *The Monuments of Mars: A City on the Edge of Forever.* Berkeley, California: North Atlantic Books, 1992. 348 pages.

Hobson, Christine. *The World of the Pharaohs.* New York City, New York: Thames and Hudson Inc., 1987. 192 pages.

Janetski, Joel C. *The Ute of Utah Lake.* Salt Lake City, Utah: The University of Utah Press, 1991. 81 pages.

Kang, C.H. and Nelson, Ethel R. *The Discovery of Genesis: How the Truths of Genesis were found Hidden in the Chinese Language.* St. Louis, Missouri: Concordia Publishing House, 1979. 139 pages.

Kephart, Calvin. *Races of Mankind, their Origin and Migration.* New York City, New York: Philosophical Library, Inc., 1960. 228 pages.

King, Edward, viscount Kingsborough. *Antiquities of Mexico.* 8 Volumes. London, England: James Moyes, 1831-1848.

Lundquist, John M. "Was Abraham at Ebla?" *Studies in Scripture, Volume 2: The Pearl of Great Price.* Salt Lake City, Utah: Randall Book Co., 1985. 446 pages.

McConkie, Bruce R. *Mormon Doctrine.* 2nd ed. Salt Lake City, Utah: Bookcraft, 1966. 856 pages.

Millet, Robert L., and Jackson, Kent P. *Studies in Scriptures: The Pearl of Great Price.* Volume 2. Salt Lake City, Utah: Randall Book Co., 1985. 446 pages.

Nibley, Hugh. "There were Jaredites." *The Collected Works of Hugh Nibley.* Volume 5. Salt Lake City, Utah: Deseret Book Company, 1988. 156 pages.

Nibley, Hugh. "The World of the Jaredites," *The Collected Works of Hugh Nibley.* Volume 5. Salt Lake City, Utah: Deseret Book Company, 1988. 129 pages.

Noorbergen, Rene, and Jochmans, Joey R. *Secrets of the Lost Races: New Discoveries of Advanced Technology in Ancient Civilizations.* New York City, New York: Barnes & Noble Books, 1969. 228 pages.

Osman, Ahmed. *Moses: Pharaoh of Egypt: The Mystery of Akhenaten Resolved.* London, England: Grafton Books, 1990. 200 pages.

Osman, Ahmed. *Stranger in the Valley of the Kings: The Identification of Yuya as the Patriarch Joseph.* London, England: Souvenir Press Ltd., 1987. 171 pages.

Parry, J. H. *The Book of Jasher.* Salt Lake City, Utah: J. H. Parry & Co., 1887. 254 pages.

Quincy, Josiah. *Figures of the Past from Leaves of Old Journals.* Boston, Massachusetts: n.p., 1983. 400 pages.

Richardson, C. Faith. *Ebla: A New Look at History.* (Baltimore, Maryland and London, England: The Johns Hopkins University Press, 1991. 290 pages. Originally published as Pettinato, Giovanni. *Ebla: Nuovi orizzonti della storia.* Milan, Italy: Rusconi Libri, S.p.A., 1986.

Romer, John. *Valley of the Kings.* New York City, New York: Henry Holt and Company, 1981. 293 pages.

Rottenberg, Dan. *Finding our Fathers: A Guidebook to Jewish Genealogy.* Baltimore, Maryland: Genealogical Publishing Co., 1986. 401 pages.

Spence, Lewis. *The Civilization of Ancient Mexico.* Cambridge, England: Cambridge University Press, 1912. 121 pages.

Talmage, James E. *A Study of the Articles of Faith*. Salt Lake City, Utah: Deseret Book Co., 1984. 482 pages.

The Church of Jesus Christ of Latter-day Saints. *History of the Church of Jesus Christ of Latter-day Saints*. 7 volumes + 1 volume index. Salt Lake City, Utah: The Deseret Book Company, 1969.

The Church of Jesus Christ of Latter-day Saints. *Birthright Blessings*. Salt Lake City, Utah: Deseret Sunday School Union Board, 1942. 149 pages.

The Church of Jesus Christ of Latter-day Saints. *The Doctrine and Covenants of The Church of Jesus Christ of Latter-day Saints*. Salt Lake City, Utah: The Church of Jesus Christ of Latter-day Saints, 1981. 298 pages.

The Church of Jesus Christ of Latter-day Saints. *The Pearl of Great Price*. Salt Lake City, Utah: The Church of Jesus Christ of Latter-day Saints, 1981. 61 pages.

The Church of Jesus Christ of Latter-day Saints. *The Book of Mormon*. Salt Lake City, Utah: The Church of Jesus Christ of Latter-day Saints, 1981. 535 pages.

The Church of Jesus Christ of Latter-day Saints. *The Holy Bible*. Salt Lake City, Utah: The Church of Jesus Christ of Latter-day Saints, 1979. 1590 pages.

The University of Chicago, editor. *Encyclopaedia Britannica: A New Survey of Universal Knowledge*. 23 Volumes. Chicago, Illinois; London, England; and Toronto, Canada: Encyclopaedia Britannica, Inc., 1945.

Thompson, George A. *Faded Footprints*. Salt Lake City, Utah: Roaming the West Publications, Inc., 1969. 120 pages.

Toynbee, Arnold J. *A Study of History*. 12 volumes. London, England: Oxford University Press, 1961.

Unity School of Christianity. *Metaphysical Bible Dictionary*. 2nd edition. Kansas City, Missouri: Unity School of Christianity, 1942. 714 pages.

Velikovsky, Immanuel. *Worlds in Collision.* Garden City, New York: Doubleday, 1950. 401 pages.

Velikovsky, Immanuel. *Earth in Upheaval.* Garden City, New York: Doubleday, 1850. 301 pages.

Verrill, Alpeus Hyatt, and Verrill, Ruth. *America's Ancient Civilizations.* New York City, New York: G. P. Putnam's Son, 1953. 334 pages. Reprinted New York City: Capricorn Books, 1967.

Weaver, Muriel Porter. *The Aztecs, Maya, and their Predecessors: Archaeology of Mesoamerica.* New York City, New York: Seminar Press, 1972. 347 pages.

Wilkins, Harold Tom. *Mysteries of Ancient South America.* New York City, New York: Citadel Press, 1956. 216 pages.

Wilson, Clifford A., Dr. *Ebla Tablets: Secrets of a Forgotten City.* 3rd edition. revised and enlarged. San Diego, California: Master Books, 1979. 130 pages.

Manuscript

Aaronson, Lisa. *The Care & Feeding of Revision Hypotheses.* Jerusalem, Israel: Internet, 1995. 10 pages.

Downes, Samuel. *The Testament of the Twelve Patriarchs, the Sons of Jacob.* Manchester, England: Ralph J. Bradshaw, 1843. 28 pages.

Ginenthal, Charles. *The Flood.* n.p.:Internet, 16 March 1995. 56 pages.

Periodicals

Kelly, Allen O., and Dachille, Frank. "Tunisia and Algeria," *Target Earth.* (1953). Carlsbad, California.

LaFay, Howard. "Ebla, Splendor of an Unknown Empire," *National Geographic 154* (1978): pages 731-757.

Lemonick, Michael D. "Secrets of the Princes' Tomb," *Time: The Weekly Magazine,* May 29, 1995, pages 48-54.

McQuown, Norman A. "The Classification of the Maya Languages." *International Journal of American Linguistics 22* (1956): pages 191-195.

The Church of Jesus Christ of Latter-day Saints. *Improvement Era* (1968): page 14.

Taylor, John. "Ancient Ruins." *Times & Seasons 5 #23* (December 15, 1844): page 746.

Trifil, James. "Whale Feet," *Discover* (May, 1991): pages 45-48.

Woodward, Scott. "Genealogy of New Kingdom Pharaohs and Queens." *Archaeology 49 #5* (September-October, 1996): pages 45-47.

Newspapers

Jerry Spangler. "Researchers say Aztec Homeland was in Utah." *The Deseret News.* Salt Lake City, Utah. March 24, 1990, B1, B6.

INDEX

17,000 tablets 77
18th dynasty 7, 135, 154
19th Dynasty 135, 154
1st and 2nd millennia 77
1st Babylonian dynasty 87
21st Dynasty 33
22nd Dynasty 33
2nd century B.C. 228
2nd Intermediate Period 96
3rd century B.C. 221
3rd dynasty of Ur 96
3rd Intermediate Period 96
3rd millennium B.C. 77
4th century B.C. 221
5,000 places 77
60,000 10, 28
6th century B.C. 222
7th century A.D. 222
A land out of the depth of the sea 69
A. Scharff 32
Aakheperkarē 125
Aakheperurē 125
Aakherperenrē 125
Aamu 146
Aaron 157, 186, 188, 191, 192, 197, 236, 240
Aaronic Priesthood 191
Ab-ra-mu 79
Aba 201
Abba Eban 53
Abbey Mine 49
Abel 65, 226
Abia 120
Abijah 120
Abimael 109
Abimelech 203
Abkan 95
ABO system 93
Abraham 7, 8, 11, 53, 64, 77, 79, 82, 86, 91, 173, 193, 194, 196, 198-200, 202, 204, 205, 207-210, 212, 234, 236, 243
Abram 18, 84, 86, 137, 202, 206
Abram's dwelling in the land of Canaan 204
Absolute chronology 123
Abu Simbel 96

Abydos 44, 57
Abydos King List 58
Abyssinians 108
Accad 87, 88, 112, 114
Acco 147
Achaeans 105
Achon 104
Acropolis 90
Ad-da 87
Adad-nirari I 131, 132
Adah 67
Adam 8, 12, 14-16, 18, 20, 26, 51, 55, 58, 65, 66, 70, 71, 82, 113, 117, 121, 122, 195, 214, 215, 226, 243
Adam Clarke 230
Adam-ondi-Ahman 13, 58
Adamic 214
Adan 115
Adbeel 209
Admah 78, 83, 84, 113, 116
Adonizedek 206
Aedorachus 26
Aegean 95, 96
Afghanistan 222
Africa 44, 45, 54, 68, 79, 81, 93, 94, 112, 114-116, 207,
African 40
Afro-Asiatic 224
Agade 90
Agate 50
Age of Metals 55
Ager 44, 45
Agriculture, 22
Ahah 236, 240
Ahmed Osman 136, 155
Ahmose 125, 189
Ahmose-Nefertari 125
Ahmosides 125
Ahmosis 139
Aka 89, 90
Akhenaten 91, 123, 125, 155, 162, 166, 167, 177, 180-182, 184-187, 189, 191, 244
Akhmin 165, 171
Akkad 80, 89, 114, 219

Akkadian 201, 219, 222, 226
Akurgal 89
Al-Ubaid 76
Alabama 229
Alaska 38
Albanian 108
Albert T. Clay 75, 78
Albright 96, 127, 189, 204
Aldred 123, 124, 135
Aleppo 200, 220
Alexandrian astronomer 128
Alfonso Rivas-Salmon 232
Algeria 45
Allan O. Kelly 45
Alleles 92
Allelic genes 93
Alma 175, 207
Almelon 26
Almodad 109
Alonzo de Posada 231
Aloparus 26
Alorus 26
Alpeus Hyatt Verrill 229
Alphabet. 239
Alps 28
Altai Mountains 100
Altaic 98
Alvin R. Dyer 13
Amada 143
Amalekites 84
Amanus 201
Amar-Sin 91
Amarna 96, 182-184, 186-188
Amegalarus 26
Amempsinus 26
Amen-hir-khopshef 135
Amenemhet 168
Amenhotep 168
Amenhotep III 141, 158, 162, 163, 166,
        167, 171, 177, 179,
        181, 182, 184, 188,
        191
Amenhotep IV 167, 185
Amenipet 168
Amenophis 125, 189
Amenophis III 244
Amenophis IV 189
America 13
American 236
American continent 116
American Indians 93

American Research Center 40
American University in Cairo 126
Americas 54, 227, 228, 230
Amharic 226
Aminadab 193
Amman, Jordan 228
Ammenon 26
Ammi 87
Ammisaduqa 126
Ammon 109
Ammonite 222
Ammu 87
Amnigaddah 236, 240
Amori 115
Amorite 84, 113, 220, 226
Amorites 80, 84, 91
Amoritic 87
Amosis 125, 189
Amram 138, 156-158, 186, 187, 191, 192,
        197
Amraphel 83, 84, 86, 210
Amun 147, 165, 171, 180, 181, 189
Amun Temple 146
Amunite 180, 181
Amurrite 148
Amurru 87, 148
Anamim 113
Anamin 114
Anar 110
Anasazi 233
Anatolia 95, 96, 110, 116, 200, 201
Ancient artifacts 239
Ancient civilizations 11
Ancient Egypt 42, 139, 154, 177
Ancient Jewish scroll 120
Ancient Near East 123, 126
Ancient of Days 12
Ancient One 24
Andaman Islands 112
Andes 28
Andrea Dorfman 125
Andrew Jensen 13
Anedjib 58
Anen 165, 171, 176
Aner 84, 85
Angel Gabriel 120
Angelin 228
Angels 70
Angoli 102
Animal husbandry 22
Ankhesenamun 125

Ankhkheperurē 125
Anom 63, 114
Antediluvian 22, 25-27, 51
Antediluvians 51
Anthony and Cleopatra 119
Anthropologist 232
Anthropologists 215, 238
Anthropology 92, 231
Antonio Lebolo 6
Aper-el 188
Apocalyptic literature 8, 9
Apocrypha 115
Approximately 204
Arab 187, 222, 225
Arab (partially) 108
Araba 149
Arabia 109, 115
Arabian 77, 79, 110, 220
Arabic 87, 223, 225, 226
Arabs 109, 208, 222
Aram 79, 109, 111
Aramaean 108
Aramaic 220-223, 226, 233
Ararat 34, 73, 74, 93, 116
Archaeological 46, 123, 140, 204
Archaeological finds 13
Archaeologists 21, 32, 48
Archaeology 31, 36, 48, 127
Archaic Period 230
Archangel 58
Archeological 36, 75, 77, 94, 104, 215, 230
Archeologists 204, 238
Archeology 97
Architecture 22
Arctic 44
Arioch 83, 84, 86
Ariphi 106
Ark 10, 17, 23, 25, 27, 33, 34, 73, 74
Arkee 116
Arkite 113
Arman 201
Armenia 99
Armenian 200
Armenians 108, 110
Armenians, 98
Armies 65
Armor 239
Arodi 116
Arom 193
Arphaxad 17, 19, 63, 64, 79, 98, 108-110
Arrowhead 47

Artaxerex 119
Arthur J. Brandenberger 33
Artic Ocean 100
Artifact 51
Artifacts 10, 21, 239
Arts 22
Arvadite 113
Aryan 98, 100, 215
Aryans 102, 215
Ascalon 149-151
Asenath 163, 165
Ashed 110
Ashkelon 144
Ashkenaz 99, 100
Ashkênâz 100
Ashmua 67
Ashteroth 83
Ashtoroth 77
Ashur 110
Asia 23, 38, 39, 53, 54, 94, 100, 102, 108, 116, 145-147, 150, 212, 218, 224, 233, 238
Asia Minor 99, 105, 144, 146
Asiatic 98, 104, 108, 148, 149
Asiatic shepherd rulers 138
Asshur 109, 112, 114
Assur 79, 96
Assyria 10, 67, 71, 79, 104, 110, 126
Assyrian 35, 108, 129, 131, 219, 220
Assyrian King List 127
Assyrians 97, 110
Assyriology 32
Astour 123
Astronomer 34
Astronomical 34-36, 123, 127
Astronomy 22, 36
Aswan 56
Aten 162, 181, 187, 188, 191
Aten Gleams 162
Aten-it 187
Athens, Greece 229
Athothis 57
Athribis Stela 143
Atlantic Ocean 38
Atlantis 10, 70
Attica 105
Augustus 119, 121, 128
Auriferous quartz 49
Australia 93
Australian aborigine 111

Australopithecines 75
Austrian 49
Auxiliary hypotheses 123
Avaris 138, 139
Ay 125
Aye 163, 171, 176, 182, 184-186, 191
Azathim 115
Aztec calendar 232
Aztecs 109, 218, 231, 232, 239
B-t Phar'a 177
B-y-t Phar'a 177
Ba-en-Re 143
Ba-en-Re Meriamon 144
Babel 75, 88, 112, 114, 206
Babylon 28, 78, 81, 87, 91, 96, 126, 129, 138, 193, 217
Babylonia 81, 87, 126
Babylonian 26, 27, 108, 123, 129, 131, 219, 220
Babylonian chronology 127
Babylonian King List A 127
Babylonian Talmud 223
Babylonians 26, 27, 218
Bactriana 219
Badarian 95
Baghdad 77
Baines 94
Balgar 102
Balulu 89
Banefre 61
Bantu 112
Baptize 69
Barges 238
Barrier Canyon 232
Barrier Creek 232
Bartonia 101
Bartonim 101
Bashemath 196
Basque 111
Basra 76
Battaks 25
Battle 68
Bedawiye 225
Bedouin 151, 152, 186
Bedouins 153
Beeri 196
Beersheba 195
Beirut 79, 149
Bel-Marduk 27
Bela 83, 84
Bera 83

Berah 115
Berber 81, 224, 225
Bering Strait 38, 230
Bermant 35, 36, 89, 203
Bernard Grdseloff 149
Bernardino Drovetti 6
Berosus 27
Beruit 75
Bes 167
Beth-Shan 147-150
Beth-pe-or 175
Bible 25, 32, 34, 46, 77, 95, 104, 118, 135, 138-141, 151-153, 157, 186, 187, 191, 194
Bible Dictionary 19
Biblical 26, 34, 36, 46, 78, 82, 87, 97, 118, 129, 138, 139, 141, 145, 151, 152, 154, 155, 176, 178, 186, 197, 200, 204, 208, 209, 221, 230
Bid 102
Bieneches 59
Bierbrier 129, 135
Bint-Anath 136
Birsha 83
Bishop Lightfoot 206
Bizayon 110
Black 68, 70
Black Dragon Canyon 232
Black Sea 103, 106
Blackness 68
Blood groups 93
Bloodshed 65, 69
Boat 25
Boaz 193
Bohemia 101
Bolor 100
Book of History 103
Book of Jasher 18, 210
Book of remembrance 214, 226
Book of the Dead 7, 33, 159
Bosnia 101
Boston Transcript 47
Brahmins 102
Brandenberger 33
Brass 229
Brass and copper plates 229
Brass Plates 176
Braun 49

Brewster 49
Brigham Young University 77, 231
Brinkman 129
Britain 49
British 141
British Association of the Advancement
　　　of Science 49
British Columbia 231
British Isles 29
Bronze Age 55, 123
Brownrigg 115
Buddhist 103, 229
Budge 33
Bukhara 219
Bunefer 62
Bur-Sagale 35
Burmese 98
Burnt offering 23
Bushmen 112
Buzar 102
Byblos 75, 79, 96
Byblos Syllabic 221
C. Faith Richardson 88
C. H. Kang 103, 227
Cain 65-68, 70, 71, 112
Cainan 16, 20, 26, 55, 58, 59, 66, 68, 71
Cairo 45, 143
Cairo Museum 141
Cal State Fresno 232
Calach 110
Calah 112
Calendar 118
California 28, 49, 50, 238
Calligraphy 226
Calneh 88, 112, 114
Caluhim 113
Calvin Kephart 94, 218
Cambridge Ancient History 89
Cambridge University 44, 231
Canaan 18, 68-70, 74, 86, 98, 108,
　　　　112-115, 144, 146,
　　　　147, 150, 151, 158,
　　　　195, 196, 199, 202,
　　　　204, 205
Canaanite 66, 108, 144, 204, 220-223, 226
Canaanite-Phoenician 221
Canaanites 68, 108, 113, 115, 199
Canaanitic 87
Canada 38
Caphtorim 113
Caphturim 114

Carbon-dating 32
Carboniferous 48
Caribbean 109
Carpathian Mountains 101
Carthage 221
Carthaginian 108
Casloch 115
Casluchim 114, 115
Caspian Sea 39, 100, 101, 104
Cassuto 156, 183, 193
Castellemonte 6
Cataclysm 46
Cataclysmic 47
Catal Hüyük 95
Catalonian 108
Catastrophe 21, 27, 29, 30, 52, 78
Catastrophes 37, 151
Catastrophic time 242
Catastrophism 44
Caucasoid 93
Caucasus Mountains 106
Cecilio Orosco 232
Censorinus 127, 128
Central Africa 93
Central America 236
Central American 109
Central Asia 94, 100, 217, 218
Central Australia 93
Central Mexico 238
Ceramic 50, 51
Černý 129
Chad 81, 224
Chadic 226
Chaim Bermant 35, 36, 89, 203
Chaires 59
Chalcolithic 55
Chaldea 104, 111, 198, 201
Chaldean 26, 67, 81, 113, 201
Chaldeans 81, 111, 198, 219
Chaldees 77, 199
Chamothi 116
Chaphtor 114
Chariots 153
Charles Ford Society 50
Charlesworth 65
Chasloth 114, 115
Chazoni 104
Chedorlaomer 83, 84, 86
Cheops 61
Chephren 42, 61, 90
Cherokee 109, 239

Chiapas, Mexico 229
Chichen Itzá 229
Chief Queen 125
Childress 44
China 23, 93, 102, 116, 198, 226
Chinese 23, 32, 64, 98, 103, 199, 218, 226, 229, 235
Chou 24
Christ 9, 12, 55, 118, 193, 204, 208, 222, 232
Christian 117, 124, 220, 224, 233
Christian Father 119
Christian Palestine Aramaic 222
Christianity 82
Christians 223
Chronographers 124
Chronological 89, 94, 117, 123, 156, 157, 191, 193
Chronologies 5, 197
Chronology 22, 32, 33, 35, 36, 46, 55, 77, 80, 88, 89, 95, 124, 126, 127, 152, 153, 158, 183, 192, 200, 204, 239
Chul 111
Church 204
Church Historian 13
Cities of the Plain 78
City of Enoch 10, 58, 85
City of Holiness 70
City of Zion 10, 72
City-states 10, 89, 90, 146
Clarke 230
Classical 221
Clay 75, 78
Clay tablets 27
Cleopatra 119
Clifford A. Wilson 78
Coal 31, 48, 49
Coffin 31
Colbert 30
Colorado 28, 47
Com 236, 237, 240
Comay 115
Compiled sources 5
Confucius 103
Confusion of tongues 64, 199
Consecutive dynasties 124
Construction 22
Continents 39
Copper 50, 51, 76

Copper age 47, 55
Copper and stone 55
Copper arrowhead 47
Copper battle axes 101
Coptic 147, 225
Coriantor 236, 240
Coriantum 236, 237, 240
Cornelius 127
Corom 236, 240
Coso 51
Coso Mountains 50
Costa Rica 231
Council of the Indies 232
Covenants 204
Creator 25
Cretan 96
Crete 74
Croat 98, 108
Croatia 101
Cromarty 29
Crowns 239
Crucified 122
Crystals 50
Culp 48
Cuneiform 220, 221
Cuneiformist-astronomer 127
Cunning craftsman 48
Cura 104, 106
Curse 10
Curson 104
Cush 63, 88, 102, 109, 112, 114, 207
Cushitic 225
Cushni 107
Cyclades 105
Cylinder 50
Cyril Aldred 123, 124
Cyrus Gordon 200
Czech 99, 108
D. Sidersky 127
Da-u-dum 79
Dachille 45
Dagan 80
Dagon 201
Dalmatia 101
Daly 38
Damascus 78, 84, 110, 111, 148
Dan 84
Dan Rottenberg 53
Dane 108
Daniel 12, 118, 121, 122, 222
Danubian 101

Daonus 26
Dapur 148
Darius I 228
David 53, 79, 83, 117, 122, 192, 193, 196,
    198, 244
David H. Childress 44
Davidovits 40
De Lubicz 42
De Witt 49
Dead Sea 145, 149, 151, 228
Debata 25
Dedan 112, 114, 223
Dedon 106
Delta 95, 148, 152
Deluge 22, 23, 25, 28, 31, 37, 40, 52
Demotic 225
Den 58
Derek Ager 44
Descendants 12, 23
Descent 137, 138, 155, 158, 176, 191, 197,
    244
Deshret 56
Desolation 239
Destruction 23
Deuteronomy 82, 121, 149
Devonian 29
Diamond saw 50
Dilah 109
Dinosaurs 27, 30
Diocletian 128
Discrepancy 204
Dispersion of the nations 64
Djedefhor 61
Djedefra 61
Djedefre 61, 62
Djedkare 63
Djer 57
Djeserkarē 125
Djeserkheperu 125
Djeserkheperurē 125
Djet 58
Djokha Umma 229
Djoser 60, 96
Dnieper River 100
Doctrine 204
Documented 12
Dodanim 99, 105
Dodwell 34
Dor 77
Dorchester, Massachusetts 47
Dorfman 125

Dravidian 111
Drought 18, 235
Drovetti 6
Dubness 102
Dumah 209
Dungi 89
Dutch 108
Dynasties 32, 33, 89
Dynasties XIX and XX 133
Dynasty 32
Dynasty XIX 132
Dynasty XX 132
Dynasty XXI 132, 133
Dynasty XXII 129, 132-134
Dynasty XXV 129, 134
Dynasty XXVI 129
E. A. Wallis Budge 33
E-sa-um 79
Eannatum 89, 90
Early Bronze 96
Early Classic Period 230
Early Dynastic Period 96
Early Post-Classic Period 230
Earth time 242
Earthquakes 27
East Africa 75, 225
East Aramaic 222
East Slav 99, 108
Eastern Delta 139, 153, 180, 181
Eastern Europe 93
Eastern Hamite 112
Eastern Semitic 220
Eban 53
Eber 17, 19, 64, 79, 109, 110, 212
Ebla 10, 11, 28, 36, 74-78, 80, 82, 90, 91,
    198, 200, 201, 205,
    207, 210, 241
Eblaite 220, 226
Eblaites 80, 218
Ebrium 79
Ecuador 238
Ed. Meyer 128
Edel 130
Eden 74
Edessa 223
Edom 149-151
Edomite 150, 222
Edomites 203
Edward King 229
Edwin H. Colbert 30
Egypt 6, 10, 11, 28, 32, 33, 35, 40-46, 55,

63, 67, 71, 74, 80-82, 86, 90, 91, 95, 96, 112-114, 119, 124, 126-128, 130, 135-137, 139, 143-146, 148, 153, 158, 173, 182, 188, 190, 195, 197, 222, 224, 225, 244

Egyptian 32, 35, 36, 42, 44, 45, 75, 81, 101, 112, 123, 129, 130, 137, 138, 141, 145, 146, 149, 151, 176, 179, 181, 184, 185, 189, 221, 224

Egyptian history 57, 124

Egyptians 11, 26, 32, 44, 97, 113, 114, 136, 141, 146, 149, 150, 216, 218, 219, 227

Egyptologist 32, 141, 149

Egyptologists 81, 126, 140, 141, 151, 156, 224

Egyptology 33

Egyptus 32, 46, 56,63, 67, 71, 72, 81, 112-115, 207

Ehoboth 112

Eighteenth and Nineteenth Dynasties 138

Eighteenth century B.C. 221

Eighteenth Dynasty 125, 139, 141, 182

Ekronim 115

El 188

El-Hadr 222

Elam 83, 84, 86, 109

Elamite 96

Elamites 80

Elamitic 87

Elbe 39

Eleazar 188

Electrical 51

Eli 188

Eliakim 67

Elicanum 102

Elichanaf 103

Elishaa 67

Elishah 99, 105

Elizabeth 120

Elkenah 212

Ellasar 83, 84, 86

Elohim 175, 188

Elon 196

Elparan 83

Emer 237, 240

Emims 83

Emperor Shun 103

Empirical data 5

Empirical proof 123

Emutbal 87

Enakale 89

Enannatum 89

England 48, 137

English 108

Enkhengal 89

Enlil-nasir II 127

Enmishpat 84

Enoch 8, 10, 16, 26, 56, 58, 65-72, 85, 214

Enos 16, 18, 20, 26, 55, 58, 59, 65, 66, 71, 226

Entemena 89

Ephraim 163, 170, 176, 184, 186, 191

Er 203

Erech 88, 112, 114

Eridu 76

Errors 5

Esau 79, 195, 196, 203

Eshcol 84, 85

Esrom 193

Eternal Father 9

Eternal truths 6

Ethel R. Nelson 103, 227

Ethem 236, 240

Ether 208, 216, 217, 236, 240

Ethiopia 10, 67, 71, 187, 220

Ethiopian 223

Ethiopians 114

Etiological 78

Etruscan 233

Euphrates 10, 37, 55, 67, 74, 76, 87, 99, 166, 200

Europe 53, 54, 79, 94, 100, 101, 106, 116, 218

European 53, 98, 101, 108, 109

Eusebius 119

Eve 65

Evolution 14, 47, 215

Evolutionary 47

Evolutionary process 21

Evolutionary theory 14

Evolutionary Time 21

Evolutionist 28

Evolutionists 21, 28

Exile 138, 188

Exodus 135, 138-141, 145, 146, 150-153, 174, 176, 178, 183, 197
Ezra 138, 188, 222
F. Cornelius 127
Faith 9
Faiyum 95
Fall 103
Fall of Adam 14, 117, 242
Famine 18, 71, 140, 199
Far East 217
Father 69, 70
Father of Church History 119
Father to Pharaoh 155
Feast of the Tabernacles 121
Feldspar 49
Ferghana 219
Fertile Crescent 55, 74, 77, 82, 116
Fifth century B.C. 138
Fifth Dynasty 33
Fifth millennium 37
First Dynasty 32, 90
First Dynasty of Babylon 126
First millennium 123, 204
First millennium B.C. 35
Flavius Josephus 140, 230
Fleming 108
Flood 9, 17, 19, 20, 22-27, 30, 32, 34, 36, 37, 39, 44, 46, 51, 52, 55, 63, 67, 70-72, 75-77, 81, 82, 88, 94, 99-101, 103, 116, 202, 213-215, 234, 235, 238, 241, 243
Flood deposits 37
Floods 37, 38
Forefathers 71
Forest of Cedars 80
Formosa 98
Fossil 29, 31, 50
Fossil-encrusted 50
Fossilized 45
Fossils 28, 37
Four hundred and thirty years 138
Fourteenth century B.C. 139, 146
Fourth generation 137
France 229, 233
Frank Dachille 45
Freedman 78
Fremont 233
French 151, 217

French Provençal 108
Frisian 108
Full moon 121
Gabriel 120, 121
Gaelic 218
Galilean Aramaic 222
Galilee 148
Galla 225
Ganges 102
Garber 75
Garden of Eden 12-14, 71
Gates 95, 98, 104, 106
Gather 111
Gaza 77, 79, 113, 144, 147
Gaza Strip 136
Ge'ez 224
Gebul 115
Geisental 30
Gemara 223
Genealogical 83, 202
Genealogies 8, 13, 208, 209
Genealogists 218
Genealogy 51, 104, 239
Generations 14
Genesis 8, 9, 14, 17, 19, 22, 25, 27, 46, 51, 55, 66, 71, 72, 75, 78, 79, 83, 96, 105, 109, 110, 112, 113, 139, 140, 149, 155, 157, 158, 177, 183, 188, 195, 203, 204, 206, 217
Genetic classification of the races 93
Genetic repertories 92
Genome 93
Genotypes 92
Geode 51
Geographical races 93
Geological 31, 47, 48
Geologist 22
Geologists 28, 47, 48, 51
Geophysical 37
George A. Thompson 232
George F. Dodwell 34
George Gaylord Simpson 30
Gerar 113
Gerarim 115
Gergashi 116
German 108, 215, 233
Germany 30, 100
Getae 98, 100, 219

Geté 100
Gether 109
Gezer 144, 151, 221
Giants 10, 25, 69, 71
Gibson 125
Gihon 10, 67, 102
Gilgah 237
Gilgamesh 79, 90
Gillayon 230
Gilman, Colorado 47
Giovanni Pettinato 88, 201
Girgasite 113
Githim 115
Given 204
Giza 10, 61
Gizeh 42, 44
Glaciers 39
Glyphs 11
God 9, 10, 16, 23, 26, 55, 69-71, 73, 84-86, 181, 199, 214, 215, 226
Goiim 87
Gold 48
Gold chain 48
Gold thread 48
Golden Book of the Mayas 229
Gomer 98, 99, 102, 219
Gomorrah 78, 83, 84, 113, 116, 210
Gordon 200
Goshen 139, 180
Graeci 106
Grand River 13
Granite 48, 49
Grdseloff 149
Great 204
Great Basin 39, 233
Great Basin Native Americans 231
Great Pyramid 61
Great Russian 99, 108
Great Sphinx 61
Great Temple 96
Great tower 237
Great Year 127, 128
Greco-Latin 108
Greece 105, 215, 229
Greek 108, 111, 215, 218, 221, 222, 233
Greek islands 142
Greek mythology 99, 105
Greeks 97, 105, 107
Green River 232
Gregorian 118

Gregorian Calendar 242
Guatemala 229
Gudea 78, 90, 202
Gulf Coast 231
Gunkel 203
Gura 80
Gurls 49
Gurneh 6
H. Nissen 89
H. R. Hall 32
Habu 172, 177
Habuba-el Kebira 95
Hadan 115
Hadar 209
Hadoram 109
Hadramauth 223
Hadya 225
Hagar 209
Hall 32
Ham 8, 17, 19, 51, 63, 67, 72, 74, 75, 80, 81, 83, 98, 99, 102, 108, 109, 112, 113, 115, 116, 207, 211, 212, 214, 234
Hamathite 113
Hamblin 228
Hamites 75
Hamitic 81, 111-113, 219
Hamito-semitic 224
Hamito-semitic language 81
Hammath 147
Hammu 87
Hammurabi 86, 87, 91, 210
Hanannihah 11, 67, 69, 71
Haner 11, 67, 69, 71
Hanigalbat 131
Haran 19, 77, 199, 200, 202, 205, 210, 212
Harappa 10, 11
Harmon 110
Harold T. Wilkins 229
Harris 7, 92
Harry S. Ladd 29
Harvard University 229
Hathor 56, 164
Hatra 222
Hatshepsut 91, 125
Hatti 129, 130, 144, 150
Hattushilish I 126
Hattushilish III 129-131
Hattusili III 148
Hattusilis III 136

Hausa 226
Havilah 10, 67, 71, 109, 112, 114
Hawaiian 24
Hawaiian 109
Hawaiians 72
Hazarmaveth 109
Hazezontamar 84
Hazor 77
Head of Sinbad 232
Hearthom 236, 240
Hebrew 84, 99, 105, 108, 150, 151, 158, 177, 179, 188, 217, 221-223, 226
Hebrew University of Jerusalem 156, 193
Hebrews 106, 208
Hebron 192
Hedjet 56
Helaman 118
Helen Gibson 125
Heliopolis 124, 142, 143, 165
Helix 51
Hellenistic 123
Hemon 61
Heni 11, 67, 69, 71
Henutmire 136
Henutsen 61
Herakleopolis 96
Hermon 79
Herod 119
Herodotus 105, 238
Hesepti 58
Hetep-heres I 61
Hetep-heres II 61
Hetepheres 61
Heth 98, 108, 113, 115, 236, 240
Hexagonal 50
Hiddekel 10, 67
Hierakonpolis 56
Hieroglyphic 221, 228
Hieroglyphics 33
Hieroglyphs 221
High priest 85, 86
High Priest of Re at Heliopolis 62
High Priest of the sun god in Heliopolis 124
Himalayas 28
Hindi 218
Hiram de Witt 49
Hissar Mountains 219
Historians 22, 47, 215, 218
Historic Age 55

Historical Record 13
History of the Church 7
Hithlah 102
Hittite 96, 101, 126, 127, 129, 130, 132, 146, 148, 149, 196, 200
Hittites 91, 98, 108, 112, 136, 144, 145, 147, 148, 150, 218
Hivi 116
Hivite 113
Hoagland 42
Hobah 84
Hokan 231
Holy Ghost 9, 69, 70
Hophni 189
Hor 26
Hor-Aha 57
Horemheb 153, 182, 183, 185
Horemheb 125
Horite 151
Horites 83, 145
Hornung 130
Horseshoe Canyon 232
Horus 56
Hotepsekhemwy 59
Hottentot 112
Howard LaFay 79
Hsia 24
Huastec 231
Huber 127
Hugh Miller 29
Hugh Nibley 77, 208, 210, 216, 218
Hul 109
Human bone 47
Hungary 101
Huni 60
Hur 116
Hurru 144, 145, 151
Hutton Webster 97, 215
Hyksos 91, 96, 138, 140, 141
Hyksos kings 159
Hypocephalus 7
Hypostyle Hall 147
Ibbi-Sin 91
Iblul-Il 90
Ice Age 37, 41-43, 45
Icecaps 38, 39
Idaho 239
Ideogram 23
Ideograms 226
Ideographic 227

Ideographs 227
Idrenaeus 119
II Kings 104
Ili-Dagan 80
Illinois 49
Illyrians 106
Im-r-n 187, 191
Imhotep 60
Immanuel Velikovsky 29, 37
Immunochemical 93
Improvement Era 7
Imran 187, 191
Inaccuracies 5
Incas 232
India 10, 28, 37, 93, 99, 111, 215, 218
Indo-Aryans 108
Indo-European 99, 215, 218
Indonesians 24, 98
Ini 63
Intermarriage 93
Ion 99, 105
Ionea 105
Ionians 105
Ionians Greeks 105
Iowa City 47
Irad 66
Iram 79
Iran 95, 101, 223, 228
Iranians 101
Iraq 75, 76, 220, 222, 223, 228
Ireland 99
Iron Age 55
Isaac 83, 162, 173, 195, 204, 205, 208,
210, 243
Isador Braun 49
Isaiah 230
Isesi 63
Ishbi-Erra 91
Ishmael 109, 209
Isin 87, 91
Islam 82
Islands of the sea 116
Isles of the Gentiles 99
Ispogogee Indians 229
Israel 99, 104, 138, 141, 144, 145, 151,
153, 176, 187, 244
Israel Stela 141, 143-146, 150, 151
Israelite 140, 150, 157, 177, 181, 204
Israelites 111, 135-137, 139-141, 145, 146,
151, 153, 158, 181,
183, 187, 188, 230

Istnofret 136
Italac 102
Italian 108, 217
Italians 106
Italy 6, 215
Itet 96
Itti-Marduk-balatu 130
J. Černý 129
J. van Seters 204
J. W. S. Sewell 127
Jabal 67
Jabus 104, 106
Jackson County 12
Jacob 82, 138, 154, 162, 173, 174, 177,
190-192, 195, 197,
203, 204, 210, 244
Jacom 237
Jamdat Nasr 96
James E. Talmage 12
James H. Charlesworth 65
James R. Harris 7
James Trifil 45
Janet Serlin Garber 75
Janetski 231, 239
Japan 93
Japanese 98
Japetus 99, 105
Japheth 8, 17, 19, 51, 62, 67, 72, 74, 95,
98, 99, 102, 104, 106,
108, 112, 116, 205,
214, 219, 234
Japhetic 111
Jared 16, 20, 26, 56, 58, 61, 64, 66, 104,
216, 234, 235, 237,
238, 240
Jaredite 11, 104, 109, 227, 230, 238, 239
Jaredites 109, 199, 217, 218, 228
Jarmo 75
Jaromir Málek 94
Jasper 50
Javan 99, 105, 107
Javanim 105
Jaxartes 100
Jay Pascal Angelin 228
Jean Yoyotte 151
Jebusite 113
Jehovah 11, 20, 52, 161, 175, 199, 235
Jerah 109
Jericho 32, 36, 152
Jerry Spangler 233
Jershon 199

Jerusalem 77, 118, 120, 144, 156, 176, 193, 206, 207
Jesse 193
Jesus 119, 121, 122, 204
Jesus Christ 14, 117, 118, 120, 122, 238, 242, 244
Jetur 209
Jew 121
Jewish Babylonian Aramaic 223
Jewish customs 122
Jewish Palestine Aramaic 222
Jewish records 122
Jewish traditions 121
Jews 152, 156
Joan Comay 115
Job Stone 150
Jobab 109
Jochebed 184, 186, 191, 197
Jochmans 34
Joel C. Janetski 231, 239
Joey R. Jochmans 34
Johannes Riem 22
John 120
John A. West 42
John Baines 94
John C. Whitcomb 52
John D. Lee 13
John M. Lundquist 76
John Taylor 206
John the Baptist 120, 121
John [A.] West 43
Johns Hopkins University 88
Joktan 79, 109, 110
Joktanites 79
Joppa 77
Jordan 75, 104, 121, 222, 228
Joseph 7, 13, 140, 154, 158, 162, 170, 172, 174, 182, 184, 188, 190, 244
Joseph Davidovits 40
Joseph Smith 7, 8, 12, 13, 15, 83, 190, 206
Josephus 120, 124, 140
Joshua 151, 206
Jubal 67
Jubilee 148
Judaea 221
Judah 192, 194, 196, 244
Judaism 82, 223
Judæa 119
Judith 196
Julian 118, 127

Julian Calendar 120
Juvenile Instructor 13
Ka-Nekhet Tutmes 163
Kadashman-Enlil II 129, 130
Kadashman-Turgu 130, 131
Kadesh 84, 147, 149
Kaha i 134
Kaiu 63
Kakai 62
Kaku 90
Kalat Shergat 228
Kane 24
Kang 103
Karl Gurls 49
Karnaim 83
Karnak 147, 149, 181, 185, 186
Karnak temple 147
Karnak War Inscriptions 143
Karoy 166
Kashgaria 100
Kassite Dynasty 91, 127
Kawab 61
KBo I 10 129
KBo I 14 129, 131
Kedar 209
Kedemah 209
Keith C. Seele 184
Kelly 45
Keltemin 214, 218
Kelteminarian 218
Kenneth A. Kitchen 149
Kent Weeks 126
Kephart 94, 101, 218
Kerma 96
Kesed 106
Khaba 60
Khabur River 76
Khafra 41, 61
Khafre 61
Khamaat 62
Khamazi 79
Khameremebty I 61
Khameremebty II 61
Khamermebty I 61
Khartum Variant 95
Khasekhem 60
Khasekhemwy 59
Khentkawes 62
Kheops 61
Kheperkheperur ē 125
Khephren 61

Khor 146
Khuenre 62
Khufu 61
Khufukaef 61
Kib 237, 240
Kim 236, 240
Kimmerians 219
Kindgoodie Quarry 49
King 26, 33, 83, 229
King David 117
King Herod 119
King lists 127
King of Goiim 86
King of nations 83
King of peace 86
King of Salem 210
King of Upper and Lower Egypt 143, 144
King Omri 222
King's Highway 78
King-list 124
Kings 25, 35, 36, 71, 79, 87
Kirgipa 166
Kish 87, 236, 240
Kish 89, 90
Kitchen 133, 149-151
Kittim 99, 105
Kiya 166
Koath 191
Kohath 138, 156-158, 191, 192
Kom el Ahmar Stela 143
Koptos 81
Koran 79, 153, 176, 178, 179, 187, 192
Korea 229
Korean Plates 229
Koreans 98
Kramer 32
Kudur-mabug, 87
Kunnike 22
Kurgan 101
L'Astronomie 50
Laban 149, 195
Lachish 77
Ladd 29
LaFay 79, 80
Lagash 89, 90, 202
Lake Aral 100
Lake Balkhash 100
Lake Bonneville 39, 238
Lake Lahontan 238
Lake Menzalah 148
Lamanite 11, 109

Lambayeque, Peru 228
Lamech 20, 26, 57, 59, 66, 67
Land of Moron 239
Land of promise 66
Land of Ramses 139
Land of Seir 116
Land of Shulon 12
Lane 50
Languages 26
Larsa 88
Lasha 113
Late Classic Period 230
Late Egyptian 225
Late Paleolithic 95
Late Post-Classic Period 230
Latin 215, 217, 233
Latin America 54, 230
Latter-day 204
Latter-day Saints 12
Law of Moses 121
Leah 196
Lebanon 75, 147, 221
Lebolo 6
Lebuda 65
Ledah 101
Legends 25
Lehabim 113, 114
Lehi 117, 118, 176, 225
Leonard Woolley 37, 200, 208
Lett 108
Letter KBo I 10 129
Lettic 108
Levi 138, 156-158, 184, 188, 191, 192, 196, 197, 236, 240, 244
Levite 120, 187
Levites 187
Lewis Spense 231
Lib 236, 240
Libnah 149
Libraries 22
Libya 144, 150, 152
Libyan 112, 141-143
Libyans 114, 115, 143, 144, 147, 150
Lili Nu-u 24, 72
Lima, Peru 228
Limhi 236
Lineages 11
Linguistic 81
Lions 69
Lisa Aaronson 19
Lithuanian 108

Little Russian 99, 108
Liverpool University 149
Liyn 223
Lombards 105
London 50
London Times 48
Lord 16, 25, 52, 68, 69, 71, 114, 136, 139, 153, 199, 206, 216, 236, 237
Los Angeles 238, 239
Lot 75, 84, 104, 109, 199
Lower and Middle Egypt 138
Lower Egypt 56, 139
Lower Egyptian 142
Lower Nubia 95, 96
Lowland Scot 108
Lubal 103
Lucy 21
Lud 64, 109, 110, 114, 115
Ludim 113, 114
Lugalanda 89
Lugalzagesi 90
Lugalzagesi 89
Luke 120
Lunar calendar 126
Lundquist 76, 202
Luther 206
Luxor 135, 148, 149, 181
Lydians 108, 110
Lyman D. Platt 1
M. L. Bierbrier 129, 135
M. Maspero 33
Ma 26
Ma'ada el-'Omari 95
Maat-Hor- Neferure 136
Machine-made 50
Machines 51
Machul 110
Macro-Mayan 231
Madagascar 98
Madai 98, 99, 102, 104, 108, 109
Maetkarē 125
Magillath Ta'anith 120
Magnetic 50
Magog 99, 103, 106, 107
Mahah 237
Mahalaleel 16, 20, 26, 56-58, 60, 66
Mahijah 66, 68
Mahoni 234
Mahonri Moriancumer 64, 235
Mahujah 11, 67, 68

Maidum 96
Makdonia 105
Mal-lawi 187
Malay Archipelago 98
Malay Peninsula 112
Malayo 98
Malayo-Polynesian 108
Malays 98
Male mummy 239
Málek 94
Mallevi 187
Maltese 226
Mammals 30
Mamre 84, 85
Manasseh 170, 176
Manchu 98
Mandaean 223
Mandaean Gnostic 223
Mandaeans 223
Manetho 124, 178, 181, 187
Manishtushu 90
Maništusu 89
Maoris 108, 208
Mardon 114
Margie Morris 40
Mari 80, 90
Marquesan 109
Marvin Harris 92
Mary 120
Mash 78, 109, 111
Mash-qi 79
Mashu 79
Maspero 33
Massa 209
Massagetae 219
Mastabah 33
Mathematics 22
Matthiae 80, 201
Matthias 120
Maxey 50
Maya 11, 109, 229, 231
Mayan 11, 229, 231
Mayan Calendar 57
Mayas 218, 239
McQuown 231
Mebaragesi 89, 90
Mechanical 50, 51
Mechanism 50
Medai 103
Medes 97, 98, 104, 108
Media 99, 104

Medieval Hebrew 100
Mediterranean 53, 55, 74, 76, 79, 98-100, 105, 110, 116, 144, 147
Mediterranean Sea 45
Mediterraneans 216
Megiddo 77
Mehti-em-sa-t 33
Mehujael 66
Melancthon 206
Melanesian Islands 112
Melchisedec 206
Melchizedec 77
Melchizedek 83-86, 110, 198, 205-207, 210
Melech 206
Memphis 57, 128, 139, 142, 143
Memphite 95, 128
Men 57
Men-pehti-rēc or 129
Men-pehu-rēc 129
Mena 33
Mencheres 62
Menes 33, 57
Menkauhor 63
Menkaura 62
Menkaure 61, 62
Menkheperrē 125
Menkheperurē 125
Menophres 128
Merari 188
Merenptah 133, 141-143, 145, 150-152
Merenptah Hotep-hir-Maat 143, 144
Merenre 56
Meresankh I 61
Meresankh II 61
Meresankh III 61
Merey 142
Meriamon 143
Merimda 95
Meritamun 125
Meritaten 125
Meritates 61
Meritre 125
Merneith 58
Merneptah 136
Mersin 36
Meryetamun 136
Meryre II 188
Mesalim 89
Mesanepada 89
Mesha 109, 110, 222

Mesha Stone 222
Meshech 99, 103, 106
Meshechites 106
Mesheq 78
Meskiagnuna 89
Meso-Americans 118
Mesoamerica 104, 227, 228, 231
Mesopotamia 18, 35, 36, 75, 76, 81, 82, 88, 90, 91, 101, 111, 195, 200, 215, 219, 220, 222, 223, 226
Mesopotamian 46, 52, 129, 131, 207, 221
Mesopotamian Valley 11, 74, 79, 100, 114, 227, 238
Mesopotamians 157
Mesosaurs 30
Messiah 119, 190
Metal cube 49
Metal screw 49
Metal-working 22
Metallic 51
Metallic shaft 51
Metallic vase 47
Methuselah 16, 20, 26, 56, 58, 67, 71
Mexica 232, 233
Mexican 231-233
Mexico 81, 229, 231
Mexico City 232, 233
Meydum pyramid 60
Meyer 128
Mibsam 209
Michael 58
Michael C. Astour 123
Michael Weitzman 35, 36, 89, 203
Middle Bronze 96
Middle East 81, 94, 220, 222, 224
Middle Egypt 138
Middle Egyptian 225
Middle Hittite Kingdom 126
Middle Kingdom 90, 91, 96
Midianite 151
Midianites 153
Mike Mikesell 50
Mikesell 50
Milcah 199
Millennium 242
Miller 22, 29
Min 165
Minaean 223
Minoan 101
Minoans 216

Miqqedem 75
Miras 110
Miriam 186
Miscegenation 93
Mishma 209
Mishnah 223
Mishnaic 221
Misr 81
Missouri 12, 71
Mistranslations 5
Mitanni 96, 131, 146
Mitannian 184
Mitzraim 114
Mizraim 63, 112-114
Moab 109, 150, 151, 175
Moabite 150, 222
Mohenjo Daro 10, 11
Mokil 110
Monarchs 24
Mongolian 98
Mongoloid 93, 98, 104
Mongoloids 93
Mongols 102
Montenegrin 98, 108
Montet 129
Moravia 101
Moreh 199, 200
Morianton 236, 240
Mormon 99, 104, 205, 225, 238
Moron 236, 239, 240
Moroni 236
Morris 40
Morrisonville Times 48
Morrisonville, Illinois 48
Moscow 106
Moses 27, 65, 136, 138, 139, 141, 151, 153, 154, 156-158, 175, 176, 179, 180, 183, 184, 186, 187, 190-192, 197, 204, 208, 226, 230, 244
Mosul 75
Mount Ararat 34
Mount Paran 116
Mount Seir 145, 149
Mountain of Cedars 201
Mountain of Silver 80
Mountains fled 69
Mousterian 75
Mrs. S. W. Culp 48
Mt. Ararat 53

Mt. Paran 116
Mulekite 230
Mummies 6, 239
Mummification 146
Mummy 239
Muriel Porter Weaver 230
Murshilish 127
Murshilish I 91, 126
Murshilish II 131, 132
Muscovites 106
Muslim 83, 187
Mutemwiya 125
Mutnezmet 185
Mutnodjme 125
Muwatallis 136, 148
Muwatallish 131
Mycenaean 96, 105
Mycerinus/Mykerinus 62
Myth 10
Mythological 37
Mythological origin 138
Mythology 23
Myths 22
N. P. Nilsson 105
Naamah 67, 72
Nabataean 222
Nagada I 95
Nagada II 95
Naharin 166
Nahor 64, 199, 202, 212
Nahr-el-Kelb 149
Nahua 231
Náhuatl 231, 233
Nail 49
Naphish 209
Naphtuchim 114
Naphtuhim 113
Naqada 57
Naqada II 96
Naram-Sin 80-90, 201
Narmer 56
Nasbon 193
National Archaeological Museum 228
National Geographic 79
Native American 9, 104, 109, 233
Natural disasters 18
Natural history 14
Nature 50
Near East 36, 123, 224
Near Eastern 132
Near Eastern synchronisms 129

Neb Kheparu-Re 163
Nebajoth 209
Nebettawy 136
Nebka 60
Nebkheperurē 125
Nebmaetrē 125
Nebpehtirē 125
Necho, 7
Nefer-Hebo Gereh-Tawi 163
Neferefre 62
Neferhotep 62
Neferirkare 58, 62
Neferkara 59
Neferkheperurē 125
Neferneferuaten 125
Neferneferuaten-Nefertiti 125
Nefertari 136
Nefertiti 171, 181, 184, 186
Negeb 149
Negrito 112
Negro 70, 112
Negroes 68
Negroid 93
Nehemiah 118
Neit 163
Neith 57
Nekhen 56
Nekure 61
Nelson 103, 227
Nemathap 60
Neo-Assyrian 126
Neo-Assyrian eponym list 123
Neolithic 41, 75, 95
Neolithic Age 55
Neolithic Jericho 95
Nephercheres 59
Nephite 11, 109, 228, 230
Nephites 118, 236, 239
Nergal 201
Neterka 59
Netjeri-khet 60
Neugebauer 127
Nevada 49, 239
New Guinea 112
New Kingdom 40, 96, 125, 126, 128
New Mexico 231
New moon 121
New Zealand 108
Nfirms 186
Nibley 77, 208, 212, 216, 218, 240
Nile 41, 55, 56, 81, 139, 153, 166, 180

Nile River 135
Nile Valley 82, 95
Nilsson 105
Nimrod 64, 80, 88, 112, 114, 207, 211
Nineteenth Dynasty 129, 139, 141, 145, 151, 153, 182
Nineveh 37, 77, 110, 112, 114
Nissen 89
Nithotep 57
Niuserre 63
Noachian 27
Noah 8, 10, 15, 17, 18, 20, 23, 25, 26, 33, 34, 37, 51, 52, 59, 64, 67, 72, 73, 82, 92, 93, 99, 100, 102, 112, 113, 116, 193, 197, 198, 202, 204-206, 209, 210, 212, 214, 215, 219, 234, 235, 240, 243
Nod 10, 67, 71
Nofret 61
Non-Aryan 218
Noorbergen 34, 52
Nordic 98, 100, 101, 215, 219
Nordics 215
Norman A. McQuown 231
North Africa 45, 225
North America 9, 38, 54, 230, 238, 239
North American 231, 238
North American tribes 109
Northeastern Syria 222
Northern Iraq 222
Northern Spain 111
Northern Syria 144, 146, 147
Northwest India 10
Northwestern Semitic 220
Norwegian 108
Nu-u 24
Nu-wah 23
Nubia 57, 143, 146, 187
Nubian Stelae 143
Numbers 121, 149
Numic 231
Numidian 225
Nur-Ninsubur 88
Nut 163
Nynetjer 59
O. Neugebauer 127
Oaxaca, Mexico 229
Obal 109

Obed 193
Obi River 100
Obliquity of the ecliptic 34
Oceania 54
Of 204
Ohio State University 33
Oktanites 110
Olancha, California 50
Old Egyptian 225
Old Kingdom 42, 43, 90, 96
Old Testament 22, 65, 77-79, 137, 138, 140, 145, 150, 155, 157, 179, 208, 217, 221, 222
Old World 23
Old World Mongoloids 93
Olishem 201, 210, 212
Olmec 104, 109, 239
Oman 223
Omer 237, 240
Omner 11, 67, 69, 71
Omotic 226
Omri 222
On 165
Onan 203
Ongal 102
Ongolis 107
Onitah 212
Ophir 109
Oppression 183
Oral genealogies 9
Oregon 239
Orelum 103
Orient 24
Original sources 5
Orihad 237
Orihah 237, 240
Orinoco 23
Orkney 29
Oromo 225
Orontes river 147
Orosco 232
Osarseph 162
Osiris 114
Osirus 26
Osman 136, 155
Osorkon 33
Osorkon I 132, 134
Osorkon II 133
Osorkon IV 129, 134
Oswiris 114

Otiartes 26
Out-of-place 21
Owens Lake 50
Oxidation 50
P. Huber 127
P. Montet 129
Pa-Ramses 153
Pacific Ocean 38
Pagodas 103
Paleontologists 27, 45
Paleontology 30
Paleozoic 29
Palermo Stone 58, 59
Palestine 82, 95, 115, 141, 144-147, 149, 151, 153, 174, 220, 221
Palestinian Syriac 222
Palestinians 146
Palmyra 222
Palmyrene 222
Pamirs 219
Panehesy 188
Pangrave 96
Papuan 112
Papyrus 7, 124, 222
Papyrus of Ani 33
Pariahs 102
Paris, France 50, 229
Parzunac 102
Pashiah 106
Passover 120, 121
Passover lambs 121
Passovers 121
Pathros 115
Pathrusim 113-115
Patriarch 26, 82
Patriarchal 68, 82, 113, 198
Patriarchal blessings 13
Patriarchal order 20
Patriarchal succession 15
Patriarchs 8, 15, 20, 25, 26, 52, 72, 204
Pe-Kanan 147
Pearl 204
Peat 31
Pedigree 12
Pedigrees 13
Peleg 17, 18, 64, 109, 199, 212, 235
Pelishtim 115
Peloponnese 105
Pentateuch 139, 204
Pepi 90

Pepi I 33, 56
Pepi II 33
Perez 203
Peribsen 59
Persia 12, 79, 99, 108, 110
Persian 123, 215, 218, 228
Persian Gulf 76, 77
Persians 108, 110
Persopolis 228
Peru 228
Pethor 110
Petra 222
Petrie 141
Petroglyphs 223
Pettinato 80, 88, 200, 201
Pharaoh 7, 63, 82, 113, 114, 125, 136, 139,
        153, 212
Pharaoh of the Oppression 141, 154
Pharaohs 71, 82
Pharaz 193
Philippines 98, 112
Philistim 113
Philologists 214
Phinehas 188
Phoenicia 149
Phoenician 108, 147, 148, 220, 221, 226,
        233
Phoenicians 108, 115, 230
Photogrammetry 33
Photographs 239
Phut 112, 114, 115
Pi-nehase 189
Pi-Ramses 139
Piankhy 132-134
Pictographs 215, 226, 227, 232, 239
Pictorial symbol 23
Piedmont 6
Pinehas 189
Pison 10, 67
Pithom 182
Plain of Olishem 210
Plate movements 74
Platt 1
Pleistocene 45
Plesiosaurs 30
Pole 99, 108
Polish 149
Political organization 22
Politics 26
Polynesians 98
Population 51, 52

Porcelain 50
Portuguese 108, 217
Post-diluvian 27
Post-Flood 34, 37, 68, 95, 198, 215, 234
Post-Shamarkian 95
Potiphar 164
Potiphar's Hill 201, 210, 212
Potipherah 164
Pre- Flood kings 88
Pre-Christian 221, 222
Pre-Classic Period 230
Pre-dynastic 33
Pre-Flood 31, 32, 51, 55, 68, 71, 95, 215,
        234
Pre-historical 105
Prehistoric 26, 29, 81, 218
Prehistory 232
Price 204
Priesthood 15, 82, 113, 206, 207
Prince of peace 85
Prophecies 230
Prophecy 20, 68, 119
Prophesy 68
Prophet 12, 236
Prophetic 68, 74
Prophetic cycle 119
Prophetic time 119, 242
Prophetic week 119
Prophetic years 119
Prophets 6, 7
Proto-Sinaitic 221
Proto-Indo-European 218
Proto-West Germanic 218
Protolanguage 218
Psammetichis I 129
Pseudepigrapha 9, 65
Psusennes 33
Ptah 26
Pterosaurs 30
Ptolemaic 40
Ptolemy I 124
Pu-Abi 90
Pudding stone 48
Punic 221
Purposeful inaccuracies 5
Pyramids 33
Qa'a 59
Qatabanian 223
Qedem 75
Quechua 109
Quetzalcoatl 232

Qumran 228
R. A. Schwaller de Lubicz 42
Ra 26
Ra'mose 96
Raamah 112, 114
Rabi 87
Rachel 196
Racial groupings 92
Raciologists 93
Radiocarbon 32
Radjedef 61
Ragbib 102
Rahotep 61
Rain of Fire 232
Rainbow 24
Rakhaef 61
Rameses 139, 189
Ramesses 139, 189
Ramesses I 128
Ramesses II 125, 128-131, 134-136
Ramesses III 133
Ramesses IX 133
Ramesses V 133
Ramesses XI 133
Ramesside 152
Ramose 189
Ramses 182
Ramses I 139, 141, 146, 153, 154, 158,
         182, 244
Ramses II 141, 145-152
Ramses II 150
Raneb 59
Raneferef 62
Ras Shamra 217, 220
Ray Winfield Smith 185
Rbn 149
Re 143
Re-neb Ka-w Sehetep Neteru 163
Rebekah 195
Rebu 143
Record keepers 5
Red Crown 56
Red Sea 45
Redford 177
Redjedef 61
Referencing standards 5
Reginald Daly 38
Rehobother 110
Religion 26
Rene Noorbergen 34
Rephaims 83

Rephath 101
Reptiles 27, 30
Reptilian 30
Research procedures 5
Resen 110, 112
Reu 17
Reuben 196
Reweddjedet 62
Richard C. Hoagland 41
Richardson 88
Riem 22
Riff 225
Righteous Man 24
Righteousness 23, 69, 86, 210
Rim-Sin 87
Rim-Sin of Ellasar 87
Rimuš 89
Rimush 90
Rings 50
Riphath 99
Riphath 101
Riplakish 236, 240
Rivas-Salmon 232
Rockies 28
Rocky Point Mine 47
Roman 7, 111, 121, 123, 217
Roman Empire 119
Roman Period 225
Romanian 217
Rome 81
Ronald Brownrigg 115
Rottenberg 53
Rowton 130, 131
Royal archives 80
Rumanian 108
Rushash 107
Russia 100, 106
Russian 218
Ruth 203
Ruth Verrill 229
Ruthenian 99, 108
Rutherford Mills, England 48
S. Smith 127
Sa-u-lum 79
Sabaean 223
Sabtah 112, 114
Sabtecha 112, 114
Sacred New Year 127, 128
Saf 223
Sahara 42, 225
Sahara Desert 42, 44, 45

Sahure 62
Saints 204
Sais 57
Sakae 219
Salah 17, 19, 109
Salem 78, 84, 85, 198, 205-207
Salim 77, 83, 110, 198, 207, 210
Salmon 193
Salt sea 83
Salzburg Museum 49
Samaritan Aramaic 222
Samoan 108
Samuel Noah Kramer 32
San Francisco 238, 239
Sanakhte 60
Sanpete 239
Sanpete Valley 239
Sanskrit 215, 219, 233
Saqqara 57, 96
Saqquara King List 58
Sarah 203, 209
Sarai 199
Sargon 80, 88-90,104, 114
Sargonid 96
Šarkališarri 89
Satan 65, 70
Satirna 166
Saul 79
Sbâyet 189
Scandinavia 106, 233
Scandinavians 230
Scharff 32
Schwaller de Lubicz 42
Science 21
Scientific 49, 55
Scientific American 47
Scientific method 14
Scientific methodology 5
Scientific truths 6
Scientists 28, 47, 49
Scorpion, 56
Scotland 93, 99
Scrolls 7
Scythia 101
Scythian 98, 100, 103
Scythians 106, 108, 238
Scytho-Indian Empire 219
Sea of Galilee 145, 147, 151
Seb 26
Seba 112, 114
Second millennium 123

Second millennium B.C. 221
Second Pyramid 61
Second World War 50
Secular history 118
Sedimentary 29
Seele 184
Seine 39
Seir 83, 116, 149
Sekhemkhet 60
Selah 64, 79, 110
Semenkhkare 182
Semerkhet 58
Semitic 81, 82, 87, 99, 108, 111, 138, 151,
    219, 221, 226
Semti 58
Sendji 59
Seni 116
Seoul, Korea 229
Sephar 79, 109, 110
Serb 98, 108
Serug 17
Sesostris III 36
Set 26
Seth 16, 18, 20, 26, 55, 58, 59, 65, 226,
    236, 240
Seth-Peribsen 59
Sethenes 59
Sethite 26
Seti I 136, 141, 146-148, 150, 151, 153,
    244
Setka 61
Seven Wonders of the Ancient World 61
Seventeenth century B.C. 138
Sewell 127
Shalmaneser I 131
Shalmaneser III 228
Shamshi-Adad 127
Shang 24
Shang Ti 103
Shar-kali-sharri 90
Sharon 11, 67, 69, 71
Shasu 146, 148, 150-152
Shasu-land 149
Shaveh 84
Shaveh Kiriathaim 83
Sheba 109, 112, 114
Shebashni 106
Shechem 174
Shedolamak 56, 67, 71
Shela 203
Shelach 110

Sheleph 109
Shells 50
Shem 8, 17, 19, 51, 62, 67, 69, 71-73, 79,
        98, 99, 104, 109, 112,
        116, 197, 198, 202,
        205, 206, 210, 214,
        234, 243
Shem-Re 59
Shemeber 83
Shemites 75
Shepherd 147
Shepseskaf 62
Shepseskare 62
Shez 236, 240
Shibashnic 106
Shiblon 236, 240
Shilo 190
Shimeathites 149
Shin'ar 75
Shinab 83
Shinar 75, 83, 84, 86, 88, 112, 114
Ship 24
Shos 147
Shoshenk I 129, 133
Shoshenk V 132, 134
Shu Ching 103
Shu-Sin 91
Shub-Ad 90
Shule 237, 240
Shulgi 91
Shulon 10, 12, 55, 66, 67, 71
Shum 67, 68
Shuppiluliumash I 126
Shushan 110
Siamese 98
Siberia 38, 100
Siberian 98
Siberian tribes 109
Siddim 83, 84
Sidersky 127
Sidon 113
Sihor 114
Silver 47
Silver vein 47
Simeon 11, 67, 68, 196
Simmuballit 87
Simpson 30
Simyra 148
Sinai 77, 141, 142, 144, 146, 150, 151, 153,
        175, 179, 182, 187,
        188

Sinite 113
Sinitic 98
Sinuhe 75, 180
Sir David Brewster 49
Sirius 36, 127
Sitamun 165-167, 181, 185
Six-penny nail 49
Sixth Dynasty 33, 63
Skehemib 59
Slavic 98, 99, 108
Slavs 99
Slovak 99, 108
Slovene 98, 108
Sm't 149
Smith 7, 8, 15, 127, 185, 206
Sneferu 61
Snefru 61
Snofru 61
Sodom 78, 83, 84, 113, 116, 210
Sogdiana 219
Sojourn 137-140, 151, 155, 198, 211
Solar eclipse 35, 132
Somali 225
Son 69, 70
Son of God 85
Son of Man 70
Sons of God 85
Soris 61
Sothic calendar cycle 127
Sothic cycle 127, 128
Sothis star 127
South America 9, 228, 230, 232
South American 109
South Arabian 223
South Arabic 226
South Australia 34
South Slav 98, 108
Southeastern Idaho 239
Southern China 93
Southern Ethiopia 226
Southern India 111
Southern Paiute 231
Southwestern Semitic 220
Southwestern Wyoming 239
Sovereigns 24
Spain   111
Spangler 233
Spaniard 108
Spanish 105, 217
Spark plug 51
Spense 231

Sphinx 40, 42-46, 61
Spiritually empirical data 5, 242
Spring 51
Spring Hill, Missouri 12
Springfield Republican 49
St. Matthew 193
Statistics 51
Steel-and-nickel alloy 49
Step Pyramid at Saqqara 60
Steppes 100, 116, 238
Stone Age 46
Stone battle axes 101
Styria, Greece 229
Su 26
Sub-Mycenaean 96
Sudras 102
Suebian 101, 219
Sukarlam 26
Sumatra 25
Sumer 10, 11, 32, 64, 74, 76, 87, 241
Sumerian 26, 27, 90, 101, 200, 202, 220, 226
Sumerian King List 157
Sumerians 32, 88, 114, 216, 218, 219
Sumuabi 87
Sun eclipse 123
Suphis I 61
Suphis II 61
Suppiluliuma 146
Sura 79, 187
Surim 80
Sus 156, 193
Susa Young Gates 95
Swede 108
Sword 239
Symbols 24
Synchronism 89
Syria 76, 80, 82, 95, 110, 111, 141, 145, 146, 148-151, 200, 201, 220-222
Syriac 223, 223
Syrian 80, 82, 149
Syrians 110
Syro-Palestine 220, 222
T. L. Thompson 204
Table of Nations 96
Tablet of metal 230
Tadmor 222
Tadukhipa 184
Taharqa 129, 132
Tahitian 109

Takelot II 133
Talalat 185
Talmage 12
Talmud 120, 156, 180, 187
Tamar 203
Tanis 33, 148
Tarki 102
Tarshish 99, 105
Tartars 102
Taxonomy 93
Taylor 206
Technology 21
Tefnakht 134
Tehenu 144, 150
Tehran 228
Tell el Mukayyar 200
Tell el-Amarna 181
Tell Fekheriye 222
Tell Halaf 76
Tell Hassuna 75
Tell Mardikh 76
Tema 209
Temple 27
Temple archives 124
Temple Block 13
Ten Tribes 104
Tenochtitlán 232
Tentamun 168
Tepe Gawra 76
Terah 199, 202
Tertiary 49
Tertullian 119
Testament of Adam 65
Testaments 8
Teta 33
Teti 63, 114
Teutonic 108
Teutons 99
Tey 125
Thamd 223
The 204
The Book of Abraham 7, 67, 81, 112, 113, 198, 201
The Book of Ether 216, 234, 236, 240
The Book of Genesis 82
The Book of Jasher 9, 67, 71, 102, 114, 115, 204, 206
The Book of Jasher 104, 105, 114
The Book of Mormon 6, 9, 97, 117, 207, 216, 225, 234
The Book of Moroni 9

The Book of Moses 8, 10, 14, 16, 17, 19, 65-67, 70, 71, 214
The Book of the Prophet Ezekiel 103
The Doctrine & Covenants 15, 55
The Doctrine and Covenants 6, 12, 16, 204
The Fields Of Piyer 142
The First Book of Moses 8
The Holy Bible 5, 8, 14, 55, 67, 83, 93, 96, 103, 117, 118, 122, 152, 193, 198, 203, 205, 208
The land between the rivers 77
The Millennium 117
The Pearl of Great Price 6, 10, 14, 16, 65, 67, 70, 76, 97, 112, 204, 214, 226
The Refiner's Fire 13
The United States of America 12
Theban 183
Thebes 6, 96, 128, 139-141, 146, 147, 165, 181, 217
Theon 128
Theories 5
Theorized 12
Thinite king 58
Third Dynasty of Ur 91
Third millennium 123
Third millennium B.C. 76
Third millennium BC 36
Third millennium-B.C. 201
Thirteenth century B.C. 147
Thompson 204, 232
Thrace 107
Thutmose III 128
Thuya 171
Tia 125, 168
Tiberius 121
Tiberius Cæsa 121
Tibetan 98
Tidal 83, 84, 86
Tidal waves 38
Tiglath-pileser 104
Tigris 74-76, 79, 99, 104
Tigris-Euphrates 55
Tilmaz 102
Time 242
Time prophecies 119
Times and Seasons 206
Tiras 99, 107
Titan 99, 105

Tithes 86
Titus 120
Tiy 184, 185
Tiye 125, 162, 164, 168, 171, 176, 177, 179, 180, 186, 188, 191, 244
Togarmah 99, 102
Tokhari 218, 219
Toltecs 109, 239
Tomb 33
Tomb 5 135
Tombstone inscriptions 221
Torah 189, 191, 193, 197, 244
Toshka 143
Tosorthos 60
Totonacan 231
Tower of Babel 11, 18, 19, 64, 94, 103, 116, 199, 212, 215, 234, 235
Toynbee 189
Traditions 22
Tragan 104, 106
Transjordan 148, 150
Transjordanian 149
Translation 58, 176
Transylvania 101
Treasure City, Nevada 49
Tribal memories 10
Tribal traditions 13
Tribes 23
Trifil 45
Troezen 105
Truth 9
Tuari 106
Tubal 99, 103, 106
Tubal-cain 67
Tuckabatchee, Alabama 229
Tueris 167
Tugarma 102
Tunisia 45, 221
Turanian 218
Tureg 225
Turin 124
Turkey 34, 36, 53, 76, 200-202, 223
Turkish 98, 105
Turkistan 101
Turks 101, 106, 219
Tushratta 184
Tuskanah 106
Tut 26
Tutankhamun 96, 125, 159, 163, 166, 171,

182, 187
Tuthmosis 125, 179, 189
Tuthmosis III 91, 164
Tuthmosis IV 158, 162, 244
Tutmose 189
Tuya 159, 161, 165, 171
Twelfth Egyptian dynasty 36
Twenty-four gold plates 236
Uadji 58
Ubaid 37, 95
Udimu 58
Ugarit 220
Ugaritic 220, 226
Uigurians 106
Ukraine 101
Ulisum 201, 210
Umberto Cassuto 156, 193
Umma 89, 90
Unas 33, 63
Uniformitarian 37
Unis 63
United States 28, 33, 45, 54, 236
Universal destruction 25
Universal laws 6
Universal method 6, 8
Universal methodology 5, 242
Universal principles 6
Universidad Autónoma de Guadalajara 232
University of California 45
University of Chicago 87, 106, 228
University of Pennsylvania 32
University of Utah 231
Upper Egypt 56, 139, 140, 181
Upper Nubia 95, 96
Upthrusts 74
Ur 19, 37, 76-78, 82, 88-90, 198, 199, 201, 202
Ur of Chaldea 202, 210, 212
Ur of the Chaldees 77, 80, 82, 198, 200, 202, 212
Ur-Nammu 91
Ur-Nanše 89
Ur-Nanshe 90
Ura 200
Ural Mountains 100
Ural River 101
Urfa 223
Urlumma 89
Ursu 202
Uruk 90, 95, 215

Urukagina 89, 90
Urusalima 77, 207, 210
Uš 89
Userkaf 62
USSR 54
Utah 232, 239
Utah pictographs 232
Utah rock art 232
Ute 231
Utes 109
Utnapishtim 27
Uto-Aztecan 109, 231, 233
Utuhengal 90
Uz 109, 111
Uzal 109
Uziel 192
Valley of Teguayo 232
Valley of the Kings 135, 158, 159, 164
Valley of the Nobles 159
Van Seters 204
Velikovsky 29, 37, 44
Venus 126, 127, 232
Verrill 229
Vertebrates 29
Virginia Maxey 50
Vis 52
Viscount Kingsborough 229
Vocklabruck 49
W. F. Albright 127, 204
W. M. Flinders Petrie 141
Waa- Halau 24
Wadi es Seboua 143
Wadi Halfa 146
Wadi Hammamat 81
Wallace Lane 50
Walloon 108
Wars 65, 69, 235
Washo 231
Weaver 230
Webster 95, 97, 98, 108
Weeks 126
Weitzman 35, 36, 89, 203
Weld Prism 88
Wellhausen 204
Welsh 230
Wenis 63
Weserkaf 62
West 42, 43
West Africa 93, 226
West Aramaic 222
West Semitic dynasty 87

West Semitic dynasty of Babylonia 87
West Slav 98, 108
West-Semitic 146
Western Asia 126, 226
Western Delta 142
Western Europe 93, 217
Western Palestine 151
Western semitic 220
Western Turkistan 100
Western United States 39
Whales 45, 46
Wheeled vehicles 76
Whitcomb 52
White Crown 56
White Russian 99, 108
Wilkins 229
William Albright 96
William J. Hamblin 228
William R. Vis 52
Wilson 78
Winged reptiles 30
Wolf 230
Woolley 37, 200, 208
Worldwide tidal waves 74
Written records 14
Wyoming 239
X-rays 50
Xisuthros 27
Xisuthros 26
Yale University 75
Yanoam 144, 145, 147, 151
Yarmuti 80
Year 204
Yeman 223
Yhwa 161
Yoyotte 151, 152
Yshvat 192
Yu-Seph 163
Yuaa 169
Yucatan 229
Yuya 158, 161, 167, 174, 182, 188, 244
Zachariah 120
Zaron 106
Zarw 153, 179, 180, 183, 191
Zeboiim 78, 83, 84
Zeboim 113
Zeboyim 116
Zebuc 102
Zedekiah 118
Zeelo 104
Zelekha 164

Zemarite 113
Zerah 203
Zeuglodon 45, 46
Zidon 115
Zillah 66
Zimodi 116
Zinc 47
Zion 16, 69, 70
Zoar 78, 83, 84
Zoquean 231
Zoser 60
Zuzims 83